Database Marketing
and
Direct Mail

'Every practice rests on theory even if the practitioners themselves are unaware of it'

(Peter Drucker)

'Every theory derives from practice, even if the theorists themselves are unaware of it'

(Robin Fairlie)

Database Marketing and Direct Mail

A Practical Guide to the Techniques and Applications

Robin Fairlie

KOGAN PAGE

The masculine pronoun has been used throughout this book.
This stems from a desire to avoid ugly and cumbersome language,
and no discrimination, prejudice or bias is intended

First published in 1990 by Exley Publications Ltd,
16 Chalk Hill, Watford, Herts WD1 4BN.
This edition published by Kogan Page in 1993.

Kogan Page Limited
120 Pentonville Road
London N1 9JN

© Robin Fairlie, 1990, 1993

British Library Cataloguing in Publication Data

A CIP record for this book is available from the British Library.

ISBN 0 7494 1170 8

Typeset by DP Photosetting, Aylesbury, Bucks
Printed and bound in Great Britain by
Biddles Ltd, Guildford and King's Lynn

Contents

Contents

7

Introduction

This book is about the two inter-linked – but independent – concepts of database marketing and direct mail. There is a tendency in some quarters to confuse the two. The development of direct mail, and its growing use by business houses, has been a long slow process, extending now over three generations. While the use of the postal services by businesses to communicate with customers or prospects is at least as old as the Post Office itself, the actual development of today's direct mail industry can be said to have started in the USA in the early 1900s. Yet the industry on both sides of the Atlantic is only now reaching maturity with the conscious involvement, for the first time, of the majority of business houses with the medium – and indeed with its discovery by charities, by churches, and by political parties.

Database, by contrast, was a concept born of the computer industry in the 1960s; it has hit the business world with the impact to be expected from the offspring of such parentage. Suddenly a term, coined only twenty odd years ago, and rarely heard then outside the more esoteric computer seminars, is on everyone's lips, and every computer user possessed of a handful of names and addresses is either claiming to have a database or wondering how to acquire one. (And the Commission of the European Community, never slow to recognise a new development in which it might claim an interest, is even now writing a Directive on the legal protection of databases.)

For marketing people in general, and direct mail users in particular, concerned about how to obtain and use more, and more reliable, information about increasingly fragmented markets, database seems like the answer to a prayer. We are approaching the time when every serious marketing department will have a database, and when every user of a marketing database will be a user also of direct mail, whether as a primary or a secondary way of maximising the value of his investment in information. So where does the one discipline end, and the other begin?

Direct mail means simply the sending of business communications to individual persons through the post. Database marketing means using information about individual persons in such a way as to improve the effectiveness of one's marketing techniques – whether these techniques happen to use direct mail or some other medium.

In practice, of course, if one has substantial information of marketing relevance about named individuals (which normally includes their addresses) it would seem natural to use the postal services to establish and maintain some kind of link with these persons. But there are alternatives: one can use the information available to enhance the efforts of a sales force, or of a telephone marketing service, for example.

Moreover, the uses of a database are not confined to selecting individuals to whom communications can be made, whether through the post or by other means. The opportunities offered by good database facilities for analysis of information, for example, so as to give new insights into markets, are immense. Database techniques, then, offer a means of defining and refining markets. Direct mail is one major medium through which markets so defined can be exploited.

So, the subjects of our interest do exist independently, and we will look at them, at least initially, each in turn. The excuse for dealing with both between one set of covers is simply that it is hard to envisage a database user not being moved, at some point, to use direct mail – even though that may not have been his original motivation in building his database. Similarly, most users of direct mail, if they are to use the medium effectively by targeting their promotions to qualified prospects, will increasingly have to consider database techniques as a way of giving them access to a necessary knowledge of their prospects' needs.

In old-fashioned business circles you will still hear direct mail referred to (when mentioned at all) as an advertising medium. It is not. Direct mail is a marketing medium; advertising is one function of marketing, and one function, therefore, of direct mail. Direct mail is, in turn, one arm of marketing – an arm whose muscle power is provided by information, such as can be held and ordered by database techniques.

In the beginning there were two kinds of companies – the direct mail companies and the rest. (I almost said The Reader's Digest and everybody else.) For the former, direct mail was a total way of life; for the latter it didn't exist. Those who used the medium, used it to advertise, to conduct market research, and to sell – the three classic marketing functions. And they used little or nothing else. Everybody else preferred not to know.

These days have gone, on both sides. The Reader's Digest itself now advertises on hoardings, in the Press, on television and sells its wares through retail outlets as well as by mail. And the rest of the world is learning rapidly, even with some enthusiasm, to use direct mail – not in the old way, as an all-purpose, or exclusive, device, but as one limb in a total integrated marketing strategy, deriving strength from, and contributing to, other forms of marketing activity.

So, what has caused this change, and is it likely to continue? In part, of course, it's a bandwagon effect, but that begs the real question – what started the bandwagon rolling in the first place? The largest single factor would seem to be the growing fragmentation of the consumer market, which makes it necessary for marketeers to target their efforts ever more precisely. Improved targeting has rather limited scope in the traditional media; nor has direct mail, with its mass marketing approach, always been as outstanding in this regard as its public apologists would like us to think. But direct mail does contain within itself the *possibility* of close targeting, and it is significant that as the roll-call of its users grows, so the development of more highly selective tools gathers pace. This can be seen in the growing use of demographics, and the collection of lifestyle data – as well as the development of database techniques (all of which we will be considering later in this book).

A second factor of major importance has been the year-by-year change in relative cost-performance of the different media. In 1991/2 the average cost of postage per piece of direct mail was 15.5p – compared with 12.6p in 1981/2: an increase of 23 per cent, which is far below the rate of inflation for the period. Unfortunately there is no comparable set of figures for the average cost of a minute of air-time, or a column-inch in the Press, but no one could dispute that if such figures were available, they would show a much steeper increase. The Royal Mail has done much in the last ten years to encourage direct mail growth, but its most important contribution by far has been to keep price increases to a minimum.

A further factor has been the explosion in financial services in the mid-80s, symbolised by the Big Bang in the City of London in 1986. During this period powerful financial institutions, with ample resources, found themselves quite suddenly faced with having to market an immensely widened range of services – and with a ready-made market for those services in the shape of lists of existing customers for their traditional range.

Direct mail is not immune to recession, as events of the early 1990s have confirmed. But the industry does stand up to recession better than most – and certainly better than most advertising media. This is because – as we shall see in Chapter 1 – direct mail can be judged by results; managers in a recession become ever more suspicious of all forms of expenditure whose cost-effectiveness cannot be clearly and unambiguously justified – and accordingly a greater proportion of advertising expenditure tends, at such times, to be diverted into media, such as direct mail, where the results can be measured. These gains, once made, are rarely lost with the return of better times: seeing the results of one's marketing effort is a drug which, once experienced, few marketing managers are eager to abandon.

And finally one must refer to the general perception of the direct mail industry – both by those who are daily exposed to its blandishments, and by those who are considering using it for the first time. Overall there can be no doubt that this image is improving – from a very low base, be it said. The improvement is in part due to the influx of new users, many of them well-known and respected names in the market-place; in part it is due to the efforts made by the industry itself to clean up its act. The work of the Mailing Preference Service, and the Direct Mail Services Standards Board, have contributed to this improved perception.

This book is addressed, as its title suggests, to marketing staff, regardless of the particular marketing discipline in which they may have been raised. And to those marketing staff, especially, who have learned, or recognised, or sensed, that to run a marketing department in the 1990s without reference to direct mail is rather like trying to walk on one leg: it can be done, but at some cost in efficiency of locomotion. We do not aim to instruct the reader in how to become a direct mail expert, or in how to build a database for himself. There is nothing here on how to write sales letters, or other forms of copy, nor on sampling theory or production methods, or legal obligations. Nor do we deal with the technical distinctions between hierarchical, network, and relational databases. For those who want, or need, to get involved in such matters there is a sufficiency of books already; some are listed in the Bibliography.

Rather we seek first to suggest what it is that the newcomer to these techniques might look for by way of assistance to his existing marketing effort. And having discussed what is on offer, we then discuss how best to obtain it – using in the first instance the services of others. Using direct mail, or running a database, can be an activity for an expert – and a very fascinating one too. But it needn't be. There is, within the direct marketing industry, every kind of service house offering the advertiser every kind of service, at different levels of cost and expertise. To use such service houses to best advantage requires some knowledge, and the exercise of some management skills. That is what this book seeks to provide – a basic collection of do's and don'ts for those who employ direct marketing agencies or computer bureaux, and a guide through the jungle of service houses to enable them to exercise intelligent choice in determining which are likely to be best, or least, able to meet particular needs.

Above all, this aims to be a practical book. At the beginning of the book, you will find two quotations. Each, I suppose, contains a germ of truth. But I am in no doubt about where my sympathies lie. Practice *can* exist without theory – the outcome of a continuing process of trial and error, and re-trial, and ultimate success; theory without practice, whatever its intellectual fascination, is a dead end. That is not to say that theory, in direct marketing or elsewhere, is worthless. Far from it: this book will have plenty of theories to advance, in the hope that in this way readers can shorten the process of trial and reduce the number of errors. But the theories themselves, in this field at least, are no more than a distillation of the countless trials, and only slightly smaller number of errors, made by past practising marketers.

Our first chapter, then, deals with direct mail, and our second and third with database, while four to seven might be held relevant to a discussion of either. The remainder of the book deals with services which a user in either field may require, and how to find and utilise them to best advantage.

1

Direct Mail in an Integrated Marketing Strategy

Direct mail (the sending of business communications to individual persons through the post) is one medium of direct marketing. Direct marketing is itself a specialised branch of Marketing. So let's start there: what is Marketing?

Here is one definition, suggested by the Institute of Marketing:

> Marketing is the management function which organises and directs all those business activities involved in assessing and converting customer purchasing power into effective demand for a specific product or service, and in moving the product or service to the final consumer or user so as to achieve the profit target or other objectives set by the company.

Now shut your eyes, and see whether you can repeat that without peeping. Alternatively, are you any the wiser? If we must have definitions, I prefer something more concise:

> The marketing concept says that a firm should focus all its efforts on satisfying its customers at a profit. (McCarthy & Jerome, *Basic Marketing: A Managerial Approach*)

Personally, I don't much like definitions of this kind: even the shorter ones are difficult to remember, and don't actually tell us very much. After all, 'satisfying customers at a profit' could be a definition of business just as well as of marketing. It seems to me more useful to enquire not what marketing *is*, but what it *does*. Let's try a diagrammatic representation of the marketing activity:

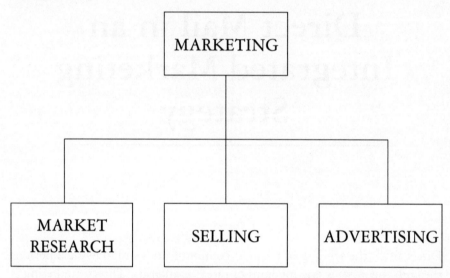

Advertising, selling, and market research are the three classic *functions* of marketing. We will be talking about how direct marketing conducts all these functions. However, I have deliberately put *selling* in the middle of our diagram, because selling is the ultimate objective towards which the other functions, of advertising and market research, are directed. And let us never forget it: the information obtained from market research, or the consumer awareness created by advertising, are ultimately worthless (indeed, they represent nothing other than a cost) unless they contribute towards profitable sales.

What, then, about a definition of direct marketing? Here is one:

> Direct marketing is an interactive system of marketing which uses one or more advertising medium to effect a measurable response and/or transaction at any location. (Roberts & Berger, Direct Marketing Management)

I don't have any quarrel with this, but I don't feel that it's very helpful. Try asking, again, what it is that direct marketing *does* – or, if you like, what tangible activities it comprises. And if we can put that in the form of a diagram again, here is a sort of family tree of the activities which are commonly regarded as forming the parts of what we mean by direct marketing.

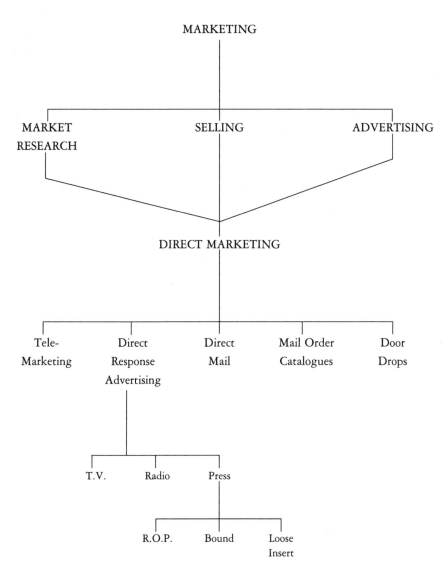

Or, to put it another way, we can regard these activities (of direct response advertising, direct mail, etc) as the *media* through one or more of which direct marketing (whether as an advertising, a market research, or a selling function) is conducted.

Since the functions performed by direct mail, and the media used by it, are the same as those performed and used by any other form of marketing, what is it that sets direct marketing apart – that makes it a special branch of marketing requiring study on its own account? Here another look at our written definition may help. This tells us three things:

i)   direct marketing communications aim at obtaining a *response*;
ii)   the results of direct marketing (or rather, *some* of the results) are *measurable*;
iii) direct marketing is *interactive*.

Let us take these points one at a time. Consider a typical direct marketing campaign:

a) *Response.* A manufacturer places an advertisement for a new product in a magazine, inviting readers to cut out and return a coupon asking for further details. Those readers who return the coupon are *responders*.

b) *Measurement.* Since the number of people responding can be counted, the response is measurable. Moreover, the response can be measured either against the readership of the magazine (giving a response rate per thousand readers) or against the cost of the advertisement (giving a cost per response obtained). However, pause at this point to note that measurable response is only *part* of the consequence of an advertisement. The primary purpose of a normal (ie non-direct) advertisement is to create awareness, build an image, arouse desire, or some such. And, of course, a direct advertisement is as capable of doing this as any other advertisement. We will return to this point a little later.

c) *Interaction.* Having obtained a response to his advertisement, the manufacturer sends back the details requested, soliciting an order. A proportion of the consumers reached in this way will respond again, this time with orders. Again, these responses will be counted, and can be measured against the number of original responses, giving a ratio normally referred to as the conversion rate – the proportion of enquiries converted into orders. Or, we can relate orders to advertisement cost, plus the cost of sending out further details, to obtain a cost per order. The manufacturer will then fulfil the order, with an invoice, and the consumer should respond with a payment. This series of *interactions* leaves us, at the end of the campaign, with a precise measurement of how effective the original advertisement has been in producing profitable orders. And, finally, the manufacturer will place the customer's name and address on his database, with a view to initiating further two-way communications with him at some future date.

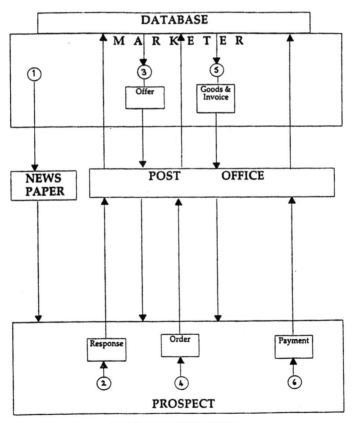

**DIRECT MARKETING
INTERACTION**

Now, it is true that direct marketing is not unique in looking for a measurable response as part of an interactive process. This is certainly the case with all types of market research, and indeed one could say it is true of, for example, retail selling also. But it is the only form of marketing that is about measurable response from the very *beginning* of the marketing process to its end.

In this chapter we will consider the use of one form of direct marketing – the direct mail medium – in advertising, in selling, and in market research. In each of these contexts we will consider how the medium can be used to reinforce other parallel efforts. Then, finally, we will look at an outline of the planning process for a direct mail campaign.

1. ADVERTISING

The early pioneers of direct mail, who built a living on the medium, thought of it as a means of selling products for distribution through the mail. The fact that it also performed an advertising function at the same time was, to them, incidental, irrelevant, and even unrecognised. The point can be illustrated by an interesting (and true) story. As late as the early 1960s, Reader's Digest – till then basically a magazine publishing house – started to produce hardback non-fiction titles for sale by direct mail. These sold well, and pretty soon some bright young man thought it would be a good idea to sell a few copies through the bookshops also. The real object of this exercise was not directly to maximise the sale of books, but to enable the Digest, by pricing books for retail sale at a higher level than direct mail copies, to claim a 'saving' for its direct mail purchasers.

The outcome was a considerable surprise: Digest books sold through bookshops, despite the higher price, like hot cakes, in numbers that greatly outstripped the expectations not only of Digest staff – amateurs in the retail business – but of Hodder and Stoughton, the experienced traditional publishers who had undertaken trade distribution of the titles. Book after book, and year after year the story went on. At last the penny dropped. When the Digest promoted a book by direct mail, an elaborate promotion shot went through anything from one to two million letterboxes. Orders would be received from a large number (but still quite a small percentage) of those promoted. The company made a profit, and was well satisfied. But what of the great majority of promotees who had not replied? Nobody thought, or much cared, about them. Yet they had been exposed, in large numbers, to *an advertisement*. Much more directly exposed, indeed, than if they had merely been buyers of a newspaper in which an advertisement had appeared. And those of them that walked into a bookshop a week, or a month, later, looking, say, for a cookery book, might see on the shelf a book, perhaps in the cookery section, somewhat familiar in appearance. That was the one they would look at first … and probably buy.

What was being seen in this unexpected way was the power of advertising to condition, and help to persuade. And it was being seen by a company which, at least until then, and indeed for some years afterwards, maintained a decidedly ambivalent attitude to 'mere' advertising, being happy to sell space in its magazine to others, but highly dubious of the efficacy of the activity for its own purposes. (Of course, the effect was heightened by the fact that very few books then, or now, are advertised to the buying public to any notable extent at all. How publishers, let alone booksellers, expect to make a living at their peculiar trade is altogether beyond me.)

Those for whom advertising is a way of life – in particular, the major advertising agencies – have been, until very recent times, at least equally blind. Some still are. How can a major motor car manufacturer, to take an example, continue to pour money into expensive, and largely undirected, advertisements on television and in the colour supplements, while failing to correspond on an individual and personal level with his own *known* customers – all of whom must be expected, at some point, to require replacements for their cars? It is, I suppose, only to be expected that the first two car companies to see the light should have been overseas manufacturers whose UK operations are not burdened by British management on a large scale – Volvo and Toyota.

Yet it is the advertising agencies, rather than the advertiser, with whom the blame for years of lost opportunities must first lie. The reasons for this state of affairs are various, and worth pondering:

a)   Direct mail isn't 'glamorous'. Trendy young account executives, copywriters, visualisers, are unlikely to feel that their favoured lifestyle, which revolves round TV studios, models, fashionable photographers and exotic locations, is enhanced by anything so square and everyday as direct mail. So, from top to bottom of every advertising agency there is a hard core of those who don't want to know about anything that is outside the main stream of their preferred experience.

b) Worse still, direct mail is – or is held to be – hard work. Knowledge is required, if a client is to be properly advised in the medium, of a kind that main-line agency personnel don't have. And there is still little facility, inside or outside the agencies, for teaching the art, or science, of direct mail to those that do want to find out.*

c) More: when one masterminds a TV and/or press campaign for a client there is normally one, and only one, crunch point – does the client like it? In direct mail there is – or should be if the medium is properly used – another and much more objective test: what is the measurable response, and what has it cost to get that response? There is, of course, good advertising to be seen on television, on poster sites, and in the Press. Some of it even produces some quantifiable results, from which it can, by and large, be adjudged a success. There is also a great deal of very poor advertising, which is almost certainly a waste, partial or total, of the advertiser's money. But so long as the client is satisfied, and the agency gets its commission, who knows, or cares? Direct mail, by contrast, has this unpleasant knack of identifying winners and losers; nobody who doesn't have to is anxious to put their head on the chopping block every time a mailing goes out.

d) Finally, direct mail doesn't fit conveniently into the agency's financial scheme. An agency handling a client's press campaign gets his reward from the 15 per cent commission allowed by the medium on the cost of space booked. In direct mail the medium 'owner' is, if you will, the Royal Mail. And although the Royal Mail has changed a great deal in the last 15 years, and offers a whole range of rebates, discounts, special

---

* The Direct Marketing Centre, 21 Eden Walk, Kingston upon Thames is the industry's first attempt (set up in 1987) to create a broad educational facility. It has done a first-class job in creating learning opportunities for people already working in direct marketing. It has been less successful, so far, in introducing direct marketing concepts into general marketing, or business, courses. It is this integration that is now badly needed: direct marketers have a lot to teach, and to learn from, their general marketing colleagues.

terms and services to encourage use of the post, all of these are available, not to the agency (to whom the Royal Mail is not, or not yet, in the business of offering a commission) but to the ultimate advertiser.

So, if the client is knowledgeable enough, and brave enough, to insist on having direct mail included in his schedule, the creative cost must either be carried by the agency as an unwanted overhead, or, contrary to practice with other media, a basis must be found for charging a fee to the client.

Change is coming, with all the heady, exciting speed of a glacier rushing downhill to the sea – but also with some of its inevitability. The most hoity-toity of agencies can't forever go on ignoring the fastest growing source of advertising in the business. So there are now not only a few agencies that specialise in direct mail, and that operate (without the world coming to an end) on a fee basis; there are also direct marketing arms, or subsidiaries, of most of the main-line agencies, created in the last few years in an attempt to jump, late in the day, on the direct mail bandwagon before it accelerates out of sight.

So far, these direct marketing subsidiaries are still sitting not only 'below the line' but also well below the salt, as far as the parent agency personnel are concerned, but this may not last. The whole idea of having a direct marketing subsidiary is itself a fairly pathetic attempt to solve the problem caused by the ignorance of most agency personnel of an important branch of their trade. Pathetic, because it attempts to answer yesterday's problem of how to provide a service for those who wish to advertise by direct mail, without addressing today's problem – which is how to provide an *integrated* multi-media advertising service to clients who want to co-ordinate their activity across all forms of outlet. Any advertiser looking for a new agency today would do well to seek out an agency that can offer, within a single organisation structure, skills across the board. There are not too many of them about, and they are not today's big names either. Their turn will come.

So, what are the advertising functions that this medium, ignored for so long by the main-line agencies, can be expected to perform for the advertiser? Clearly, the primary function of any advertisement is to deliver a message from the advertiser to those he wishes to address. This function we must consider in two parts. First, as to conveying a message, it is plain that direct mail is well-equipped – its centre-piece being that oldest of all devices for the purpose, namely a letter. Secondly, there is the question of the audience to be addressed – what the direct mail industry has traditionally referred to as the list. Here direct mail has a potential advantage over all other media. There is no way, using newspaper, television, radio, poster advertising, in which the advertiser can deliver a message to all the people and only the people that he wishes to reach – achieving maximum impact and optimum economy at one and the same time. To be honest, there are not that many direct mail campaigns that come close to this ideal either – but the possibility is there. An advertiser, or an agency working on his behalf, may well be able to compile a list of precisely those people, and no-one else, likely to be interested in this product or service. No newspaper or collection of newspapers can offer such a profile. And if they could, a high proportion of those 'reached' in this way would never see the advertisement.

As we shall see later on, it is in this whole area of list compilation that we move from the first subject matter of this book – direct mail – to its second – database. The traditional direct mail list is a fairly static entity, consisting of names and addresses and a minimal quantity of information about the source of the said names. A database is a dynamic affair, where the information stored changes continually; it includes information about the on-going behaviour of people, and it enables its owner to keep day-by-day track of changes in his market-place. Database techniques bring closer to reality the dream of being able to achieve perfect targeting for one's advertising message.

Next, an advertisement, having delivered a message, must persuade at least a proportion of those reached. Persuade them to hold, or change, or modify, a view, or to remember something – a name, or a fact – or to act in a certain way. As a persuader, direct mail has a number of advantages; above all it is not pressed for time. The reader of a newspaper or magazine advertisement is, ten to one, trying to get to the leader page before his coffee gets cold, and glances impatiently at intervening advertisement headlines, anxious to move on. The television camera, burning hundred pound notes as the motor turns, dare not linger. Direct mail moves at a more leisurely pace. Newspaper and television advertising is, for most of its audience, an intrusion on the true purpose of the medium in which it appears – an irrelevance at best, an impertinence at worst. Direct mail advertising stands, or falls, on its own.

Finally, an advertisement, having reached the right parties, or some of them, and having persuaded a proportion to the end desired by the advertiser, must be cost-effective. Or must be believed to be so. Indeed, this last criterion really embraces the other two as well: an advertiser can, eventually, reach all his audience by dint of repeated saturation coverage in any one medium or media-mix. And he can do a marvellously persuasive job if time and/or space is no problem. But cost is likely to run riot. Direct mail doesn't avoid these problems, but it is remarkably adept at minimising them. A sharply profiled list avoids the cost of advertising to parties devoid of interest in your subject. The medium itself, by being directly addressable to individual persons by name ensures the best possible chance that the material will be seen, and read, by those to whom it is addressed – thus minimising the wasted cost of material that is never seen. The cost of each extra hundred words of persuasion, each additional illustration, is tiny: 60 gram (the basic postal weight step) is a whole lot of paper.

But most important of all is the fact that direct mail is a response-oriented medium, and because it has this facility, it is possible to measure and evaluate the effects of a direct mail campaign, as of few others. And thus to know if it was cost-effective, and at what level. Of course, any advertisement in any medium can invite response – even radio or television. But no other medium (except the telephone) makes it so easy as direct mail. So much so that we may safely lay it down that the first and cardinal sin in the use of direct mail is to send out material that does *not* demand a response.

So, a direct mail advertisement must be a verifiably cost-effective way of delivering a persuasive message to a chosen audience. And in order to do that properly, any direct mail shot must contain these elements:

a) A letter. A direct mail shot without a letter is like a car body without an engine – it will get you nowhere. It is still truly remarkable how many such shots get sent out.

b) A response medium which the addressee can return to indicate whatever type of response the advertiser is seeking – or just to indicate the effect of the promotion overall.

At a less essential level, most direct mail shots also contain:

c)   An outer envelope or wrapping. But it is possible to have an all-in-one self-mailer which dispenses with this item.

And sometimes:

d)   A leaflet, to give a more visually dramatic impact to the offer.
e)   A reply envelope, pre-addressed and pre-paid; this should only be dispensed with where the response medium is itself a reply card which can be dropped straight in the letter box, or some kind of self-mailer device.

To which can be added as many others as the imagination can devise.

Armed with these items, what types of persuasion can a direct mail advertisement seek to exert? It is common to think of direct mail in two distinct categories – business mail, which is addressed by one business house to another – or to individual persons in their business or professional capacities; consumer mail, which is addressed by a business house to individual members of the public at their private homes. It is true that in some significant respects the two types of approach are different – but not in all respects. So, for example, direct mail, whether business or consumer, can be used to:

a) **Qualify prospects**. The principle here is the same in either case. For example, a company dealing direct with consumers may wish to send a heavy, expensive catalogue to a substantial number of really good prospects – but to avoid the considerable cost of sending it to numbers of people who are not really interested. So a first direct mail shot will go to a large audience, seeking to elicit a response only from those who will be interested in buying from the catalogue. This is the kind of operation that the mail order houses – GUS, Littlewoods, Grattans – undertake in looking for 'agents'. Alternatively, a sales manager may wish to determine which business houses in a given area are worth the time of a salesman in making a call. Every year salesmens' time becomes more expensive in real terms; direct mail (whose largest single cost element is postage) has tended for some years past to become cheaper. Consequently, the use of direct mail to persuade businessmen to identify themselves as good, or less good, prospects, can turn a team of salesmen into a very much more productive and cost-effective unit. (Note, please, that it is no part of our contention that direct mail can substitute for, or replace, a sales team; the two operate quite differently, and have different strengths and weaknesses. Here, as elsewhere, the emphasis should be on the use of direct mail to complement and enhance other sales and marketing efforts, not to replace them.) And, as we shall see, the harnessing of database techniques to an integrated system, employing both salesmen and direct mail, gives an even sharper cutting edge to a company's efforts.

Again, direct mail can be used to:

b) Supply information – perhaps to a customer list (of business people or consumers) about a new product or service. This of course is the type of information the marketeer most often wants to impart. But it is worth pausing for a moment to ask what kind of information the customer most wants to receive. For example, if you bought a new Volvo last year from your local dealer, would you be more impressed by a letter from the company's sales director extolling the superior merits of this year's model, or by a polite letter from your local dealer reminding you that your car is due for servicing in two weeks' time, and offering you an appointment? (With, of course, a brochure about the new model enclosed.)

Here too it should be remembered that, even where the supply of information is the major marketing objective, direct mail should not be a one-way street; it is important to have the addressee respond, because only so can one measure the effectiveness with which information has been conveyed.

Or to:

c) Distribute samples. It should be remembered that, while a letter is a necessary part of any direct mail shot, it is not the only possible component, and that things other than words and pictures on paper can be conveyed by mail. This characteristic again sets it apart from other media.

There is a multitude of particular functions that a direct mail advertisement (considered only as an advertisement, not as a sales medium) can be called on to perform; most of them can probably be subsumed under one of these headings – the qualifying of prospects, the conveying of information, the distribution of samples. (And of these functions, the traditional advertising media can offer equivalent if different advantages in only one – the conveying of information.) Too many advertisements – regardless of the medium they use – fail because the advertiser has not begun by asking himself two vital questions: what, precisely, does he wish to accomplish with this advertisement, and what kind of message is his intended audience likely to listen to. It is only when these questions have been answered that it becomes relevant to ask which particular medium – or mix of media – is best qualified to achieve the stated objective.

2. SELLING

The use of mixed media becomes an even more interesting possibility when the objective is not simply to advertise a product or service, but to sell it. The combined use of television and direct mail contains some interesting examples: a well-known television personality will be used to advise viewers that they may be the lucky recipients, next day by post, of an exciting new offer, which they should be sure to read and deal with straight away. This approach combines the strengths of the two media instructively: the TV spot creates interest and a point of recognition for those who receive the mailing (or a proportion of them, since not all will have seen the TV advertisement). The announcer, if well chosen, lends the reassurance of his familiar personality to the necessarily impersonal mailshot.

It is a curious fact that consumers appear to regard television as a more credible and trustworthy source of advertising information than other media, even when the same information is being conveyed by each. This has, perhaps, something to do with the use in television of people with faces and voices, where the print media have only silent pictures, and the written word. It is also, sadly, the case that direct mail is widely regarded as the least trustworthy of the media; the effect of reinforcement by television is therefore to lend it a greater credibility than it would otherwise achieve. Then again, television has its weaknesses:

a) time is short – complex messages can't be conveyed;
b) television is not a response-oriented medium – viewers are not sitting in large numbers with pencils poised ready to jot down reply addresses;

c)   the message, once delivered, is retained only as a memory in the viewer's mind, not as a physical document that can be referred to again.

Direct mail's strengths lie in just those areas: the medium can convey whatever complexity of message the advertiser desires, with minimum impact on cost; response facilities can be built in; the message can be easily retained and re-examined any number of times.

Because television is a largely indiscriminate medium, addressing mass audiences, its use to bolster a direct mail sales campaign will only appeal normally to a large organisation with a mass market. Which is not to say that direct mail is exclusively, or even primarily, a medium for that kind of situation. Indeed it can be a valuable partner in small local sales activities as well as in large national ones.

Take by way of example a marketing operation selling by traditional retail methods – through one corner shop, or a national multiple chain, it doesn't matter. The retail trade has traditionally regarded direct mail (and direct response, or off-the-page, advertising) in those areas (such as book-selling) where it is aware of its existence, as the enemy, competing – by methods frequently categorised as 'unfair' – for a share of a fixed-size cake. Personally I have always regarded this as an unattractive, and usually erroneous, view of almost any market: the more people are persuaded, by whatever means, to buy books (or shoes, or computers, or jam doughnuts) the larger the market for books (or shoes, or computers, or jam doughnuts) will become, to the benefit of *all* those selling these things. (I am reminded of the 1951 estimate by Remington Rand that the world-wide market for general-purpose digital computers was 27.) The experience, quoted above, of Reader's Digest discovering, albeit accidentally, that direct mail sales effort enhanced the sale of its books in bookshops, is striking evidence of this simple truth. But if direct mail and retail can reinforce each other by accident, they can achieve a great deal more when integration is planned and deliberate. Again, the possibilities for integration can best be seen by examining some of the principal strengths and weaknesses of each medium, and considering how they can best complement each other:

a)   The weakness of the retail trade is that it is, in relation to its customers, an essentially *passive* medium. That is to say, the *customer* decides to 'go shopping'; he makes the trip to the High Street, surveys the stores, decides which one to enter, and views selectively the goods on display. (Nowadays he probably has to pick them off the shelf and carry them to a check-out counter as well.)

b) Direct mail, by contrast, is an *active* medium: the *seller* determines which prospects to approach, when, and in what numbers, in their own homes or offices. He determines which product(s) to offer to whom, and which aspects of those products to highlight.

c) As against this, direct mail has two major weaknesses. First, the customer buying by mail must make up his mind to order, and sometimes pay, in whole or in part, before seeing the goods. In some cases this doesn't greatly matter – for example, where the product is fairly low priced, so that 'shopping around' for a bargain, or a slightly superior brand, is not a high priority for the consumer. The same may be true where the product is in some respect demonstrably unique: books, for example, or records, are not (except, perhaps, Mills and Boon) interchangeable one with another. For that matter, uniqueness may lie in a very clear price advantage, as in the case of off-the-page offers of luggage, cutlery, cooking utensils. But in the case of high-priced consumer durables, the consumer's desire to see, touch, try out before making a commitment is likely to be paramount. It is to answer that desire that direct mail so often offers goods 'on approval' or alternatively with money-back guarantees. But the consumer knows as well as the seller that to order on approval is more than half way to buying, and may remain reluctant.

Second, direct mail is widely distrusted – much less so than ten years ago, but still significantly. This is in part because direct mail transactions do not take place face-to-face between two people, but impersonally. This makes it difficult to cater for unique individual circumstances, to answer particular questions, to provide reassurance, and so on.

d) The retail trade is well placed to overcome these problems. It offers premises where samples of the goods on offer – and frequently of other similar, competing goods – can be seen and evaluated. And it provides staff who, at least in theory, are equipped to answer questions, deal with customers' problems, and provide a human context for the sales transaction.

So, how can these strengths and weaknesses be combined to produce a selling effort that makes the most of both worlds? One answer is to use direct mail as the initial approach to potential customers, with retail premises as the back-up where the sale is consummated. On this basis, a direct mail shot can be used to tell people of the existence of the shop (in particular where new premises are being opened) and its range of products, to advise them of a particular product, or a special offer, or to advertise a sales promotion scheme run by the shop. In this context the direct mail shot itself is not selling; it is being used as an advertising medium, supplying information – but with a very specific purpose directly related to the selling function. It is the purpose of such a direct mail piece to attract people to the shop concerned, at a time chosen by the seller, and in pursuit of objectives suggested by the seller. Used in this way, direct mail becomes an arm by which the retailer reaches out to his public, makes, and retains, contact with them. Direct mail becomes the retailer's second, mobile, shop window, with a potential audience many times larger, and more attentive, than his real window. (Argos is one example of a mixed-media sales operation distinct from the conventional retail pattern.)

But, although the use of direct mail in ways of this kind is growing, it takes a while to wean people to new ways. Much more common than this form of integrated marketing (which is still the wave of the future) is the use of a direct mail offer as a straightforward selling medium. And in this connection the question one most often meets from marketeers who have not used direct mail before is: how do I determine whether my product is suitable for sale by direct mail – what are the characteristics of a direct mail product?

2.1 Selling Consumables

It is astonishing, in all that has been written on direct mail and how to do it, in all the seminars and workshops that are held every year, that little or no attention has been devoted to this question. Perhaps this is because it doesn't seem like an easy one to answer: after all, London Bridge was, I am assured, sold by direct mail (although no doubt some form of conveyance other than the postal service was used for its actual delivery), so what does that exclude? Nevertheless, if we leave out extreme, or one-off, examples of this kind, it is possible, with a little thought, to lay down some useful rules of thumb. Like any other rules in business, they are valid only until someone finds a sensible way of circumventing them.

By far the most desirable characteristic of any product from the seller's point of view – and regardless of the medium through which it is to be sold – is that it should be, in some sense, consumable. Prime examples of consumable goods traded through the mail are those offered by the mail order catalogue houses (Littlewoods, Freemans, JD Williams, GUS) being clothing, soft furnishings, and the like. Even more quickly consumable is a periodical, and although, in contrast to the USA, the UK sells the bulk of its periodical journals from news-stands, there are still some notable exponents among them of direct mail expertise (Reader's Digest, Consumers' Association, Automobile Association).

Books are one of the staples of the direct mail industry, as, to a lesser extent, are records. Books are an interesting case: their *contents* may be said to be consumable: reference books date, and have to be replaced, while most other books are read not more than once by any one person. Moreover, the medium-term consequence of buying, and reading, a book is probably to stimulate the appetite for books rather than to satisfy it. But the artifact itself tends not to be consumable: books, unlike magazines, are not thrown away, but gradually collect on shelves.

2.2 Selling Collectables

For the key fact about books is that, while they are in one aspect consumable, they are in another aspect collectable – and if your direct mail product cannot have the one characteristic, then it is a useful second best if it has the other. After all, the greatest cost in any form of marketing lies in locating your customers. What better then, having located them, than to have them spend the rest of their lives re-ordering the same consumable product or, alternatively, slightly different, collectable versions of the same product.

The market in collectables is a large one. The Royal Mail has carved out a lucrative slice with its commemorative stamps. This slice is worth some attention, because it illustrates a major dilemma inherent in this kind of market. A collectable owes some of its fascination for the collector to its scarcity – or better still its uniqueness. (In this sense London Bridge fits into our pattern after all: it was bought as a unique collectable.) Tied to this also is the expectation of a rising real value, which in turn is a result of demand exceeding supply – ie effective scarcity. The producer of collectables, then, who saturates his market is undermining his own future position since, once he has met total demand there can be little prospect of values rising. In the case of the philatelic market, this is so large, and so international, that the number of stamps of a given issue sold by the Royal Mail is not a serious problem – though the period of issue is still restricted. What does cause concern is how many new issues a given postal administration puts out in a year. The philatelic world keeps a close watch on this, and postal administrations which become greedy quickly find themselves black-listed.

Producers of other collectables do not usually have this kind of externally imposed discipline, and many of them find the exercise of self-discipline rather demanding. So we live in a world, as it sometimes seems, rapidly silting up with commemorative medals, royal wedding mugs, silver ingots engraved with vintage cars, and such-like bric-a-brac. The idea being, as with a book club, to transform a single transaction for the sale of one product into a continuing relationship where the once-captured goose goes on laying golden eggs for ever and ever.

One form of added incentive deployed by direct marketers in the collectable field is the concept of the 'limited edition'. This description is intended to stimulate the prospect's acquisitive instincts by implying that the product concerned will quickly gain scarcity value. The British Code of Advertising Practice – that arbiter of what claims are, and are not, acceptable in advertising copy – has attempted to curb the more blatant excesses of the 'limited edition' school by insisting that the term must be accompanied by some form of qualification. The results to date have not always been enlightening – as one can see in the case of the 'collectable' plates, whose editions are 'limited' to, for example, '100 firing days' – whatever that may be thought to mean.

In sum then, it is highly desirable to have a product that is consumable, the craving for which is renewed automatically at regular intervals. Failing that, find something that is collectable; if it can also be fairly represented as likely to gain in value, that is a bonus. Not an easy recipe. But failure to observe it means a lot of hard work, and perhaps ultimate failure. Direct marketing in the seventies – particularly through the burgeoning colour supplements – took off into a whole new realm of watches, luggage, clocks, radios, clock-radios, cassette-radios, cassette-clock-radios ... Items neither consumable nor, normally, collectable. Many of these were very good value for money. Indeed the whole phenomenon (led in particular by one firm, Scotcade) did much to redeem the previously rather sleazy image of direct marketing. And in doing so sowed the seeds of its own destruction: if you sell Mrs Jones a six-piece suite of luggage, then the better it is, and the more she likes it, the less likely you are to sell her a second one. So you will have to find something else for encores. And then something else. And then ...

2.3 Selling One-Offs

What then can we say about 'one-off' items for sale by direct mail? Other than urging that you have an inexhaustible fund of new ideas? Well, there are some simple points of economics with which to start. First, do not pay too much attention to all that direct mail propaganda about how goods sold direct to the public are better value for money because they cut out the middle man. The economics of direct selling are different from those of retail selling – and not necessarily more favourable at all. What they do demand is a very healthy mark-up – something like three times. That is, if you have a product you are buying in, or manufacturing, for £5, you are going to have to sell it for not significantly less than £15. (As the absolute sum of money increases, the required percentage mark-up will lessen somewhat – say to $2^1/_2$ times.) Consider an illustration:

> Product x is bought in at £5, and offered to an audience of 100,000 people by direct mail at £15. The resultant response rate, in terms of orders, is 5%. Then:
>
> | | £ |
> |---|---|
> | Cost of 100,000 pieces @ £400/thousand | 40,000 |
> | Cost of 5,000 products @ £5 | 25,000 |

Reply postage on 5,000 orders @ 18p	900
Handling 5,000 orders @, say, 50p	2,500
Despatching 5,000 products @ 75p	3,750
	72,150
Revenue from 5,000 orders	75,000
Contribution to overheads and profit	2,850

Bearing in mind that this calculation makes no allowance for bad debts, returned products, etc, this is clearly not a recipe for getting rich quickly. If the prospect list is very good, and pulls 10% rather than 5%, things are, of course, better. Promotion cost doesn't change; other costs double, making a total cost of £104,300. Revenue doubles to £150,000, leaving a more sensible contribution of £45,700. But not that many direct mail promotions can be confident of pulling a response of 10% from a list of any size.

Again, promotion material need not cost £400/thousand. But with postage alone varying from £122 to £180 per thousand (depending on the rate of discount available) it isn't easy to get large reductions without reducing the impact of the promotion, and hence the response rate.

What we can deduce from examples of this kind is that, over and above the requirement for a three times mark-up, it is unlikely that a one-off product can be profitably sold by direct mail at a price significantly less than £20. (Unless, of course, you are prepared to pay a premium to build a list – or a database – of customers for future products.)

The ideal direct mail product, selling at £20 or more, and with a three times mark-up, will also be a unique product, or have important unique features, or be part of a unique proposition. If this is not so – if the product is simply a slightly different version competing with many others of essentially like kind – then the prospect will be less likely to buy it sight unseen. The seller, in fact, must produce a compelling reason why the prospect should do something so unnatural as to order an item he hasn't seen – and this can most easily be done by convincing him that only by doing so can he obtain such-and-such a unique benefit.

2.4 Distribution

Finally, consideration must be given to how the product, once sold, is to be conveyed to the purchaser. Distribution is an area where retail stands at a distinct advantage to direct mail. The manufacturer or wholesaler who requires to distribute in bulk to a limited number of retail outlets has an altogether more manageable problem than the direct mail seller, who must deliver single items to single addresses anywhere in the country. Retail shops that will deliver to consumers' homes are nowadays a rarity: such service is confined to bulky (and expensive) items. For the most part, the retail trade has solved its distribution problem by ignoring it; the customer is now himself, aided by his private motor car, the shopkeeper's distribution agent. Direct mail has no such assistance. Most practitioners, already heavily involved with the postal service for the distribution of promotion material, turn naturally in the same direction for product distribution. This means that thought has to be given, from the inception of the campaign, to postal distribution costs, security of packaging, and such-like matters. Clearly a direct mail product will benefit by having a low weight-to-price ratio; at the extreme end of the spectrum items which are too bulky for transmission by post carry a built-in disadvantage, unless a suitable national distributor can be found.

3. MARKET RESEARCH

This is the function in which direct mail differs most radically from other marketing media. Every marketing person preparing to launch a new product, or contemplating an attack, with an established product, on a new market, faces essentially the same problem: how does he determine the size of demand for the product? Worse still, since demand is presumably a variable affected by other factors, such as price, credit terms, guarantee, etc, how does he fix upon the optimum combination of variables that will produce the greatest profit?

The truth probably is that very few products or services are in fact sold on anything like optimal (from the seller's point of view) terms. If the product is being sold through traditional retail outlets, there are really three avenues to explore in trying to fix on the best set of terms for an offer. These are:

a) Discover what the competition is doing, and then decide whether to:
   i) undercut them, and risk a messy price war; or
   ii) stress the improved features of one's own product;
b) Establish a unit cost for whatever number of products
   i) the sales manager says he can sell over a given period; or
   ii) the warehouse has space for and add a percentage to cover selling costs, overheads, perhaps (if you think the market can stand it) profit.
c) Commission a market research survey.

This last option has the advantage of getting the problem off the marketing manager's back for a few weeks, and into the hands of 'experts' who can be relied upon to produce an impressive-looking report for the Board, suitably dressed up in Adspeak, and who can conveniently be blamed if anything goes wrong afterwards.

By contrast, market research in a direct mail context is not a separate area of endeavour employing different techniques from those familiar to the marketing department. The direct mail marketing manager doesn't rely on what people say they will do in a set of interviews, or on learned analyses of gaps in the market and disquisitions on 'positioning'. Market research in direct mail consists in actually selling your product to a sample of your intended audience in order to see how many takers there are on a given set of terms – or to several samples, varying the terms for each. And the conclusions derived from this are based upon what real people actually do in real circumstances – not on what they say they will, or might, do in quite different circumstances. Direct mail practitioners, in fact, don't talk about market research at all, in the sense of a separate set of techniques for assessing demand. They do talk, all the time, about testing – trying out this or that variation of price, premium, copy, colour, on sample segments of the market, measuring the response, and drawing conclusions.

That testing has its expertise is undeniable. But it is a mathematical, or statistical expertise, based upon actual occurrences in the real world. It will tell you:

If, out of a representative sample of your audience, x% behave in a given way, then you can be 95 per cent confident that, in identical circumstances, x, plus or minus y, % of your total audience will behave in the same way.

This still begs a few questions. What does 95 per cent confidence mean? It means that the mathematics holds good 95 times out of every 100. Oh yes? And what about the other five times? Well, they're there to remind you that there is no such thing as certainty about a future event, and to keep you on your toes. And what does 'identical circumstances' mean: after all, if I do a test mailing now and then mail my total audience in a month's time, the one thing I do know for certain is that the external circumstances won't be identical. Very true.

Nevertheless, the insights given by testing in a real market, instead of asking hypothetical questions, are real and worthwhile. This is not the place in which to describe the techniques of testing: the interested reader can find a full description for himself elsewhere.* Suffice it to say that, whereas conventional market research techniques enable the marketeer at best to make a slightly more educated guess at the answers to his questions, direct mail testing enables the direct mail marketer to calculate. The calculations are not infallible, and do not guarantee success every time. But those that use them will come out on the right side over a period.

Testing, of course, is not only about sounding out the market for a new product. One of the major differences between direct mail and the other marketing media is that in other media each sale tends to be a one-off event; in direct marketing each sale – indeed each promotion – creates a packet of information about the prospect, which is fed back to the promoter's records for future use. (It is this feed back that marks the distinction between a mere passive list of prospects and a dynamic database, as we shall see later.) Therefore, the object of each promotion sent out should be to generate as much information as possible, subject, of course, to cost constraints. When we research the market for a new product, we are testing a particular product/offer against break-even – will it be profitable or not. When we do a mailing for an established product, we should be taking the opportunity to ask further questions – by comparative testing of one piece of copy against another, or of an attractive premium versus a price

---

* Eg in a Chapter by the present author entitled 'Testing and Measurement' in the *Direct Mail Handbook*, published for the Royal Mail by Exley, 1984.

reduction. Testing is a continuous process of refining the terms of one's approach to the public by observing results and trying new methods.

There are people around who find this an unnecessarily energetic approach: for them the object of testing is to find the winning formula, which they will then stick to come hell or high water. This is inadvisable. The universal law of entropy – which predicts that in time everything runs down – applies to direct mail as well as to astrophysics. Lists decay, response rates deteriorate. To combat this inexorable trend we must be continually looking for new approaches – and testing is the tool by which we can find a new formula before the old one becomes too tired to work.

4. PLANNING FOR CREATIVE DIRECT MAIL

4.1 The Product, the Market and the Media

Nobody, but nobody, can teach creativity. (I know that a number of universities and colleges run courses in 'creative writing'; I have always regarded these as a rather elaborate kind of joke that is beyond my understanding.) After all, the essence of creativity is to produce something that no one has thought of, in quite that way, before. Since no one has thought of it, clearly no one can teach it. So I don't aim to teach creativity. I do aim to indicate what place creativity should have in the production of good direct marketing material, and how to organise the planning process so as to give it proper scope.

Here, then, is an outline of the marketing planning process as applied to direct mail in particular:

a) Determine overall marketing objectives.
b) Devise a strategy for the use of advertising, selling, and market research resources to meet these objectives, with consideration of all available media.
c) Determine the functions required of each chosen medium in relation to this strategy, taking into account the nature of the product/service being promoted, the audience to be addressed, and the relative strengths and weaknesses of the medium in these circumstances.

d) Map out a series of activities through which the chosen media can carry out these functions.

e) Decide on the precise objective of each proposed activity.

f) Analyse the economics of each activity and create a budget for it.

g) Select the appropriate audience for each activity.

h) Produce the necessary material, including appropriate response media, for each activity, and implement.

i) Handle response in line with undertakings in promotion.

j) Monitor response and analyse the actual economics of each mailing; compare with budget, and use these findings to modify, if necessary, further parts of the programme.

k) Ensure that a full record is kept of individual responses, thus modifying the nature of the potential audience for further mailings – or indeed other marketing activities.

These processes can be illustrated diagramatically, as opposite. From this illustration it can be seen that the whole process contains two feedback mechanisms – a vital aspect of all direct marketing activity. The first of these is the feedback of an economic assessment of the degree of success or failure achieved by each mailing. The second is the feedback of individual data about each respondent – and, by implication, about each non-respondent. It is this second factor which makes possible the construction of a dynamic marketing database – a subject that we will be addressing in the next chapter.

It is at the strategic planning stage that we must sort out the relationships between product, market and media. For example, a £5,000 laser printer is likely to find its best market in a business environment, whereas a £500 ink-jet printer is likely to have a very large consumer market. A new model washing machine will sell to consumers – but direct mail is an unlikely medium through which to sell it (although a possible advertising medium for use by a range of stores stocking it). You would be unlikely to sell a new model car off the page, but you might feature it in press ads to familiarise your audience – if you thought the audience for this particular model could be reached through one or more newspapers with the right readership profile for you. You wouldn't sell a £500,000 computer by telephone, even to the best-targeted of business lists – but you might use

Direct Mail in an Integrated Marketing Strategy

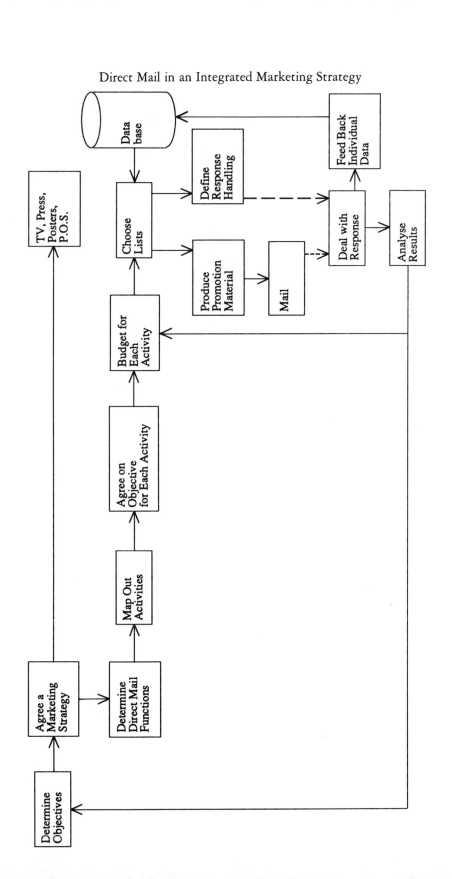

the medium to discover which companies would be the best prospects for your sales force to call on over coming months.

It may not sound as though there is anything identifiably creative involved in this part of the process. Not so. Consider: does the process start with the product, or with the medium, or with the market? Actually, there is no single answer: whichever we try to start with, consideration of the other two will tend to modify our thinking: the creative bit lies in trying to find a set of parameters that give the best 'fit' for these three components.

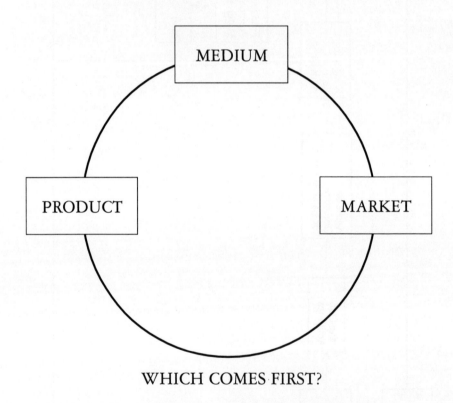

WHICH COMES FIRST?

4.2 Strategy and the Offer

There are two vital steps at this stage of the marketing process. The first is

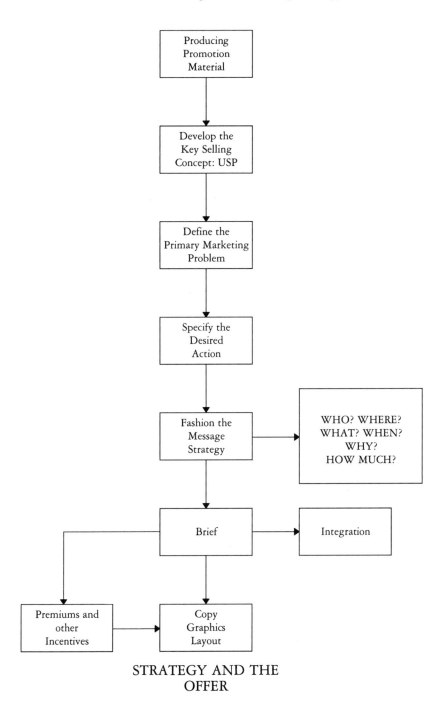

STRATEGY AND THE
OFFER

to discover what it is that your customer most wants/needs; the second is to persuade him that that is precisely what your product offers, above all others. This will be your Unique Selling Point (USP). It is to be hoped that a great deal of the work involved in determining a USP has already been done at the product planning stage – that market research has conducted interviews with customers, and that the product has been designed and built to take account of these findings. But the moment at which you are about to start creating promotion material is the time to go over this ground again, and in more detail. It is vital, at this stage in the process, to stand in the prospect's shoes, to understand his problems, and to view the product through his eyes.

Reversing the process, and asking what is the prime marketing problem from the seller's point of view, is usually easier. A particular product may be difficult to illustrate attractively; it may seem very expensive in relation to the competition; it may require expensive maintenance.

Since the essence of all direct marketing, as we have seen, is the solicitation of response, it is vital to be clear as to precisely what action we wish the prospect to take. Normally we wish him to say 'yes' to the offer we are making; it is essential to ensure that the means of doing this are kept as simple as possible. That is to say, we shouldn't be asking the prospect to provide a signature (unless there is a legal requirement to do so); even ticking a box requires him to obtain a pen or pencil, which may not be to hand.

Fashioning the message strategy involves final clarity on a number of questions:

a) WHO are our prospects?
b) WHAT are we asking them to do?
c) WHY should they do it?
d) WHERE do we find them?
e) WHEN do we address them?
f) HOW MUCH will it cost?

4.3 Briefing

Who is it that should be participating in the creative process that we have been describing so far? The senior member of the creative team should have been a party to all the discussions I have described; when we come to the briefing stage, all the creative team – copy-writers, graphic designers, lay-out experts should be there. This is the point at which the client must describe fully his product, his market, and their characteristics. It will be the task of the creative team to translate the characteristics of the market into perceived *needs*, or *desires*, and the characteristics of the product into *benefits* – benefits for the *customer*.

It has been truly said that a customer buys a product, not for what it *is* (its characteristics) but for what it can *do for him/her* (its benefits). Of course, it's the characteristics that produce the benefits, for the most part – but a good copy-writer will always sell the benefits. So at the briefing stage we must be considering not just the product's USP – but every benefit that could accrue to some part of the market from its use.

Briefing, which starts with the product, the market, and the benefits (the WHAT, the WHO, and the WHY) must go on to discuss all the other aspects of the offer, such as the price, the premium, and the payment terms. But the concept of the offer goes beyond this: it comprises such ideas as discounts, free trials, order now pay later, money-back guarantee, free sample, etc – limited only by your imagination. The briefing should also discuss product positioning, both absolutely and relative to the competition: is this a mass-market product, or exclusive; is it a fun product for to-day, or built to last a lifetime; is it used by the person who buys it, or is it bought to be given to someone else?

A representative of those who are going to have to handle the response to this offer should also be part of the briefing team – not so much to inject further creativity into the process, as to prevent unrealistic promises from being made. Thus, for example, it is a thoroughly bad idea to promise prospects the supply of goods by return of post, if habitually and una-voidably your warehouse takes 10 days to despatch.

At the briefing stage too, we should pay attention to what else is being done for the marketing of this product – or indeed what other marketing initiatives are being undertaken by the company. We should be aiming to *integrate* the image of the company, and of the product that we are putting over, with the image projected elsewhere and in other media. This may involve such things as the use of logos, or colours, or indeed particular slogans or selling messages. It will certainly involve the perceived position of the product in the market-place.

4.4 *Incentives*

Finally, we should consider, while briefing, the use of premiums, and/or other sales incentives. Incentives are, of course, another form of benefit – a benefit that doesn't derive from the product itself, but from the offer, of which product and incentive are both parts. Incentives can be as various as the products they are designed to help sell; here we will consider two types – the premium, in the form of a subsidiary product supplied 'free' with the main product, and the sweepstake, prize draw or competition.

Consider the following case. We are selling, by direct mail, a three-volume encyclopaedia to a mass consumer market. We have established, by testing, that the optimum price for the product is £99. Sold without a premium, we expect this to produce, from our house list of one million previous book buyers, 100,000 orders at a rate of 10%. Suppose that the cost of the book, from the printers, is £35, and the cost of the promotion to a million people is £1 per person – that is to say, the cost of acquiring each order is £10.

Now suppose that we have the opportunity to buy, in quantity, an attractive pocket calculator, retail selling price £20; price to us £6. We can give this calculator away as a free premium to those who order the encyclopaedia. The economics of this offer will depend upon how far the premium improves the expected response rate of 10%. Consider the comparative results if the response rate rises to, say, 11% on the one hand, or 13% on the other:

Response Rate:	10%	11%	13%
Revenue from sales	£9,900,000	£10,890,000	£12,870,000
Less product cost	£3,500,000	£ 3,850,000	£ 4,550,000
Less promotion cost	£1,000,000	£ 1,000,000	£ 1,000,000
Less premium cost	–	£ 660,000	£ 780,000
Initial contribution	£5,400,000	£ 5,380,000	£ 6,540,000

So far, it looks as though, even by improving response from 10 to 11%, the premium offer has paid for itself. But beware. Unless the offer is cash-with-order, there are going to be returns. Let us assume that the rate of returns on a straight offer is 5%. With a premium, this might rise to 10%. Moreover, if bad debts on a straight offer amount to 2%, then they might rise to 3% in our other two cases, giving these results:

Less returns	£ 495,000	£1,089,000	£1,287,000
Less bad debts	£ 198,000	£ 326,000	£ 386,000
Gross profit	£4,707,000	£3,965,000	£4,867,000

From this we can see that premium offers can be powerful tools for improving profit. Not only that, they can create a miraculous form of an 'everybody wins' situation. Consider: in the case illustrated by the third column, the publisher earns an extra hundred and fifty thousand pounds contribution to his overheads and profits; the consumer gets a product for nothing that costs £20 in the shops; the calculator manufacturer sells 130,000 calculators – presumably at a profit; his work-force earn overtime and his shareholders get a bigger dividend; the printer prints more books, on which he earns more profit – and his work-force and shareholders also benefit; even the taxman is happy, since everyone now has a higher tax liability.

Nonetheless, there are dangers in premium trading – not least from the people who order the product only to obtain the premium, and then don't pay. This makes it doubly desirable, before embarking on this course, to test very carefully the *total* effects of proposed actions.

Sweepstakes, or competitions, are another form of incentive used to improve response. In the UK there are fairly stringent laws governing the use of sweepstakes. These make it illegal to offer entry to a sweepstake *only* to those who buy your product: entry must be equally available to all those to whom the offer is addressed, whether they accept the product offer or not. Why then does a sweepstake actually have any effect in increasing the number of people prepared to order? There are two possible answers:

a)   The main problem in every direct marketing campaign is to overcome the prospect's *inertia*. Once you have persuaded him to get out of his arm-chair, and proceed down the road to the letter-box, 75 per cent of your job is done. The sweepstake offer has the effect (it is alleged) of overcoming inertia, and persuading the prospect to respond.

b) The second explanation is a good deal more cynical. It says merely that, no matter how often you tell people that they have an equal chance of winning the sweepstake whether they buy your product or not, a large number of them don't believe it. They therefore order your product so as to be able to participate in your sweepstake.

4.5 Execution

It's no part of the intention of this book to turn readers into copy-writers. But anyone involved at a senior level in direct marketing should have an understanding of how good copy is written, and be able to criticise it. So, let us look a little more closely at each of the components of a direct mail shot that we referred to above.

a) **The letter.** First and foremost, then, every direct mail piece starts (sorry, *should* start) with a letter. That's what people expect to see when they open an envelope addressed to them by name, and that's what they should get. It's remarkable how many direct mail pieces are still produced without a letter – don't do it.

Good sales letters are not all that different from good personal letters. That is, they should begin by telling the prospect something that *he wants to know*. To quote one of the UK's leading copy-writers:

> Forget what the writer wants to write – write only what the reader wants to know. (John Fraser-Robinson)

So what does the reader want to know?

1.   What's this about?
2.   Why has it come to me?
3.   Is it relevant?
4.   What's in it for me?
5.   Do I believe it?
6.   Do I need it?
7.   What do I have to do?

It is surprising how many direct mail letters start off with the personal pronouns 'I' or 'We', instead of 'You'. To take the simplest example, a letter that starts 'I am writing to tell you that . . . ' is trying to do the same job as one that starts 'You will be pleased to know that . . .' but the latter is doing the job very much better.

There is an acronym that is sometimes used by those who teach copy-writing. It is:

A   Attention
I   Interest
D   Desire
A   Action

That is to say, the copy-writer must begin by grabbing the reader's attention (and he must hold on to it). Then he must create interest, and arouse desire. Finally, he must ensure action.

I don't much like this mechanical approach to copy-writing, but so long as this acronym is not regarded as the last word on the subject, it's more useful than most things of this kind.

b) **The leaflet.** Not every direct mail piece will have a leaflet, but most do. Direct mail, like most forms of advertising, is about words *and pictures*. And the leaflet is the traditional way of illustrating your product, and your offer, in colour. The job of the leaflet is to add credibility to the words in your letter. The photographs demonstrate that what you are writing about really exists. And the words alongside the photographs tell the same story as the letter, all over again.

c) **The response medium.** As we have seen at the very start, response is at the heart of all direct marketing. Direct marketing by radio or television will often use the telephone as a response medium – if only because a telephone number is easier to memorise than an address in the few seconds that it is available to the listener or viewer on air. In direct response advertising too, a telephone number may be used, but the most frequent response medium is a reply coupon. Here are some 'rules' about reply coupons in direct response advertisements:

1. Make sure the coupon appears in the bottom right-hand corner of a right-hand page, or bottom left of a left-hand page.
2. Make sure that the material on the reverse side of the coupon isn't something the reader will be reluctant to cut up.
3. MAKE THE COUPON BIG ENOUGH. Designers hate reply coupons, because they use up space in which they would rather draw pretty pictures. Don't let them get away with it – prospects have to write a name and address on this coupon, and if there isn't room to do so, COMFORTABLY, then they won't.
4. Don't let the artist designing the reply coupon get carried away: have you ever tried to fill in your name and address on a coupon with an arty green background where the printing is reversed out in white?

In direct mail, there is more room for choice. The response medium can be a reply-paid card. (Do *not* make the prospect look for a postage stamp.) It can also be a tear-off slip from the top or bottom of your letter – in which case, be sure to supply a reply-paid envelope. In general, minimise the action necessary for the respondent to take. Normally the response device should have been pre-addressed by you with the prospect's details, so that there is nothing to do but pop it in the post.

In direct mail, it is normal practice to ask the prospect to respond, *whether he wants to accept your offer or not*. So he must be given an option – to say Yes, or No. This can be in the form of two Yes/No stamps, or two envelopes, marked Yes and No, or a tick box. The reason that we do this is simple: the greatest problem that the direct mailer (or any other marketer) has to overcome is *inertia*. Make the prospect feel obliged to *do something NOW*: there is then a good chance that he will do what you most want him to do.

d) Other material. In most forms of direct marketing, the major cost that you face is the media cost – air-time on radio or TV, space cost in direct response advertising. In direct mail, the media cost is the postage. It is usual in the UK for postage to amount to somewhere between 20% and 30% of the total cost of the promotion package. But the interesting thing about postage cost is that it doesn't rise proportionately to the quantity of material. That is to say it costs the same to post a letter in the UK regardless of whether the letter weighs 1 gram or 60 grams. Make the most of this – spread yourself. Have a large leaflet if you have a lot to show, and a long letter if you have a lot to say. And add any other pieces that will help to improve response.

2

Database: The Concept

1. DEFINITIONS

The key to good direct mail has always been perceived as access to good prospect lists. Every seminar on direct mail has had something to say about lists – how to obtain them, how to use them, how to maintain them. Now suddenly the buzz-word is database; plain ordinary lists of names and addresses have been transformed overnight, and every direct marketing agency possessed of a micro computer is offering database facilities to its bemused potential clients. (And, as usual, the European Commission has got in on the act, producing a 'Directive on the Legal Protection of Databases'.)

What is a database? The best answer might be: an exceedingly imprecise term. As frequently used, the term means nothing much more than a collection of information held on a computer and organised in some logical manner. (My old friend Drayton Bird defined it in a recent lecture as '... simply a list of people with relevant details about them placed on a computer.') On this definition, any old list of computerised names and addresses is a database. In this book we propose to use a more stringent set of criteria.

The term 'database' was first coined at an American military seminar in 1963 on 'Development and Management of a Computer-Centered Data Base'. The same seminar produced the first attempt formally to define the term:

Database: The Concept

a) A database is a set of files;
b) A file is an ordered collection of entries;
c) An entry consists of a key, and data.

In other words, if a file is a collection of data entries, each of which can be accessed by a unique key, then a database is a set (ie a related collection) of such files. But this doesn't help much: in real life the question whether a given collection of data entries constitutes (or should constitute) a single file, or several different but related files, is no more than a matter of technical convenience. It would seem more useful to define a database with rather less reference to its conceptual structure, and rather more reference to its purpose, function or potential. (Just as it may be more illuminating to define a knife as a hand-held implement for cutting things, rather than by reference to its shape, composition, size, colour, etc.) A database, then (at least for the purposes of this book) is:

a) a collection of data entries, which is
b) organised on a computer by
c) a software package, which
d) allows the user to relate, collate, summarise and reproduce such entries in accordance with any internally logical criteria.

If that sounds a frightful mouthful, let's try an example. A company is selling goods to consumers through 200 retail outlets. It is able to collect a certain amount of data about each retail transaction:

Customer name and address
Branch
Product purchased
Price
Method of payment
Date of purchase

This data, in relation to each sale, is held on a computer, which also holds further information about each customer:

Sex
Marital status

Credit limit
Current debt

and about each outlet:

Branch number
Name of manager
City/suburban/town/rural
Current year's sales target
Sales year to date
Selling area in square feet

Now, there are several different ways in which this information can be structured in a computer (or in any other filing system). Theoretically, we could have a single file in which the individual data entries consisted of customer records, each keyed by a unique customer number, and each containing details of every transaction involving that customer, including full details of the outlet or branch at which the transaction took place. Such a file organisation is perhaps unlikely, for two reasons:

a)   There is a high degree of data redundancy: ie branch data is repeated many times, wasting storage space (which costs money) and probably costing much extra processing time as well.

b)   It becomes a considerable exercise to extract branch-oriented information – eg to calculate the total sales for a given branch, one has to look at every sales transaction.

Alternatively, we could have a single file organised by branch rather than by customer. This reduces data redundancy (since there will be fewer purchases per customer than there are per branch) without eliminating it, since customer data will now have to be repeated for each branch purchase. Moreover, while it will now be simple to obtain information about a given branch's performance, it will be laborious to determine, for example, the total purchases of a single customer – who may, after all, patronise several branches.

One answer to these problems would be to have two files – one with data entries relating to customers and their transactions, and another with data entries pertaining to branches – but taking care to include in the branch file such extra items as:

Total number of customer transactions in this branch
Total value of transactions in this branch

Each sales transaction would then affect both files; data redundancy would be at a minimum; branch statistics and customer profiles alike would be easy to derive.

However, it may be that in our imaginary company there is a frequent need for the production of product-based sales statistics – that we wish to discover, for instance, what proportion of product x sales, made through branch y, were paid for by Barclaycard. Such a need, or its possible prospect, might persuade the database designer to set up this application with three files:

Customer file (containing static data)
Branch file (as above)
Sales file (with one entry per sales transaction, keyed by product, and showing customer identification).

To which one might wish to add fourthly a product file, giving static details of each product, such as:

Source
Cost
Delivery lead time

Now, the particular choice of method by which this data should be structured on the computer is a technical matter of little practical interest to the user – so long as the latter's needs have been properly identified and communicated in the first place. Moreover, the criteria for making such technical decisions themselves change over time, according to the relative cost of hardware and the relative sophistication and/or efficiency of software. What qualifies this collection of information to be called a database is not whether it is structured in one, two, or n files (which may well differ, on purely technical grounds, from one installation to another) but the fact that the computer software that controls the data is capable of data extraction, correlation, and summarisation in pursuit of any logical demand. So, in this horribly over-simplified example, we would expect to be able to learn what proportion of purchases by married women had been paid for by Access, separately by branch; or to list all the male customers whose current debt was less than 25 per cent of their credit limit, having made their last purchase more than three months previously.

To call a collection of information devoid of this facility a database is about as meaningful as to refer to a tiger-skin rug as though it were the living animal: not only is the right software a necessary integral part of a database; it is actually the part that provides the nerves, muscles, brains, and sinews of the total organism.

However, with the software as with the data itself, what matters is not what it looks like, or how or by whom it was constructed, but what it does. There is a tendency in some quarters to suppose that the term database can only be applied to a collection of data under the control of one or another piece of branded manufacturer's software listed as a Database Management System (DBMS for short). This is the opposite approach to that which would describe any old heap of information as a database – but it is equally a heresy. A variety of computer manufacturers have produced DBMSs for machines from micros to main frames, to provide general-purpose database facilities. Much of this software is expensive, both in itself and in its use of hardware – for the very reason that it is general purpose. There is no reason in the world why special-purpose software cannot be written by a user to support his own database application, and there is no reason why an application running without a branded DBMS should not be at least as effective in meeting the needs of its user (and that is the criterion) as one supported by the latest IBM offering. On the contrary, a well-written special-purpose system will normally be much more effective, and much cheaper to run (if one ignores the development cost), than its general-purpose cousin.

2. DATABASE: TOP-DOWN

We have seen, then, that a database is a collection of data entries with total inherent flexibility to meet the information needs of its users. But what users? What is the scope of the information covered, and what are the main uses to which, in a business context, it may be put? This book is primarily about marketing, and we will be concentrating in this chapter on database concepts as they are relevant to marketing needs. But it may be worthwhile to look first at the broader picture.

The earliest computer installations were each dedicated to performing a specific function. Thus, the first commercial computer installation in the USA (Univac I in 1951) was undertaken to process the results of the US census. In the UK Leo I (also in 1951) was commissioned to calculate the daily provisioning of Lyons teashops. (A nice instance, I have always thought, of differing American and British priorities.) But the typical business application of these machines' successors throughout the 1950s and into the 60s, was payroll – a well-defined operation which, if the scale was large enough, could always be performed more quickly and more cost-effectively on a computer than by previous methods. Payroll processing required access to tax tables and staff records; payment of various types of bonus might require reference to sales records at branches, or similar performance data. Files of information were built up; these could not be described as databases since they had little flexibility in use, or provision for data retrieval: they were not there to supply information on demand, but to perform a particular pedestrian and inflexible, unvarying, function.

In time the functions of the typical computer installation widened. The next candidate for computerisation would probably be a series of accounting functions (partly because these too were relatively well defined, partly because the financial director regarded the computer, originally dedicated to payroll, as part of his personal fiefdom, and its acolytes as his employees. The performance of accounting functions would require access to sales data, to branch records, to purchase orders – and, of course, to payroll data. Further files were created.

Later still, stock control became a fashionable area for computerisation as companies, in times of recession, attempted to rationalise their stock-holdings. This required a product file, stock records, a branch file, sales records, supplier records, records of purchase orders and deliveries.

And perhaps, at the end of it all, marketing had a shout: branch records, customer files, sales records, promotion records, salesmen's personnel records were required.

Somewhere along this line of development two things became noticeable:

a) Large areas of data redundancy were being opened up in the computer installation. (Of course, this data redundancy had always been implicit in the functional structuring of the company, but it had been neither so visible nor so noticeably expensive as it now became.) Thus, several different applications might require information about branch operations; if each application kept its own branch file, even where the information required might differ in detail between applications, a great deal of it would be common, and its repetition costly. Worse still, data redundancy leads inevitably to data inconsistency: the chances of a piece of data held in three different files being correctly maintained in all three over an extended period are small, and diminish over time.

b) On a more positive note, the enormous volumes of raw data being accumulated were capable, if only they could be collated, analysed, and reduced to manageable size, of providing new and valuable insights into the business.

The second of these considerations gave rise, in the 1970s, to the briefly fashionable drive (which even found echoes in government policy at the time) towards 'information systems' and 'information technology'. As is so often the case with business fashions (particularly when they are embraced by politicians) this produced a fair collection of disasters, and not too much is heard now of its erstwhile terminology. But from its ashes, with the added stimulus of the data redundancy/consistency problem referred to above, rose much of the thinking behind today's database concepts.

Unfortunately, not all of the lessons of earlier disasters have been learned – certainly not by the writers of text-books. The first principle enunciated by theoretical works on database is that the process of data analysis and database design should be a 'top-down' process: the analyst should look at all the information available to the organisation, and at the totality of its needs – not at pre-defined functions or departments. As we shall see later, this counsel is more often than not impossible to follow in practice – and is frequently undesirable in the real world beyond the text-books: it is a recipe for unmanageable mega-projects which consume large sums over long periods during which there is little or no visible result, with an almost total lack of accountability to any profit centre. But let us first see what is the rationale for this proposition, and where it is supposed, at least, to lead.

The idea is that the data analyst should begin by uncovering all of the data entities known to the organisation: a customer, a branch, a product, a sales transaction, etc. To each entity he should attach all of its proper attributes:

Entity:	Customer	Product	Branch
Attributes:	Ref. No.	Ref. No.	Ref. No.
	Name	Description	Manager's Name
	Address	Min. Order Qty	Address
	Sex	Cost	Location
	Marital Status	Lead Time	Sales Target
	Credit Limit	Min Stock Level	Selling Area
	Current Debt	etc	etc
	Total Purchases		
	etc		

Each entity, and each attribute, will appear once, and once only, in the analysis. Finally, the analyst should describe the relationship between the listed entities:

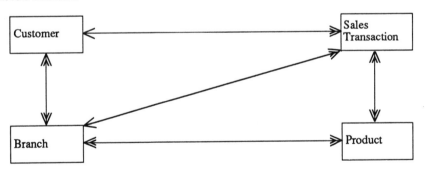

This diagram, being translated, tells us that a customer may patronise one or more branches (hence the two arrowheads between customer and branch) and may have one or more sales transactions; a sales transaction can relate to only one customer, only one branch, and only one product; a product will have one or more sales transactions and be stocked at one or more branches; a branch will stock multiple products and serve multiple customers.

However, this is clearly a picture of a small part only of a company's operations. If we are truly operating on the 'top-down' principle, then we must cover the totality, which might be shown thus:

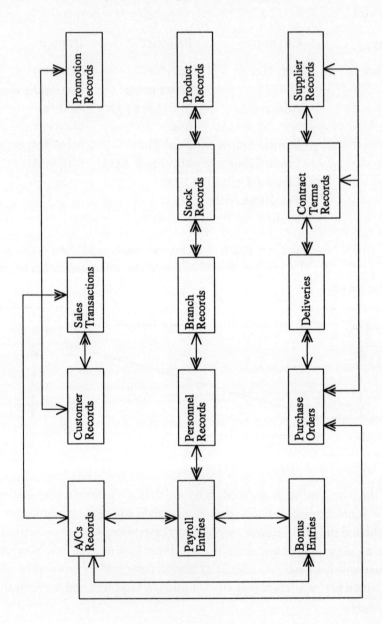

If, in our imaginary company, the first function to be computerised was payroll, followed by various accounting functions – sales ledger, purchase ledger, profit and loss etc – then, since all these functions are likely to fall within the single departmental orbit of the Financial Director, it is quite possible that by now the computer systems in which these functions are embedded have been so rationalised as to avoid *internal* data redundancy and inconsistency. It is also possible that the computer department may by now have escaped from the Financial Director's icy embrace, to become a *company* resource, headed, who knows, by a Data Processing Director. (If this has not happened, then in all probability each of the other departments, such as marketing, buying, personnel, stock control, will have acquired its own computer, and any further chance of rationalisation on anything larger than a departmental scale will have totally vanished for the foreseeable future.)

What one may be fairly certain of, however, is that when the Personnel Department computerises its functions, whether centrally or on its own equipment, it will not simply add data to the existing record of personnel used for payroll purposes: firstly, the payroll/accounting system is probably structured with insufficient flexibility to make this possible without stripping it down and starting again; secondly, such a process would raise questions regarding restrictions on data access, priority of access, and other points of inter-departmental protocol which there is no ready means within the company of resolving. So the Personnel Department will have its own personnel files, and the Accounts Department its own overlapping ones, and they will be in some degree inconsistent, which will, from time to time, drive the Managing Director to rage – but not often enough to make him take decisive action. Similarly, we may be sure that the Marketing Department and the Buying Department will have overlapping branch records and product records. And, if the Marketing Department is already using customer records and sales records for selective direct mailing, these records will certainly overlap with, and probably in some particulars contradict, the sales ledger records within the accounting system. And so on.

Elementary logic suggests that a preferable, more efficient, scenario must be one in which there is a single, central, company data resource to which all users have access for that data which they require to perform their particular functions. A company-wide database which eliminates data redundancies and inconsistencies, and which allows total flexibility in analysis, collation, and recovery of data. But elementary logic can be wrong.

First, a 'top-down' data analysis can only usefully be performed by, or at least under the close control of, someone who himself fully understands the total needs of the business and the inter-relationships of its various parts. In an ideal world the DP Director would be such a person. In addition to his understanding of the business, he would have the ability to convince his departmental colleagues of the need for a central database approach, of the advantages each stood to gain, and of the qualifications of his team of analysts to referee tricky inter-departmental problems of access and priority. Alas, we don't live in an ideal world, and there are few DP directors capable of such a role. This is not at all what one might have expected twenty years ago. It did seem at that time that the computer industry was destined to provide a ladder of advancement for its brighter staff analogous to the ladder climbed with such agility by accountants in a previous generation. It hasn't worked that way. While any number of men and women have now emerged from the chrysalis of the accountancy profession as fully capable heads of great companies, DP personnel have rarely been able to achieve this transformation. The typical DP manager, or director, today is departmentally oriented rather than company-oriented – more interested in (or worried by) the problems of hardware capacity and software performance than in user requirements, which on the whole appear to him as an imposition, and burdened by a serious communication problem with his colleagues, which arises from being so thoroughly immersed in computer-speak as almost to have lost the use of the English language. Like most successful revolutionaries, having scaled the walls of the citadel, he is now busy pulling up the ladder to cries of 'I'm all right, Jack'. He has no desire to lead a further revolution in thinking and in practice (which is what a company database is) but only to protect what he already has.

Secondly, the computer department in any large company is loaded already well beyond the point at which it can contemplate a major new project. In my first job as a computer manager, we had a staff of two analysts and six programmers. In ten months we created a marketing database with two million customer records; management insisted that in the computer purchase proposal we include a paragraph on how we would dispose of this substantial staff, which would clearly not be required in such numbers, once the computer system was working to specification. Ten years later, we had a systems staff of 30, and a six months' lead time on the start of any substantial new project. Quite simply, the task of maintaining computer systems once written is much greater than is ever allowed for, even by the 'experts'. So capacity to handle new projects scarcely ever exists in 'mature' computer installations.

Theoretically there are three ways of dealing with this bottleneck. One can recruit a new team to handle the new project. The trouble is that the state of the labour market in computer staff is – and for twenty years has been – such that a single company's chances of picking up the four or five highly qualified staff required to build a company database are nil. Or, one can take drastic measures to *make* space in the existing schedule. This will mean axing a number of projects that have already spent several months in the pipeline waiting their turn, and freezing existing systems for all but the most unavoidable changes (eg those necessitated by legislation). Neither of these measures will make the DP department, or the database project, popular with the users of existing systems, or the promoters of other new projects. More importantly, such a decision involves a substantial hidden cost – the cost of not doing a number of things one would otherwise do. Or, one can use outside assistance. And it is to those who have a need of such assistance, whether in building a database or mounting a direct marketing campaign, that this book is largely directed. So we will return to this subject later on.

The third snag in the way of developing a comprehensive, company-wide database is that such a project means not just freezing the development of existing systems, but actually changing them. The Financial Director with a smoothly functioning sales ledger system doesn't want *his* file subsumed in some corner of a huge company database; still less does he want months of picking out bugs in the new system, re-training his staff, etc. (He can still remember the last time.) And the same goes for all his colleagues with functioning systems. The cost to a company of a major systems upheaval running across several departments is likely to be extremely high, even if all goes more smoothly than the norm. And if things go rather badly, it can be catastrophic.

Finally, creation of a company-wide database is a very lengthy process.

Of course, the actual construction of the database can, if done carefully, proceed in a modular fashion, with each function converting to its use one at a time, and each in turn gaining from its introduction without having to wait for the total structure to be complete. But the data analysis and database design which must precede construction cannot be modular – and these will occupy, necessarily, 70–80 per cent of the total elapsed time anyway.

Bearing these considerations in mind, it is perhaps scarcely surprising that company-wide databases, much talked about in the text-books, are a bit thin on the ground. (To tell the truth, I don't know of any.) Rather, what one is accustomed to find is the function-oriented database, filling the needs of one function, or perhaps one department. Of these partial databases, the most common is the marketing database. And since this book is essentially about various aspects of marketing, this is the type of database we will now consider at greater length. Its visual representation at a conceptual level might look something like this:

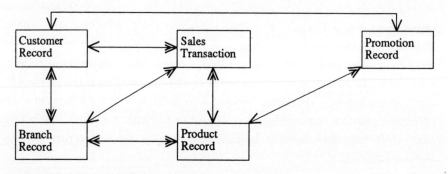

Its relationship to the organisational structure of the company, could look like the diagram on page 65.

3. DATABASE: KNOW YOUR CUSTOMER

At the heart of database marketing lies the collection of information about customers and prospects, their characteristics, tastes, habits, and lifestyles. For marketers who have a long-standing involvement with direct mail, such collecting has long been an important part of life – since, indeed, well before modern database techniques became available to help with the flexible use of such information. For many others, lacking the direct mail

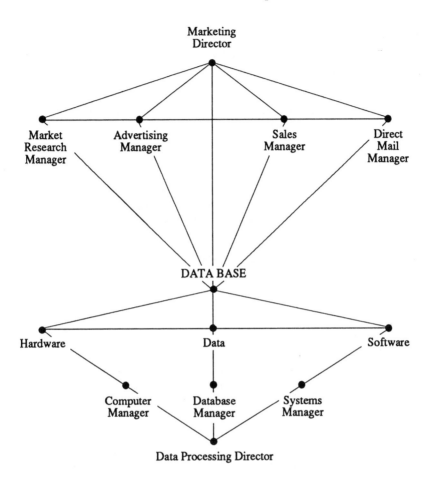

addict's necessity to think of his customers as individual entities each living behind a separate letter-box, the penny has been extraordinarily slow to drop. Over every marketing director's door should appear, in letters of fire, not the ancient Greek admonition to 'Know Thyself' (perhaps few of us would altogether care to do that), but rather:

KNOW YOUR CUSTOMER

Know him, that is, not simply as a reader of the *Sunday Times* colour supplement, of whom, by virtue of his reading habits, certain characteristics can be predicted, in the sure knowledge that, wildly inaccurate though they will be for a high proportion of the individuals concerned, they are correct for a larger proportion than in the case of *News of the World* readers. Know him, not as a member of some artificial statistical entity from whose normative characteristics many members of that entity will in practice diverge widely; know him, rather, as an individual person, with a name, living in a house, employed in a job, buying certain products, pursuing certain interests.

It's a strange thought when you consider it: shopkeepers who run corner shops and number their customers in scores, or perhaps hundreds, know their customers in just this way. Direct mail marketers, who number their customers, in many cases, in millions, can at least be said to be trying. But in between are the big department stores, for example, who neither know nor attempt to discover anything at all about their customers – unless they are account customers, who, boringly, have to be billed. In the Good Old Days when I first had a bank account, my bank manager knew me as a person (rather better than most of my friends). Today I have accounts at two banks and two building societies; I haven't so much as met a branch manager from any of them, and they (or rather their systems) know nothing more of me than the bare requirements for keeping my accounts more or less arithmetically correct, and sending statements.

This has to be crazy. We are sometimes told that the UK has the world's most efficient retailing network. (This has been alleged, for example, as a major reason for the UK's high propensity to import foreign goods.) If true, this says something pretty awful about the retail trade in other countries, because in the UK it has scarcely yet begun to understand what marketing is about.

Retail shops, for the most part, are idle, unimaginative, and almost entirely passive institutions. They squat in the High Street waiting for anonymous customers to overcome their own natural inertia and walk in through the doors. They undertake a little, impersonal, local advertising to encourage store traffic – but for the most part expect manufacturers to create demand by national brand advertising. And when a customer, acting on his own initiative, does venture inside their premises, he is, in an ever-increasing number of cases, expected to discover for himself what is on sale, at what price, to serve himself, to transport his own purchases to a cash desk, and, after queuing (a necessary British ritual on all occasions) to carry them thence to wherever he wishes to go – a destination of no interest whatever to the store.

That this process should have gone furthest in food stores is scarcely surprising, since it is there that the phenomenon of the repeat customer can be most completely relied on, with minimal encouragement required from the store. People need to buy food regularly; there is little to choose in quality between the stocks of one multiple food retailer and another, nor a great deal in price. So repeat visits become a matter of convenience first, and then of habit. It is much more surprising that shops selling products that demand less frequent replacement should show so little – almost no – interest in securing repeat custom, or in increasing the frequency of repeat visits.

It isn't only in the matter of reinforcing customer loyalty and encouraging repeat visits that retail stores appear to be blind to the need to know who their customers are, individually. In getting new custom also, they are equally unimaginative. I bought a house recently in a reasonably prosperous part of North London, which is served by a department store that is part of the John Lewis empire. The house was marketed through an estate agent. It would not have been difficult, or unreasonable, for the estate agent to have advised the department store of completion, and for me to receive a promotion offering the store's services in relation to new curtains, carpets, light fittings, etc. No such thing occurred. If I want to buy new curtains, it is up to me to find where my local department store is, and to visit it in person. If I am *very* lucky a sales assistant will condescend to take an order from me – although of course I will not be allowed to obtain any actual goods costing more than a fiver in anything under six weeks.

The behaviour of our great financial institutions is even more extraordinary. Retail stores can (and do) excuse their own idleness by remarking that it is very difficult to collect names and addresses from their customers, and liable to cause resistance. (We will return to this point later.) But banks, building societies, insurance companies, finance houses, all require names and addresses – together with an immense amount of personal information – as a condition of doing business, and they at least encounter no measurable resistance to its collection. Yet David Ogilvy could still say:

I have life insurance policies with three companies. None of these has ever written to me suggesting that I buy more insurance from them. Bloody fools.

Admittedly that was in 1965, and it is true that things are now, slowly, changing. One of the most powerful catalysts is the Big Bang of 1986, which is changing the nature of the marketing problem for financial institutions from that of selling a single range of services *extensively* to the population at large, to that of selling a much wider range of services *intensively* to existing customers. And in order to sell with maximum effect to named persons, it follows that one should know as much as possible about each one, and should use that knowledge in determining what to offer to each, and how to persuade each prospect to buy.

It doesn't greatly matter what one is selling, or what marketing media are in use – the following rules apply:

> Know *who* your customers are, individually, not just as statistical groups;
> Know *what* each has bought from you, at *what cost*;
> Know *when* each has bought, and *how often*;
> Know as much as possible of *how* each lives, in terms of lifestyle.

Those lecturers on direct mail who like to have their admonitions wrapped up in some easily memorable formula refer to this as the Recency, Frequency, Monetary formula. Personally, I find it easier to remember the admonitions than the formula – but each to his own taste.

Why is this so important? Basically there are two reasons. The first has always been true, and is no more than a matter of common sense: people buy more readily products they know from suppliers they know – provided they have had a reasonable experience the first time round. So, reactivating old or existing customers is always easier – ie more effective per unit of cost – than obtaining new ones. What may be less immediately obvious, but has also been repeatedly found to be true, is that even lapsed customers – for example those who cancel their subscriptions to a magazine, or a club, or a charity – can, at least in the aggregate, be persuaded back into the fold more readily than cold prospects.

Of course, it is much easier to make repeat sales if one is selling a consumable product which requires regular replacement, but the same criteria apply to cross-selling, where the problem is to turn purchasers of one product into buyers of a range of products: in both cases the more one knows about one's customers the greater one's ability to target a sales message to the right people at the right time, and the more cost-effective one's efforts.

The second reason why knowledge of this kind is important is of relatively recent, and still increasing, significance. The years after the last war saw, in every developed country, an explosion of pent-up demand for consumer goods (and indeed capital goods) that were in short supply. For many years it was possible to make a lot of money by selling relatively undifferentiated products to a hungry, not very discriminating, mass market. With the gradual satisfaction of the most obvious consumer wants, and the attainment of a much higher level of overall prosperity, the situation has changed radically. The days when Ford could promise their customers a car in any colour, so long as it was black, are gone for good; the market is no longer characterised by an excess of demand over supply. The mass market, in consequence, has for some years past been breaking down for product after product, into a whole series of sub-markets. A food-store today can't just stock instant coffee as an alternative to the real thing. It must stock coffee beans as well as ground coffee, both from a variety of different locales and in numerous varieties of strength and flavour; the ground coffee must also be in varieties suitable for several different methods of preparation. Instant coffee will be stocked in several different brands, decaffeinated or ordinary, and again in several varieties of taste and price. Motor cars must be available as manual or automatic, petrol or diesel, differentiated by colour and trim, as well as the presence or absence of some twenty different accessories permeated every which way. Even the nation's cats have got in on the act, so that their food is sold in a dozen different brands, each available in ten flavours and two sizes.

This fragmentation of markets is still continuing, in virtually every product area, and demands from the marketer a much deeper understanding than before of a much more knowledgeable, more choosy, and less extensive market.

4. DATABASE: BOTTOM-UP

As we have seen, one of the major problems of designing a comprehensive, top-down, database is the level of complexity (and indeed of political shenanigans) that customarily accompanies such an exercise. And some organisations, wishing to avoid such a situation, go to the opposite extreme, where each clerk in the organisation, sitting at his own terminal, controls his own little database – leading to endless data redundancy, and contradiction.

My own preference is somewhere between these extremes: I firmly believe that every organisation should possess a single, comprehensive, unduplicated database, from which all of its computerised activities should depend. But I also believe that in constructing such a database it is better to build from the bottom up, rather than to try to work from the top down.

What is encouraging – and may also be surprising – is that when we approach the problem in this way, it becomes apparent that a marketing database – incorporating a single record for every customer and prospect known to the organisation – is a first-class starting point for almost anything that needs to come afterwards.

Contrast this vision with the situation of the average large insurance company today. Such a company will possess a file of motor insurance policies, another of house-and-contents policies, another of life policies, and so on. These files – I hesitate to call them databases – are separate and unrelated, with a rate of duplication that is large but unquantifiable: nobody knows, or can tell, whether Mr Smith, who has a motor policy with the company, does or does not have a life policy.

The reason for this appalling state of affairs is that insurance companies, without exception, built computer systems for the benefit of company accountants and administrators, whose job was to look after policies, to post premiums, to obtain renewals, to process claims. Such persons are interested in policies, not in people. Consequently, any attempt to use such systems for marketing (which involves understanding the overall needs of individual customers) or indeed for customer service, was – and still is – impossible.

By contrast, had an insurance company built a marketing database first, there would have been little difficulty in adding to it any accounting functions that might be necessary. The same upside-down development has taken place at our banks and building societies, with the result that they have customer service facilities which are, by the standards of the 1990s, of unparalleled inefficiency. This is also why, as we have noted above, their entry into direct marketing has been late, and why, even now, their ability to undertake *targeted* direct marketing is undeveloped.

3

Database Applications

The information contained within a database may be used for a wide variety of marketing purposes (bearing in mind that non-marketing purposes lie, on the whole, beyond the scope of this book). It may be useful to take two or three typical sets of circumstances, and see how database facilities might be used to further the needs of the organisation in each case.

1. RETAIL

Having already decribed above, in very broad terms, some of the characteristics of a retail marketing database, we will start there. Let us suppose a company with a chain of 100 garden centres, selling plants, seeds, fertilisers, pesticides, implements – everything connected with gardening. These centres are spread through the southern half of England, mostly in suburban areas; individual purchases can range from a pound or two to two or three hundred pounds; centres range in size from small shops with an annual turnover barely reaching six figures to substantial nurseries which take that much in a good weekend. This small chain is the result of rapid growth in the recent past: when it was a much smaller outfit, management had a fairly clear view of the dynamics of each centre – who shopped there, for what, and why; to what extent repeat visits could be looked for, and how frequently; what products were likely to do better in one centre than another, and so on. But with the rapid expansion, this instinctive 'feel' for the market in each centre is no longer possible, and there is nothing much yet to replace it. Of course, when considering opening a new centre, management looks at the demographic structure of the surrounding area: are the houses old or new; are the gardens large or small, mature or not; are the inhabitants young, middle-aged, or elderly; is the soil acid or alkaline; what are the figures for rainfall and sunshine. All of this will condition a decision to open in an area or not, and/or what type of centre, dealing in what range of products, to set up. But after the decision is made, and the centre opened, there is very little feedback of hard quantified data about who uses it and how frequently. Certainly, a pattern of product demand will emerge: management will know how much potting compost is sold in one outlet rather than another, and so on. But about the people who buy the potting compost, or the Rotavators, there is no information, beyond the unquantified impressions of local staff, at all.

Moreover, medium-term results at some of the newer centres have been disappointing. Centres set up within reach of well-to-do new housing estates have turned in splendid early results as the first occupiers of the new houses have laid down lawns and bought lawn-mowers, planted fruit trees and herbaceous borders, dug and mulched and sprayed. Naturally, it wasn't to be expected that the initial level of activity from such a source would continue indefinitely, but the fall-off has been greater than can be explained simply by the satisfaction of early need for heavy investment: it is almost as though interest in the whole pursuit of gardening has come to occupy a much lower place in local priorities.

Management has determined that it needs to know a great deal more about its customers. In the short term it has employed some 'snap-shot' surveys, using face-to-face market research conducted with its customers. Long term, however, management is convinced that it must build a permanent customer database which will comprise all available information about its individual customers. The objectives which it is hoped the database, once in use, will achieve, are several:

a) By telling management who its customers are and where they live, it will make post-purchase communication possible. The purposes of such communication will be:
    i) to obtain direct customer feedback of satisfaction or dissatisfaction, and reasons for same;

ii)   to establish or enhance customer loyalty;

iii)   to encourage more frequent visits and thus increase turnover.

b)   By examining which groups of customers respond most readily to such communications, it will be possible to target such approaches more precisely, improving their cost-effectiveness.

c)   From close examination of customers' individual characteristics, buying habits, etc, it will be possible to form hypotheses about which products should most appropriately be offered to which persons, about the most suitable tone and emphasis of promotion, and so on. Moreover, such hypotheses can be tested, and refined, over time.

d)   By analysing sales according to age, sex, frequency, value, etc, it will be possible to establish whether the 'instinctive' criteria hitherto used for establishing new centres continue to make sense, or whether there are previously unrecognised factors at work in determining purchasing habits. In particular, it will be possible to build a demographic 'model' of a centre's customers, to compare this with the demographic profile of the area that the centre serves, and to derive from this comparison new criteria for locating outlets. (For more on demographics, see Chapter 4, Section 2.)

e)   Although a prime purpose in communicating with customers is to increase traffic in the centres, it may also be possible, for part of the product range at least, actually to sell by mail – more particularly where offers are going to those who have already experienced and approved the quality of the company's products.

f)   Communication by mail can also be used to solicit and obtain additional information about customers, their families, their gardens, and the purposes for which they use them – information which many customers will gladly volunteer if they believe it will be used to help the company structure its product range and its advertising in a more relevant way.

g)   By enabling management to identify frequent visitors and/or high spenders, the database opens the possibility of all sorts of added-value schemes – gardening clubs, discount cards, competitions, and shows.

The conceptual framework of a marketing database to pursue these objectives can be represented as shown already on page 64. There will be a record for each customer, and a record for each sales transaction. Sales will be related to customers, and both customers and sales will be related to branches (ie individual centres). Promotion transactions will also be recorded, indicating the promotions sent to particular customers. Sales and promotions relate to records of products, and product records in turn relate to individual centres, so that product movement can be analysed either overall, or by individual centre – or indeed in relation to customers living in a certain type of area and incurring expenditure in a given range over a specific six-month period (for instance).

It is, of course, a pity that the company, having been in operation for a number of years already, has irretrievably lost all the customer-related information that passed through its hands in that time. (As one might expect, much of the product-related information has been retained.) But that is water under the bridge; the vital thing now is to staunch the continuing haemorrhage of information. This brings us to a problem that confronts all would-be builders of databases – a problem that is, however, particularly acute in a retail environment – how does one collect customer data for one's database in the first place?

Clearly, data relating to branches, to products, and indeed to promotions, is totally within the company's control, and can be retained and formatted in any required way. The data that the company has never retained in the past is that relating to customers, and to sales at an individual transaction level. Each sale is rung up at a till, which produces a receipt for the customer, and records the product bought, and the payment, for accounting and stock analysis purposes. This, in future, will not be enough. The minimum information required now in respect of each sale is:

Customer name and address
Date
Branch
Product
Price
Method of payment

Of these items, by far the most troublesome is the first – the customer's name and address. The difficulty has two sources: the customer, who may be unwilling to provide the data, and/or irritated at being asked, and the assistant, who regards this as an unnecessary and time-consuming chore at the best of times and, in busy times, as an imposition getting in the way of the real job of serving customers and keeping queues to a minimum.

Different circumstances will suggest different ways of coping with customer reluctance. Customer credit accounts, or store discount cards dispose of the problem for those purchases where they are used. Normally it makes sense to ignore customer data in respect of purchases below a given minimum amount. Customers paying by cheque can usually be persuaded to write their address on the back (their name being already pre-printed on the front). Filling in a product guarantee card for the customer can be another way of acquiring the desired information. Anything that has to be delivered produces the data automatically. A promise of a full refund within 28 days for any product returned together with an invoice bearing full customer details, may also do the trick.

Staff reluctance is another matter. Sometimes it amounts to little more than laziness; often it springs from a feeling that there is no immediate benefit the assistant can see from this chore to offset the disbenefit of keeping customers waiting, and perhaps irritating them as well. A staff incentive scheme may help – where staff are rewarded with a bonus on a sliding scale according to the proportion of sales where a full name and address is captured. Even more important is a training programme which will show branch staff what the database can achieve *for their branch*, and why it is therefore vital to keep it supplied with accurate information.

In the case of our illustrative garden centre company, each centre will be equipped with an electronic till incorporating a micro-computer. 'Regular' customers will have discount cards and/or credit accounts – and their names and addresses will be stored permanently in the micro. Other customers, buying goods worth £15 or more, will be given a refund guarantee which holds good on the production of a full sales invoice, and will be asked to give names and addresses for this purpose. Staff at each branch will attend a full two-day residential course on database as it affects branch dealings with customers, and there will be a bonus scheme for all branch employees, based on monthly success in improving store takings over the previous year.

2. WHOLESALE

Consider the case now of the wholesaler (or manufacturer for that matter) selling to business outlets. Interestingly, this user's database does not look very different in outline from that which we have been examining in the retail case above:

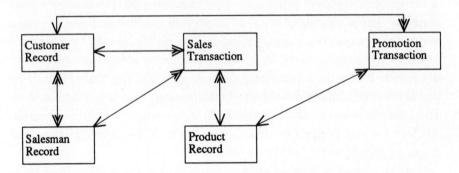

In this instance the salesman has replaced the branch; since a salesman, unlike a branch, doesn't stock products, there is no relationship expressed between salesman's record and product record; otherwise the relationships are unchanged.

For our hypothetical case this time let us take a chemical company selling industrial cleaning materials to hotels, hospitals, schools, and other such large institutions. The materials are, over a large part of the range, consumable, and therefore require fairly frequent re-ordering. The client does not wish to attempt a mechanical re-ordering system: there is strong competition in the field, and he feels compelled to maintain a personalised customer contact through a team of salesmen who are trained to provide an advice service in all manner of cleaning problems, as well as to cross-sell further products to customers who take less than the whole range.

Each of the company's salesmen has, on average, 80 active customers within his territory; he also has a further 200 prospects, each of them using one or more products from a rival manufacturer to which he has a valid alternative. The sales force has a higher turnover of staff than it should have; training is not very good and customer knowledge rather poor; morale is low.

Although the outline of available data and its relationships is little different from the retail case, the purposes for which management wishes to use a database are rather different:

a) By analysis of individual customer orders, service calls, usage rates, etc, to be able to provide an information and advisory service to the salesmen, enabling them to schedule their calls on existing customers more productively.
b) By maintaining a register of prospects, with all available details, to provide a similar prospect service to the salesmen.
c) To be able to retain all available customer and prospect information within the company, regardless of the comings and goings of individual salesmen.
d) To target relevant promotion material to customers and prospects by mail in a manner and time-scale programmed to enhance the activities of the salesmen.

In order to build and maintain a database that will fulfil these purposes, the following information will be required for each sales call made by each salesman:

Name and address of organisation called on
Contact name and position
Date of call
Product code and quantity of each item ordered
Servicing functions performed
Index of customer satisfaction
Principal competitors

In this type of application there is little or no problem in acquiring information from the customer; the problem lies in motivating the salesmen, who have an in-built dislike of paper-work, head offices, routine, directives, computers, and so on. A number of companies have in the past tried to use computer systems to dictate to their salesmen their daily, weekly or monthly pattern of calls – often with poor results. Salesmen are by definition loners, and highly individualistic; let them suppose they are being scheduled by a machine and most of them will start to treat the computer as an enemy, ignoring its schedules, and failing to feed back the information it requires. What is therefore essential is to convince the salesman that the computer is his assistant, not his would-be master. To this end, in our above example, the computer's first function will be to provide, from its database, a printed memorandum regarding the affairs of each customer or prospect on its *suggested* list of forthcoming calls. The information on this memorandum will include:

Name and address of organisation
Name(s) and position(s) of contact(s)
Date each contact last visited
Products currently in use
Date and quantity of last order for each product
Average usage rate for each consumable product
Other products deemed relevant to this customer
Chief competitors
Promotion material sent since last visit, with date(s)
Any responses received to above
Servicing problems over last six months
Index of customer satisfaction on last call

Of course, the salesman can ignore the computer's recommendations on calling and anyway, the computer can't take account of emergency servicing calls that the salesman may receive to disrupt his schedule. But once he finds the computer is working with him, not against him, attitudes will change; if the computer is the only source of information that can help him sell, and if that information is most readily available on accounts/prospects selected by the computer, then he will learn to co-operate.

When a company like this has a sales force that trusts its computer database, there is a further possible stage. One can give each salesman a terminal, at his office base or his home, on which he can interrogate the database, and view customer or prospect data on his screen. One large pharmaceutical company already does this with its sales force of over 400 salesmen, who are able not merely to access customer data remotely, but also to initiate such actions as delivery of samples, or of printed promotion material, by post. Or, again, one can give each salesman a portable terminal and modem which he can take by car to his customer's premises, plug in and interrogate the database in front of the customer – an impressive demonstration of technical expertise.

For a lot of companies that have traditionally employed salesmen, a prime question must nowadays be whether this is still the most cost-effective way of selling, given the changing cost structures of recent years. There is no real point in trying to deal with this question in general terms – beyond pointing out that, of all the marketing media available, direct mail has had the lowest cost escalation over the last ten years, or any part of that period. Direct mail is not, however, an adequate *sales* instrument for all occasions or all products. What it can do, as in the case illustrated here, is to provide invaluable backing to render the time of the prime (and expensive) sales instrument – the salesman – more cost-effective. And it can do this through the discriminating power of a good database, which can be used selectively to mail customers and prospects, to analyse their responses, and to determine which are most likely at any given time to repay a salesman's effort in calling.

3. DIRECT MAIL SELLING

So far we have looked at one example where the function of the database, operating through direct mail promotions, is to bring more trade into retail shops; and at another example where the database exists to facilitate analysis of customer information so as to assist the efforts of the sales force, and also, via direct mail promotions, to determine which prospects are most worth calling on. In both instances direct mail plays a subsidiary role in the actual selling function, while being an integral part of the overall marketing scheme. We will consider now the function of the database in the classic direct mail operation where postal communication is the sole link between seller and buyer, and where direct mail is not merely a medium for advertising and/or for market research, but also for selling.

Let us take as our example a company that has for some years past been selling, by direct mail, books, prints, video tapes, records – a whole range, in fact, of leisure material. The company's first introduction to the direct mail market was by way of renting other peoples' lists, and sending its promotion material to those names. Early on the question arose whether it was best to aim one's promotion for a given product at a list of people who had bought some analogous product from someone else – eg to promote records to a list of guarantee-card holders on a range of record players – or at a list of people who had previously bought *by mail*, regardless of product. And early on the lesson was learned that, while there is never a 100% answer to a generalised question of this kind, nevertheless time and again the factor of having previously bought by mail proves to be the most powerful single discriminator of those who are likely to purchase anything else at all by that medium.

This having been found to be the case, the conclusion was very quickly reached that the names of those who bought the company's products by mail would be the most valuable future asset of all – having the double bond of being mail purchasers and customers, for related products, of the company. So, from an early stage of operations, the names and addresses of orderers, which were already being passed through a computer system for the purpose of achieving despatch of goods, handling of accounts receivable, and so on, were retained so that they could be promoted later for other products.

This idea that one's own past customers were by far one's best future prospects was triumphantly vindicated, so that as the company's own list of buyers grew, so the need to rent outside lists diminished. But quite quickly a snag appeared. As the company's range of products increased, it wanted to offer new products to old customers, and old products to new customers. At first this wasn't too difficult: since each name and address was allocated a sequential customer number, it was possible to deduce how long a given customer had been on file, and the time for which each product had been on offer was also known. But, as time went on, the range of products widened, and the pattern of promotions became more complex. Shortly, it was impossible to tell with any certainty which individual customers had, at one time or another, been offered what products. And it became clear that the list of names and addresses had to carry information also about purchases and promotions, in order to avoid repetitiously offering the same product to persons who had either already bought it or who had indicated, by non-response to a promotion, a lack of interest in it.

So, what had started as a simple list of names and addresses of buyers, began to accumulate packages of more specific information. There was now recorded, for each customer sale:

Date of purchase
Product
Price
Method of payment
Speed of payment

And for each promotion sent out:

Date of promotion
Product
Offer
Response

Moreover, it was clearly convenient, as well as holding details of these individual transactions, to have a summary for each customer, showing:

Date of origin
Total number of purchases
Total value of payments
Total promotions sent
Date of last order
Promotions since last order

The accumulation of this information not only made it possible to perform the relatively simple exclusions that had motivated this development, so that customers were not promoted for products they had already bought, etc. It also encouraged the marketing department to look again at the old question of product affinities. They had already proved to their own satisfaction that undiscriminated buyers-by-mail were better prospects than retail purchasers of related products – and that their own customers were the best prospects of all. But given that their own customers, now almost their total marketing universe, were all mail buyers in the first place, might it not also be true that segments of this universe might be better, or worse, prospects for a given product according to the nature of what they had bought before?

Unsurprisingly, this proved to be the case. In addition, other factors were found, by trial and error, to be significant too – speed of payment for example. So that quite quickly the company was faced with the need to select prospects for mailings on the basis of quite complex algorithms. The original programmes for handling the early name and address list had provided merely for its reproduction on labels. Simple options had been introduced to allow for printing out a 1 in n sample instead of the whole list, or to print only one or more geographically defined areas. Further modifications had made possible a certain amount of personalisation, so that addresses could be printed at the head of letters, and appropriate salutations added. But a requirement to address all male customers who had purchased more than one product, including either product x or product y, but excluding those who had already bought product z, those who had received more than five promotions since their last order, and those who had not yet paid in full for their last purchase – this required a major programming effort, and this effort had to be repeated for each such new requirement.

What was required, and what was provided, was a general purpose piece of software that would accept any logical algorithm (or collection of logical algorithms) and produce the required results (counts, labels, or promotion letters) without further ado. And with the production of this piece of software (but not before) the company found itself with a functioning database.

For a while the facilities provided by this new software were more than enough to meet the demand for their use. But not for long. The desire for discriminatory information about individual customers grew as it fed. It wasn't enough to infer a customer's tastes, habits, income, lifestyle from the limited number of products he bought from the company; rather the company wanted to have access to direct information on those and similar subjects. What kind of house does the customer live in? What sort of car does he drive? How many children does he have, and in what age range? Has he a garden?

How could such information – demographic and psychographic as it is customarily referred to – be obtained? Worse still, how could it be used? For the point had now been reached where the sheer volume of data becoming available on individual customers was too great for the construction of selection algorithms by mere common-sense methods. And the number of possible permutations of data made controlled testing of alternatives – if conducted on anything like a comprehensive basis – horrendously expensive. What was required was a set of techniques whereby the *computer* could be persuaded to construct the selection algorithms for itself — predicting, in effect, which groups of customers were the best prospects for which products. And by great good fortune a set of techniques, developed for a quite different purpose, but suited to this one, lay ready to hand. These techniques are most commonly referred to in the direct marketing industry under the generic label of regression analysis, and we will describe their use, as well as considering the source and application of demographic and psychographic data in a later chapter. (See Chapter 4.)

Despite the extended quantity of information made available by tapping sources other than the simple occurrence of a sale or a promotion, and despite the extra complexity involved in the use of regression analysis, the actual picture of a direct mail database such as we have been considering is extremely simple:

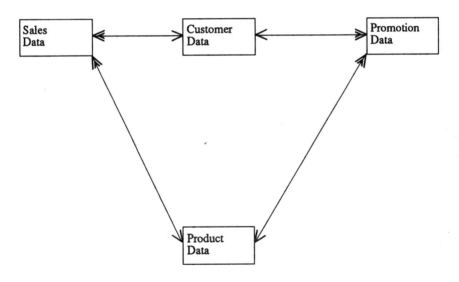

Where the file is a very large one, relative to the total population (ie running into millions) problems of data redundancy may suggest a slightly more complex arrangement, where the data common to all customers living in a given area is held once only in a record of that area, giving a picture like the one on page 84:

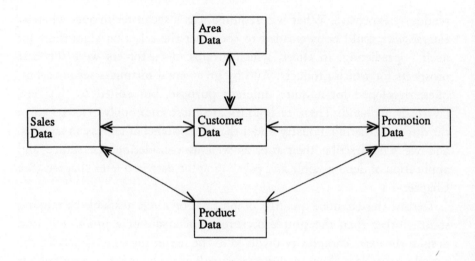

4. ANALYSIS

The use of a database, via the medium of direct mail, to support a retail operation, or to complement the activities of a salesman in the field, is a highly targeted form of advertising, based on a knowledge of the *individual* customers that one is trying to reach. Use of a database to select individuals as targets for a direct mail sales offer is, of course, a form of selling. So we have seen examples of the use of database to support two of the classic marketing functions. The third such function is market research, and, to an extent, the wholesale example we discussed above touches on this function too, since this database is being used to analyse customer needs so as to structure an advisory pattern of activity for each salesman. However, a further example of a database being used purely for analysis purposes may help to make the point that in research, as in the other marketing functions, database can play a vital part — whether or not in conjunction with direct mail.

Consider the case of an organisation running 300 slimming centres around the country. Some of these establishments are fully residential — but usually short-stay — places, others are simply clubs offering exercise facilities of various sorts, and advice, medical and paramedical, for members, all of whom have a common concern — albeit in varying degrees — to lose weight.

Members will belong to one only club – clearly close to their home or workplace – but any member may from time to time visit any of the residential establishments, or change the club to which he/she belongs on the occasion of moving house or job.

The clubs offer a variety of regimes of diet and exercise which they try to tailor to the desires, physical condition, and staying power of individual members. The capacity of members to stick with their regimes, once started, is enhanced by group activities, rather after the fashion of Alcoholics Anonymous.

The organisation is anxious to monitor the performance of individual clubs, and residential centres and, indeed, the success rate of different regimes. To this end they keep a full computerised record of each member of each club, showing:

Name and address
Club
Date of joining
Weight on joining
Target weight (set by member, with medical agreement)
Date to reach target weight
Prescribed diet
Prescribed exercise
Weekly record of diet
Weekly record of exercise
Weekly weight loss
Medical indications noted
Record of residential visits
Attendance at club
Record at any previous club

This mass of data is analysed regularly in order to see whether there are any significant differences in the success rates achieved by different clubs, and/or by different regimes. (Of course, there are individual factors unknown to the database, such as the extent to which some members cheat and don't tell – but over the large numbers involved this is probably not a statistical problem.)

5. FUND-RAISING

The number of marketing databases held by charitable institutions has grown enormously in recent years – and the number of mailing pieces sent out from them is now enormous. Fund-raising by direct mail is, of course, no different in principle from any other kind of selling: the trick is to sell an idea, rather than a product or a service, and no doubt there are some forms of marketing activity that might be considered inappropriate for a charity. But the basic techniques are the same. And the rules for data collection (with which we will deal in the next chapter) and for maintaining a clean database are no different for charities than they are for commercial organisations.

6. GOODWILL

Advertising, selling, fund-raising, and market research do not exhaust the list of marketing activities – nor the list of functions in which a marketing database can form a major resource. To quote an example alluded to earlier in this book, a car manufacturer who enables dealers to write regular personalised letters to all buyers of a particular marque – to advise them of servicing requirements, and other such matters – is not selling, or conducting market research primarily; nor even, except in a secondary sense, advertising. First and foremost, that manufacturer is seeking to cement customer loyalty, to buy goodwill. This is done by indicating that the business – indeed its managing director – knows of this customer as an individual person who bought a car, of a particular model, on a certain date, and who has been running it for just so long since it was last serviced – at which time certain specific items were attended to. It really doesn't much matter whether the dealer's service manager is able to write to Mr Jones in those terms – and to greet him appropriately when he arrives on the appointed day – simply because the dealer's well-trained memory retains a vivid impression of Mr Jones and his vehicle, down to the last optional extra – or because the manufacturer's computer has regurgitated full details on Monday morning of Jones, Smith, Brown, and Ramsbottom whose cars are all due for servicing that week. Actually Mr Jones, who wasn't born yesterday, is perfectly well aware that the latter is the case – but is *still* pleased and comforted by the degree of care and trouble taken to give individual treatment to him, and all the other manufacturer's customers.

4

Data Collection

---

1. SALES-RELATED DATA

We looked, in the previous chapter, at some of the problems involved – particularly in a retail environment – in obtaining name and address information from individual customers. For present purposes we will assume that all information arising directly from the database user's dealings with his customers – which broadly, if not wholly accurately, we will refer to as sales-related data – is readily available. Nor do we need to become involved in detailed discussion of methods of data capture. But it may be worth saying a few words about some of the consequences of holding sales-related data, which, though they may not be immediately obvious, do require to be recognised and catered for at the start.

a) **Data protection.**   The UK, unlike a number of other countries, has never had a law of privacy; despite the continual outrages committed in this area by the gutter press, there is a singular reluctance in political quarters to depart from this position. There is, however, a law on data protection. Any person or organisation that holds, on a computer, personal information about one or more other individuals must, under the terms of the Data Protection Act of 1984, register his related activities with the Data Protection Registrar. For the purposes of the Act, any data that relates to an identifiable individual person is personal data; this means that even a bare list of names and addresses falls within the scope of the Act, when computerised. Registration consists in obtaining a form from the Registrar* and filling it in so as to show the nature of the data held (and/or to be held) and the purposes for which it is, and/or will be, used. To hold personal data on a computer without registering, or to use it in ways that fall outside the terms of registration, is a criminal offence (since 11 May 1986).

It is therefore to be recommended that the database owner, in registering, specifies not only presently planned uses of his data, but also whatever future uses might reasonably arise. (One can of course, amend a registration, or enter a new one, but this minor nuisance can be avoided by some forethought.)

The Data Protection Principles, as enshrined in the Act, are worth quoting, together with the Registrar's own gloss on each. In each case the principle is printed in quotes, with the Registrar's comments below:

1. 'The information to be contained in personal data shall be obtained, and personal data shall be processed, fairly and lawfully.'
   In considering whether information is obtained fairly, the Registrar will consider whether any person has been deceived or misled as to the purpose for which it is to be held, used, or disclosed.
2. 'Personal data shall be held only for one or more specified and lawful purposes.'
   Specified purposes are those described on the Register.
3. 'Personal data held for any purpose or purposes shall not be used or disclosed in any manner incompatible with that purpose or those purposes.'
   Incompatible use or disclosure means otherwise than as described on the Register.
4. 'Personal data held for any purpose or purposes shall be adequate, relevant, and not excessive in relation to that purpose or those purposes.' (No comment here)
5. 'Personal data shall be accurate and, where necessary, kept up to date.'
   'Accurate' means correct and not misleading as to any matter of fact. You

---

* Mr Eric Howe, Office of the Data Protection Registrar, Springfield House, Water Lane, Wilmslow, Cheshire SK9 5AX.

may be unable to ensure the accuracy of data received from the Data Subject or a third party. There are provisions in the Act where by marking and processing such data appropriately you will not be considered to be in breach of this principle. Such marking or processing will also absolve you from any liability to pay compensation for damage caused by the inaccuracy of the data. Data should be kept up to date except where the purpose for which it is held does not require it to be.

6. 'Personal data held for any purpose or purposes shall not be kept for longer than is necessary for that purpose or those purposes.' (No comment here)

7. 'An individual shall be entitled:

    (a) at reasonable intervals and without undue delay or expense:

        (i) to be informed by any Data User whether he holds personal data of which that individual is the subject, and

        (ii) to access any such data held by a Data User; and

    (b) where appropriate, to have such data corrected or erased.'

    This principle introduces the right of subject access which is fully described in Section 21 of the Act. 'Reasonable intervals' will vary with the nature of the data, the nature and frequency of processing, etc and is not defined. The Act stipulates that subject access requests shall be met in 40 days after receipt or determination of additional necessary information. The Secretary of State will make an Order fixing the maximum fee which may be charged for subject access, thus ensuring that no 'undue expense' is incurred by Data Subjects.

8. 'Appropriate security measures shall be taken against unauthorised access to, or alteration, disclosure, or destruction of, personal data, and against accidental loss or destruction of personal data.'

    In considering whether security measures are appropriate regard should be had to the nature of the personal data and the potential harm which could result from unauthorised access, etc. It will be necessary also to consider the place where data are stored, security measures programmed into the equipment and measures taken for ensuring the reliability of staff having access to the data. This eighth principle applies to Computer Bureaux as well as Data Users.

    There are special dispensations for data held for historical and research purposes, where their use is such that it does not cause, or is not likely to cause, damage or distress to any Data Subject. Such data shall not be regarded as unfairly obtained merely because the historical or research purpose was not declared when it was obtained, and it may be kept indefinitely without breaching the sixth principle. Where a breach of any principle comes to the Registrar's attention he may serve a notice requiring you to take steps to comply with the principle or principles in question. Failure to comply with the terms of such a notice will be an offence.

You may feel, as I do, that this is a pretty pointless Act of Parliament, combining the maximum of bureaucratic hair-splitting gobbledegook, and inconvenience for the trader, with the minimum of intelligible or useful protection for the consumer. Unfortunately this does not make it unique, or even particularly unusual; the Act belongs to a large class of legislation whose object is not so much to achieve anything positive as to remove an irritating and intractable subject from the political agenda. At all events, fourteen years after the setting up of the first (Younger) committee on the subject, the Act reached the statute book, and must now be heeded. Copies of the Act may be acquired from HM Stationery Office. However, a mere reading of the Act, necessary as that is, will raise more questions than it answers; a great deal depends upon how the Act is interpreted – in the first instance by the Registrar's office, and subsequently by the Data Protection Tribunal and the Courts. The Registrar has issued sundry pamphlets of explanation and elaboration; these can be obtained from his office. The Advertising Association has also published (with the approval of the Registrar) in March 1987 a Code of Practice 'Covering the Use of Personal Data for Advertising and Direct Marketing Purposes'. The latest version of this Code has been incorporated in the British Code of Advertising Practice (BCAP), which is monitored by the Advertising Standards Authority, from whom copies can be obtained.*

The general expectation of those who have studied the Act, and discussed its implications with the Registrar, originally was that the Act was not likely to interfere substantially with normal accepted practice within the direct marketing industry *provided that* the purposes for which personal

---

* The Advertising Standards Authority, Brook House, 2–16 Torrington Place, London WC1E 7HN.

data is used were fully covered by the terms of registration. However, anyone collecting personal data which he intends (or might in future wish) to disclose to a third party – eg in a list rental, or list swap arrangement – does need to consider the implications of the first principle with particular care, and should give close attention to the AA's code of practice on this subject. During the second half of 1988 the Registrar's office began to concern itself more closely with the concept of 'fair' collection and use of data within the first principle. At the time of writing a prolonged debate is in progress between the industry (represented by the Data Protection Committee of the Advertising Association) and the Registrar on this subject, and it would appear that in the outcome more stringent duties are likely to be laid on data users than the BCAP currently enforces. The Registrar's interpretation of the Act is that personal data should only be used by a data user with the 'informed consent' of the data subject, and that this means full disclosure of the uses to which data will, or may, be put, at the time of collection. The implications of such an interpretation for the wide variety of different methods of data collection are the subject of current discussions. The Registrar's view of the matter was contained in the now notorious Guideline 19 issued by his office. This document was impossible to implement literally in its original form, and final resolution on this subject awaits the outcome of two cases now pending hearings before the Data Protection Tribunal. Meanwhile, the Advertising Standards Authority (or the Data Protection Committee of the AA) can advise on the best means for an individual to protect his position in his own particular circumstances. A fairly typical example of the sort of foolish confusion that arises when the law attempts to intervene in matters which are no part of its proper concern.

b) Data protection and Europe. The UK Data Protection Act was itself a restatement of the principles contained in the Convention of the Council of Europe on this subject. But the failure of a number of European Community countries to ratify the Convention, or to legislate domestically on data protection, persuaded the European Commission to produce its own Directive. The Draft Directive on Data Protection must rank, in its original form, as one of the most deplorable documents to come out of Brussels: there was no prior consultation with business or industry, and the text ran the gamut from the ambiguous to the comical to the deeply damaging. The direct marketing industry believed, with some justice, that at least some of the authors of this text had been motivated by extreme prejudice against direct mail, and probably read into it even greater threats than it actually contained. Certainly no one in Brussels had expected the outburst of rage that struck the Commission: lobbying on this Directive was greater than on any other previous subject.

At the time of writing it does appear that the second draft of the Directive will be cleansed of the worst features of its predecessor; moreover, it may be that the Commission has learned a valuable lesson about consultation. At any event, once the new draft has been through its second reading in the European Parliament, and been approved by the Council of Ministers, it will be necessary for the UK to review its existing legislation in the light of the Directive. It seems probable that not a great deal of modification will be required. (Probably the biggest single change will be the extension of data protection legislation to cover manual data files as well as computerised ones.)

c) **Duplication.** Most organisations that collect individual customer information are obliged to identify customers by reference simply to name and address. Banks, insurance companies, and a few others, are fortunate in being able, most of the time, to rely on account numbers, policy numbers, and so on: others lack this advantage. Names and addresses are notoriously hard to handle, being liable to numerous human errors in transcription, and – in the case of addresses at least – often not written the same way twice running. As a consequence, a single customer is liable to have his name and address recorded twice, thrice, or four times, with variations, on a single database. Where the database is being used to generate communications, such an occurrence on any large scale is a disaster, resulting in wasted costs, and customer irritation – as well as destroying just that sense of individual attention which the mailer wishes to engender. And even where the purpose of the database is primarily statistical, wholly misleading results may follow.

All of this makes duplication a major headache. A strategy for dealing with it has to be decided on right at the start of data collection, if the ensuing problems are to be kept within bounds. The problem is basically this: when the database receives notice that a sale has been made to Mr X living at such and such an address, how does the computer decide whether this is the first record of Mr X, or whether the database already holds a record for him? Or, more problematical still, if the database then gets to hear of Mrs X, living at the same address, should it hold two separate records for these two persons, or amalgamate them into one?

A whole variety of logical systems (going under the horrible generic title of merge-purge systems) exist for examining names and addresses in order to determine whether they belong to the same person or not, and these logical systems are incorporated in computer programmes. These can then be used either by a service bureau, which will take $1,2,3,\ldots n$ files of names and addresses and match them together, eliminating duplicates both within and between files, or by a database user, to determine in relation to each incoming name and address in turn whether or not it is already present on the database. All of these systems are to a greater or lesser extent imperfect: there is, after all, no logical method available for determining whether:

JAC Smith
12 Laburnum Grove
Newbury
Berkshire

is or is not the same person as:

Arthur Smith
Dunrovin
Laburnum Grove
Newbury
Berkshire

unless access can be had to further extraneous information. (And this is only one of an immense range of potential ambiguities.) So that all systems that rely on the content of names and addresses alone must end by 'taking a view' – just as a clerk would in a similar situation, with the major difference being that a clerk's 'view' will tend to differ from one occasion to the next, whereas a computer will at least be consistent – and this 'view' will in some circumstances result in two separate customers being treated as one, and in others will create two separate records for the same person.

The safest system for the avoidance of duplication lies in the use of postcodes. A single postcode embraces, on average, 15 households, so that the appearance in an address of a correct postcode already gives a high degree of discrimination. But how to be sure that the postcode *is* correct – bearing in mind that customers misquote them, and staff mistranscribe them? Well, again there are computer bureaux that undertake to postcode files of names and addresses by reference to the Postal Address File (PAF) created, and maintained, by the Royal Mail. And the same rules used by the bureau for this purpose can be incorporated in database maintenance programmes by any database user to deal with single name and address transactions.

Postcoding has a number of advantages:

i)   It makes deduplication of addresses (names are another matter) simple: every valid address in the country is represented once and only once on the PAF; if an address can be found on the PAF, it will always give rise to the same postcode; if an address cannot be found on the PAF the implication must normally be that the address given is incorrect. However, there are problems, even with the PAF: these relate both to the accuracy of the file itself, which has been a matter of considerable unease to its users ever since its inception, and to the speed with which changes – caused, for example, by the erection of new housing estates – can be communicated to the file. The record of the Royal Mail on the maintenance of the PAF has not, to date, been anything like as good as it ought to be; that said, it is an invaluable, even if imperfect, tool.

ii)   Within limits, addresses can be corrected by reference to the PAF: missing towns or counties, and sometimes districts, can be added and a wide range of mis-spellings corrected. Some of these corrections will improve the deliverability, or speed of delivery, of the mail; all of them will help improve the general presentation and image of the mailing piece.

iii) Addresses that cannot be found on the PAF, and cannot be corrected, will be output for clerical scrutiny – preventing incorrect, and perhaps undeliverable, items from reaching and corrupting the database.

iv) Under the Royal Mail's bulk mailing system, Mailsort, postal rebate or discount will only be available to mailers who achieve a high level of postcoding on their outgoing mail. (See further in Chapter 5, Section 4.)

v) As we shall see in the next section, the postcode is the key to externally available demographic data about addresses throughout the country, which may be of marketing value.

The postcode, then, narrows an address down to approximately 15 households. Adding to that postcode a house number will define the household virtually uniquely.* A database that uses the postcode as its prime household identifier, that allows no unpostcoded records on the database, and that checks all incoming addresses, already postcoded or not, against the PAF, will ensure that no duplicate, and no incorrect, addresses can appear on the database, ever. (As always, there have to be exceptions. It is by no means unknown for new housing estates, or individual houses, to be occupied before postcodes are assigned, and certainly before the new postcodes have been added to the PAF. Clearly some allowance must be made for such circumstances, short of refusing to recognise the existence of the households concerned.)

The database user must still decide what he wants to do about duplication of surnames. Are Mr and Mrs Smith, living at the same address, to be treated as one person (ie to be allotted only one record on file or as two? What about AC Smith and JA Smith? Or indeed, is the system to allow two different surnames to exist at the same address? In fact, is the basic record in the database a person or a household (ie for practical purposes a postal delivery point)? And if a household, can it, like a real household, contain multiple persons? And if so, what are the limitations?

The answers to these questions will vary with the nature of the business that the database exists to serve. The point of posing them here is simply to

---

* Theoretically ambiguities are still possible – but in a trivial number of cases, eg where a postcode covers a part of two streets so that 1 High Street and 1 Church Street could share the same postcode. This happens in one or two areas where postcoding was erroneously handled at the outset.

indicate that there is a good deal of planning regarding the basic structure of the information one wishes to hold, that needs to precede the collection of database information. Many of the problems of database structure are technical problems, which we will not attempt to deal with in this book. But the questions arising from problems of duplication, and how to overcome them, are fundamental to the marketing objectives of the database user: they are a good deal too important to be left to the 'experts'.

d) Expansion. Data, like the universe itself, is in a state of continual expansion – and at a very similar speed, as it sometimes seems. The problems that arise from this are not primarily problems of storing data, since the storage capacity of computers has at least kept pace in recent years with the growth in data to be stored. Nor is there a problem in accessing individual pieces of stored data: today's computer systems are well adapted to this purpose. Rather the problem occurs when very large, and continually increasing volumes of data require to be sequentially accessed – for example for analysis purposes. Even with the processing speeds achieved by today's equipment, the amount of work required, and the time taken by it can, with an expanding database, quickly overwhelm the computer.

The consequence of this is that, in any given marketing application, there is likely to be a need first to settle for recording something less than the total available information, and second to accept that stored data, after some lapse of time, can be deleted, or subsumed into a summary. Let us consider an example of each process.

A company is selling a range of units for fitted bedrooms, kitchens, bathrooms. It has in its range 150 different units. Units are available in (on average) four different sets of dimensions, eight different finishes, and ten different styles. Now, what is to be the basic product building block under which we record marketing data? If we record full data about each sale, we have potentially 48,000 product variants. Moreover, a given style lasts on average for two years, and is then replaced – giving an additional 24,000 items a year. Does the marketing department truly require to record and analyse each individual sale according to one of 48,000 current variants, plus a growing number of past ones? Or can we settle for coding our products, so far as the marketing database is concerned, by unit and style only, giving a mere 1,500 possibilities, and an extra 750 a year?

Indeed, do we need to keep past sales records, at this level of detail, indefinitely? Could we not, once a given style goes out of use, simply summarise the sales data pertaining to it under the 150 basic units – which are fewer in number and subject to much less frequent change?

Clearly the answers to questions of this kind will vary with each individual case. The important point is that this question must be asked early on, before data collection starts: what are the basic building blocks of data that will be used in our database structure? Are they:

The household?
The individual person within the household?
The basic product?
The individual product variant?
The region, or branch?
The individual salesman, or assistant, in a region/branch?

To get answers that will stand the test of time demands the utmost co-operation, understanding and mutual respect between those – the marketing staff – for whose use the database is being built, and the construction team of systems people. It is because these qualities of understanding and respect are so frequently, and sadly, lacking, and because, consequently, serious co-operation is often not forthcoming, that so many database enterprises turn out to be either substantial disasters, or much harder work and much greater generators of frustration in their latter stages than they need be if properly planned at the beginning. We will revert to this theme at a later stage in this book.

2. DEMOGRAPHIC DATA

Ideally, the marketing person who has absorbed the admonition 'Know Your Customer', wants as much information as is available about past customers and about future prospects, as individuals. We have already seen the need to preserve the data available within the company on sales and promotions; we will see in the next section what additional individual data can be obtained, and how. But here we will first consider the acquisition and use of statistical data, relating not to individuals but to groups.

During the last fifteen years a number of companies have started to offer demographic data, and/or demographic services, which are alleged to be capable of improving the targeting, and hence the cost-effectiveness, of a very wide variety of marketing efforts. If these companies are to be believed, the intelligent use of demographics can guide a user in choosing the optimum site for a new store, in deciding what products to stock in a given area, in maximising response to a promotion, whether in the Press or by mail, and in planning distribution systems or allocating sales territories. Our purpose here is to examine the origins, development, and present status of demographic systems; to indicate what types of system are on offer; to discuss the similarities and differences of competing systems, and to give some evaluation of the claims made for demographics as a marketing tool.

Demographic data is, simply, statistical information about population groups. It is extremely important to bear this in mind: although some of the systems we shall examine do use some information about individual persons or households, the basis of them all is the group. Information about the group can be ascribed to individuals in it only on the basis of probability. Thus, if we know that 35 per cent of the people in a given group are retired, we also know that the chance of any one individual in that group being retired is slightly better than 1 in 3. And we know that a promotion directed to retired persons will be 250 per cent more effective in reaching its target if addressed to this group rather than to a similar sized group of which only 10 per cent are retired. What we must *not* do is to think of the first group as though it consisted solely, or even mainly, of retired persons, since 65 per cent of it does not.

Of course, in an ideal marketing world, we would have a wealth of available information about individuals. In the real world, collection of such information across a population of 43 million adults (or 20 million households) is inordinately expensive. What we do have, readily, cheaply, and plentifully, is information about groups. The most plentiful source of such information in the UK is the decennial census.

a) **The census.** The last UK census was taken in 1991. Every householder is obliged by law to complete a census form; the data from these forms is collated by the Office of Population Censuses and Surveys (OPCS). Clearly no data for individual households is available from OPCS. However, responsibility for collecting census forms lies with an army of enumerators, each of whom deals with a small geographic area containing an average of 150 households and known as an enumeration district (ED). The ED is the smallest available building block of census data: anyone can buy from OPCS a library of magnetic tapes containing full census data about the 130,000 EDs in England, Scotland, and Wales. (Northern Ireland is excluded from consideration here: its data at the 1991 census was very imperfectly collected, and this, added to differences in presentation, makes it extremely difficult to interpret. The systems considered here do not deal with it, unless on a one-off basis for a particular client.)

This data is broadly of three kinds. It describes:

i) The people who live in the ED: total numbers, numbers by age band and by marital status, for example.

ii) Socio-economic conditions, such as numbers in certain types of occupation; levels of car ownership, etc.

iii) Types of housing.

The amount of data available is very large indeed: for each of the 130,000 EDs there are some 4,000 variables, or pieces of data, plus a further 1,500 that apply only to parts of the country (eg Scotland, Wales). Before we discuss how this mass of information can be reduced to manageable proportions, it may be sensible to pause and consider in what basic ways this type of data about groups of households can be used in a marketing context.

The root problem of all marketing effort is the problem of targeting: whom are we trying to reach. This problem underlies the siting of a new shop, the stocking of a range of products, the placing of a newspaper or TV advertisement, the sending of a direct mail promotion. Targeting means ensuring that our message reaches as many as possible of the people we are interested in, while wasting the least possible effort in reaching people we are not interested in. So the object of looking at information that describes groups of people is to be able to differentiate one group from another: what we hope is that differences in the demographic make-up of groups will be reflected in differences in all types of purchasing behaviour. We must begin, then, by establishing population groups that are demographically different; we can then consider how to test any marketing hypotheses about those groups.

On the other hand, our chosen population groups, whatever their demographic differences, must not be so small that observed behavioural differences between them have no statistical significance. An example may help. Suppose we were to use 130,000 EDs as our population groups, and were then to apply to those groups data from a random national survey of 30,000 consumers showing what brand of toilet soap they habitually bought. The majority of EDs would not contain any person from our survey; those that did would have one or two persons. It would therefore be impossible, from this survey data, to use the demographic differences between EDs as a way of differentiating peoples' purchasing behaviour regarding toilet soap. If, however, we had only 30 population groups instead of 130,000, then each group would contain on average 1,000 persons from our survey, and this should be enough to observe differences in brand preferences between groups with different demographic characteristics.

The first problem, then, is to band together EDs with similar demographic profiles so as to form groups whose demography is significantly different each from the other, and whose populations are sufficiently large that even quite modest research samples will show up at significant levels within each of them.

But before we can do this there is another problem: 4,000 variables is far too large a mass of data to handle for each ED – the more so when we recognise that much of the data is either of no interest for marketing purposes, or repetitive. All demographic systems therefore begin by reducing this number to a more manageable total of significant items. These pieces of data are then expressed proportionally – eg:

Proportion of ED residents aged 15–24
Proportion of permanent dwellings rented unfurnished

The systems we shall be looking at use between 40 and 100 principal items of data from among the 4,000 census variables.

Having determined which census variables to use, the demographic system will then examine how best, by reference to these variables, the 130,000 EDs can be banded together in groups whose members have broadly similar characteristics. The five systems we will be looking at derive (by a computerised statistical process known as cluster analysis) 40 to 150 groups of EDs. In all five cases these groups can be further aggregated into smaller numbers of super-groups.

So we now have a limited number of groups of EDs, where each group has a substantial population, and all the EDs in each group have broadly similar demographic profiles as determined by the most significant of the census variables. So far, so good.

b) Enumeration districts and postcodes. One serious theoretical problem remains. Let us suppose that a marketing manager possesses data – from market research sources or whatever – about the behaviour of a number of people. He wishes to relate this behaviour to the known demographic characteristics of the areas in which these people live, in order to see whether demography is a significant predictor of this particular behaviour. How does he discover in which ED each person in his survey lies?

The key to this whole process is the post code: if we know an individual's postcode (for which we have a map reference) then we can 'allocate' him to an ED (for which we also have a map reference). However, the migration from postcode to ED is not easy. The average postcode comprises 15 households – ie there are ten average postcodes to the average ED. But the boundaries of each have been allocated independently; consequently a postcode area may well lie in more than one ED.* As we shall see, different systems use different methods to relate the two entities; there is as yet no perfect answer. All systems end up by allocating each and every postcode to an ED, and hence to a group of EDs with a common demographic profile. By this means a demographic profile can be assigned to any individual household in the country. It does need to be stressed again that there is no guarantee that that profile will be in any way accurate for that household: if we say that a given address falls in a neighbourhood of 'private houses, well-off elderly' it may still be the case that every member of that household belongs to the 40 per cent of people in that neighbourhood who are under 45: the neighbourhood description deals only in relativities, and indicates

---

* Except in Scotland, where things are organised, as ever, more logically. Possibly at the next census a touch of logic will arrive south of the Border.

merely that well-off elderly people living in private houses are characteristic of this neighbourhood.

c) **Additional data.**   All five systems considered here use, sometimes in different ways, further data. Some of this data, unlike the census statistics, is about individual persons; it is broadly of two types:

i)   Sample data. There is a wide range of market research data available, from such sources as the Target Group Index (TGI) or the Financial Research Survey (FRS). This indicates the relationship of a sample of individuals to one or more items in which the survey is interested. Thus, FRS will tell us who, and what proportion, of a national sample are shareholders; by allocating these individuals to their appropriate ED groups, based on their postcodes, we can determine whether one ED group holds significantly more shareholders than another.

ii) Universal data. Above all the electoral register, which tells us the names of the individuals who live in each ED (via their postcodes). The next most frequently encountered example is the Lord Chancellor's list – of County Court judgements, satisfactions, Bills of Sale, and bankruptcies. Since all of these phenomena are recorded on the list, it is possible to know the total number occurring in each ED, or group of EDs.

Finally, it is possible to obtain information about road networks and journey times which can be related to the areas in which people live. This can be used to indicate how many people, in what groups of EDs, live within a given area, or within a given journey time of a particular spot. A major value in linking demographics to postal geography consists in the ability to take virtually any data that can be mapped and to express it in a way that relates to population – and to population groups differentiated by demographic characteristics. What we must now consider, first as a general principle, and then separately for each of the methodologies in use, is whether the differentiation given by clustering enumeration districts on the basis of census variables can in fact produce usefully differentiated markets for products and services.

d) Overview of theory.   There are a number of reasons for being sceptical about the concept of using demographics in this way:

i)   Most obvious of these is the fact that a census happens only once every ten years. At the time of writing the 1981 census data is already more than eleven years old; the 1991 data will not be available in these systems till mid to late 1993, by which time the 1981 data will be twelve years old; since it is generally reckoned that some 12% of the population moves house every year, it is clear that after 12 years we are not looking at anything like the same population in the same place as represented by the census. (Consider how London Docklands looked demographically in 1981, and now; think how many times, albeit on a smaller scale, this type of change has happened round the country.) How much this matters will vary from one application to another. Clearly EDs in which significant numbers of new houses (and even 15 houses constitutes 10% of the average ED) have been built since 1981, will be incorrectly described by census data. The sale of council houses, which only started in the 1980s, has substantially swollen the ranks of owner occupiers. City centre EDs can change their demography radically in a few years – through slum clearance, or by gentrification. Areas which had, in 1981, a high proportion of children aged 0–4 (eg new housing estates, or new towns) are likely to show different characteristics five and more years later. And so on. Nor is the pace of change likely to be any less in the 1990s.

ii) As noted already, there is a theoretical problem with the central function of relating postcodes to EDs, caused by the non-coincidence of their boundaries. The real problem is worse: the whole process of matching depends upon using the Central Postcode Directory (CPD), which gives a grid reference for every postcode, in conjunction with grid references for EDs. Difficulties arise in three ways:

First: The CPD map references are imprecise: they define only a square on the ground of 100 x 100 metres. In the case where one or more ED boundaries run through this square, a postcode can be allocated to an ED in which no part of it actually falls. This can be shown to affect up to 50% of the postcodes in city centres. (The effect is less where EDs are geographically larger.)

Second: A substantial number of CPD map references are actually wrong, due to mistranscription of data and careless or non-existent verification. This can result in postcodes being allocated to EDs not just yards, but many miles, astray.

Third: While the GLC, before its demise, had produced digitised grid references for the boundaries of all its EDs, no such information exists outside London. Although ED maps exist, the only digital reference for EDs is a grid reference for the centroid of each. This means that the computer system, when allocating a non-London postcode to 'its' ED, must choose the ED with the nearest centroid to the (imprecise) grid reference of the postcode. Since EDs do not have regular shapes, this causes more errors.

It is extremely hard to assess how much difference these problems make in practice. Where a postcode, for instance, is allocated to the ED next door to its 'true' ED (certainly much the most common error) the probability is that the two EDs are sufficiently similar to end up in the same cluster anyway – in which case no harm is done. For the future, work is in hand to enhance and correct the CPD – which will benefit all systems discussed here – and since ED boundaries will have to be re-drawn for 2001, it may be possible to make them co-terminous with postcodes throughout the UK. However, the vast job of digitising ED boundaries will still have to be done if perfect matching is to be achieved.

These are serious theoretical problems but, in the last analysis, marketing is a pragmatic art rather than a theoretical science: the real test of this methodology is how well it works in practice. Beyond doubt it has worked well for some users; it is also capable of very considerable improvement; ultimately however it is liable to be limited by the ageing of its base data.

e) **Overview of practice.** There are a number of different kinds of marketing purpose for which demographic systems can be used.

i)   The owner of a list of names and addresses can have the codes for demographic clusters (as determined by one system or another – or even more than one) added to each record on his file, and can use these codes as a discriminating factor (on their own or in conjunction with other data) to determine whether or not to mail individuals with a particular offer. It is in practice unlikely that the very generalised and imprecise data underlying these codes will make more than a marginal difference to the particular and precise information that a list owner should have about his own customers. But circumstances can alter cases. There can be no harm, and only small cost, in mounting a test to discover whether the extra discrimination offered by one of these systems results in extra response.

ii)   The user of an outside list on which there is little discriminatory information except codes for demographic clusters, may use this data to choose groups of people to mail. He may determine which clusters to use by one of a variety of methods:

Either: Subjectively, by looking at the demographic profile of each cluster and comparing it with his knowledge of his own product.

Or: By taking a profile of his own customers, to see which clusters they preponderately fall into, and choosing from those. (There is danger of a circularity in this method. If, for example, it is found that a user's customers come dominantly from 'affluent suburban housing' this may mean merely that he has been advertising exclusively in media confined to such households. This own-list-profile method will work properly only if the source from which that list was recruited is compatible with the list being researched.)

Or: By running a test to a sample of the proposed list, and seeing whether response is conditioned by the clusters in which promotees live.

This is one of the most frequent uses of demographics to date, so let us pause and consider it. There is no question but that all five systems surveyed do succeed in creating population clusters with widely differing demographic profiles. There is also ample evidence that a wide range of purchasing behaviour is significantly different from one cluster to another. What these statistically significant differences amount to in terms of profit and loss is another matter. Let us try a hypothetical example.*

There were, in 1982, 1,524,000 readers of *The Guardian*. Allocating a representative sample of these readers to the ED clusters produced by one particular demographic system indicated that the cluster categorised as 'High status non-family areas' scored 271 for *Guardian* readers, against a national average of 100, or a penetration of 9 per cent against 3.5 per cent. Suppose that we have a product known to be attractive to *Guardian* readers; we mail the 1,874,000 households known to be in this cluster, knowing we will reach 169,000 *Guardian* readers. Let us further suppose that the response pattern is:

Guardian readers: 5% = 8,450
Others   : 1% = 17,050
                      25,500 = 1.36%

If we had mailed a similar number of households from random EDs containing an average number of *Guardian* readers (ie 65,590) we would have achieved:

Guardian readers: 5% = 3,280
Others   : 1% = 18,084
                      21,364 = 1.14%

Now, the difference between 1.14 and 1.36 could represent a lot of money, or even the difference between profit and loss – it is, after all, a 19 per cent difference. The improvement may, or may not, be sufficient to pay for the costs incurred. But it isn't anything like as large as the difference between 271 and 100, or between 9 per cent and 3.5 per cent. The reason for this, of course, is that the phenomenon at which we are looking is only a fairly small part of the whole. If we had an ED cluster in which *Guardian* readers had a 90 per cent penetration, against a national average of 35 per cent, then, on the same

---

* Data used in this example is derived from application of a 1982 National Readership Survey to Acorn Groups.

assumptions, the difference in response would be 4.5 per cent versus 2.3 per cent – an improvement this time of 96 per cent.

Each potential user of a demographic system will have to do his own sums, and to look not merely at the relative discriminatory power of this or that system, but at the absolute number of real prospects it will deliver, and at the cost of reaching them.

Finally, it would appear that demographic systems are rather better at distinguishing bad marketing prospects than good ones. To return to the 1982 National Readership Survey, households of Social Grade A have, unsurprisingly, a score of 1 in 'Poorest Council Estates' compared to a norm of 100. Yet the highest ED cluster achieved a score in this context of only 253. One of the highest scores in the whole survey was 367, for households with oil-fired central heating in 'Agricultural Areas'; yet another cluster had a low score of 17 – one sixth of the norm. This is probably just a way of stating the fairly obvious – that poor areas are more homogeneous than affluent areas – but it has implications for demographic marketing which are worth thinking about.

iii) Demographic systems were first developed in this country for direct mail use. But in recent years other uses – for some of which they may be far more valuable than for direct mail – have been developed. Some of these uses – such as optimal siting of a new store – are highly specific; others are about offering a deeper insight into the nature and composition of one's market – a benefit that may be hard to quantify, but that no marketing person would turn down out of hand.

The general principle is that one can define a geographic area in a number of different ways – as a collection of postcodes, or postcode sectors, or enumeration districts; as everything within a certain radius of a given point, or anywhere within a certain journey time of such a point; by county, or local authority, or constituency, or ward, or TV region – and any or all of these can be related via grid references and postcodes to the people who live in these geographic expressions. Through market research surveys, existing or specially commissioned, one can characterise the buying habits of people in these areas against the national norm and subdivide by demographic clusters if required. One can map the propensity of people in urban or rural areas to travel for their shopping: the more expensive the product, the farther people travel for it; wealthier people travel longer distances for more things than poorer people. None of this is surprising, but being able to express it in precise numerical terms, and to plot its incidence on a map, is new.

From this welter of data one can draw all manner of inferences about shopping patterns; these may help determine policy on the siting of a store, or become ammunition in discussing rental levels. They are certainly a basis for a scientific approach to optimising stock-holdings of different lines.

In sum then, I am not an enthusiast for including demographic data, or codes, on advertisers' own customer files – certainly not without testing their value first. For lists devoid of other discriminants, demographic clusters are an advance on nothing: whether the advance is great enough to recoup the cost is an open question, whose answer will vary from case to case: again it can be tested. In non-direct mail situations, as an aid to defining market areas or giving an insight into market characteristics, I believe demographics have a great deal to offer.

That, however, is a generalised picture: when we turn to specific systems we will see that one practitioner or another has taken this or that approach in an attempt to eradicate, or lessen, some of the problems alluded to above. I am not sure that matters have changed greatly between 1990 and 1993; I am confident there will be considerable advances in the mid 90s, and that those who have gained experience in the meantime will be the first to benefit.

f) **Acorn** (an acronym for A Classification Of Residential Neighbour-hoods) is a demographic system offered by CACI – an international consultancy founded in the USA in 1962. CACI was not, as its literature claims, 'the first to obtain (census statistics) from the census office' which they did in 1977 some years after the Reader's Digest had taken this route. They were, however, the first company to use these statistics to build a generalised system that could provide a national demographic profile. The other systems discussed below have all built on CACI's experience – although each has added something of its own.

The current Acorn system dates from 1983, and uses the 1981 census statistics. (It will move to the 1991 data in due course.) From among the 4,000 census variables, Acorn uses 40 in order to group the 133,000 EDs, by a process of cluster analysis, into 38 'neighbourhood types', which further coalesce into 11 'groups'. CACI offers the following range of services, connected more or less closely with Acorn:

i) *Acorn Profiling.* CACI will take a random sample of a client's own postcoded list of customers (minimum sample size 5,000), apply Acorn codes to each record, and provide a profile of that sample indicating what proportion of its total falls within each Acorn type, compared with the generality of the population. This exercise can give a valuable insight into the make-up of one's customer list. It *may* also help in deciding how to structure future marketing campaigns (but see the comments on page 106).

Sub-profiles of groups of separately identified names within the total sample can also be provided at the same time (minimum number 2,000).

ii) *Acorn Test Mailing.* CACI will take a list of postcoded addresses and separate them according to Acorn codes which the client has predetermined he wishes to mail and those that he does not. Codes will be added to the selected records on this file, which is returned to the client, only for the purpose of analysing the response.

iii) *Acorn Coding.* CACI will lease to a client the Acorn directory, enabling him to add permanent Acorn codes to his own postcoded file. He can then analyse, by Acorn type, any customer behaviour recorded on his file. Minimum lease term is three years; there is a fixed annual charge plus a price per 1,000 records on the client's file. Automatic annual directory updates are supplied (eg where the Royal Mail changes postcodes).

iv) *The Acorn List.* CACI offer selections from the 43 million electoral register, as computerised and postcoded by UAPT-Infolink – a leading credit reference agency. This list is Acorn coded, therefore Acorn-based selections are possible.

Possession of this list also enables CACI to select 'neighbours' of a client's existing customers – those who live in adjacent houses, or the same street.

v)   *Spectra*.   This is an added service offered by CACI, and described as a direct mail response improvement system. The initial part of the process is not very different from the Acorn profiling described above: it simply uses more data, of a kind chosen to meet the specific needs of each client, in order to provide an individual model of a market, instead of using merely the generalised Acorn segmentation.

Spectra starts with a postcoded sample of client addresses about each of which we have either a yes/no variable (they have/have not responded to a given offer) or a continuous variable (they have spent x pounds in the last year). Any further available client data will be added to this file – purchase data, accounting data, etc. Also added will be CACI data – Acorn codes, individual census variables, travel data, retail data. From this mixture of data Spectra will produce a profile showing what factors affect response, and will then calculate a 'score' for each record on the client's file: the higher the score the greater the propensity to respond. The culmination of this process is a 'gains chart' which shows how the 'best' 10 per cent, next best 10 per cent, etc, of the file will respond.

vi)   *Site*.   This system enables a CACI client to define one or more geographic areas; Site will then produce, for each area, population statistics broken down by Acorn type, details of local work-force, unemployment statistics, and a profile of households derived from the census data. This system can also produce a quantification of the local market for goods or services across 15 standard retail fields.

vii) *Local Expenditure Zones*.   CACI has divided the UK into 1,100 LEZs each with a shopping centre and crown post office. For any LEZ CACI can provide reports as for Site (see above) together with an analysis of sales potential for any product, an estimate of total market size, and details of retail competition.

viii) *Drive Time Zones*.   CACI has modelled the main road network so as to facilitate calculation of journey times, and estimation of numbers of persons (categorised by Acorn) within x minutes of a given point.

ix)   *Door-to-Door*.   CACI will define postal sectors that best meet a client's definition of Acorn types to be targeted. This definition can then be used by a door-to-door distributor – an improvement on blanket coverage.

x)   *Monica*.   CACI has pioneered a system for estimating the likely age group of an individual from his/her first name. This system is claimed to give a good age indication for 75 per cent of UK adults, and to add therefore to discriminatory potential on the electoral register.

g) Pinpoint.   Pinpoint Analysis Ltd is a small independent company which was the first to challenge (in 1983) the early monopoly in demographic systems held by CACI. Its primary product is PIN (Pinpoint Identification of Neighbourhoods) which attempts, like Acorn, to group enumeration districts with like census characteristics in clusters, and to assign to them postcode areas, using the Central Postcode Directory (CPD) as a link.

Pinpoint was the first to point to the extent of error arising from the use of the CPD. (See page 104 for details.) Pinpoint is now playing the leading role in correcting the CPD (where this is feasible) and hopes to go further by producing an accurate grid reference for every household in the country (Pinpoint Address Code, or PAC). This will effectively by-pass the CPD, and possibly the whole postcode system (although the problem of precise definition of ED boundaries will still exist). Correction of the CPD benefits all current systems equally; grid-referencing houses will be a further significant enhancement.

Pinpoint in its early days made a lot of noise about the inaccuracies of earlier ED/postcode linkages. It is probable that they ascribed too great an importance to these inaccuracies, and that their claim to have a system that, by correcting (some of) these inaccuracies was greatly superior to Acorn were too sweeping. Moreover, it is doubtful if any system's methodology in this linking area is *now* inferior to any other's. However the dismissive attitudes struck by Pinpoint's competitors are too reminiscent of the treatment of the little boy who insisted on remarking that the emperor was insufficiently clad. Pinpoint does have an obsession with precise accuracy of data, and although that may be costly for them, it can't be bad for their clients. And it is this drive for precision that is behind PAC, which could be a real benefit to demographic users.

The standard PIN classification began with 104 census variables, selected judgementally from the 4,000 total. These were subjected to a principal components analysis, and the first ten principal components were selected. These in turn were used in a cluster analysis against all 130,000 EDs to produce 60 ED clusters, which in turn reduce to 25, or twelve, super-clusters.

The basic services offered by Pinpoint are:

i) *Postcoding.* Pinpoint is one of the Royal Mail approved suppliers of computerised postcoding services; as such it is able to postcode client files to standards approved by the Royal Mail.

ii) *Profiling.* Pinpoint will profile a sample of a client's file against the standard PIN codes. The process is analogous to Acorn profiling (f.ii) above).

iii) *Test Mailings and Prospect Scoring.* Again as with Acorn, Pinpoint can code a list of names for a test mailing, and can analyse the results of the test to 'score' the master list from which the test names were taken.

iv) *PIN Directory.* Alternatively, PIN codes can be added to all records on a client file, either through Pinpoint itself, on a once-for-all basis, or through the lease to the client of the PIN directory for use on his own main frame.

v) *Electoral Register.* Pinpoint does not itself own a computerised electoral register, but has an exclusive arrangement with Grattans, who do. Names can be supplied from PIN-selected areas.

vi) *Finpin.* This is the first of what is planned as a series of specialised systems for specific market sectors – in this case the financial sector. Finpin starts with market research data from 65,000 interviews conducted by Financial Research Services (FRS – an NOP sub-sidiary). This data is applied to the census information to identify 58 significant census variables; these are subjected to a principal components analysis which produces 20 principal components; these are used in a cluster analysis to provide 40 ED clusters, which in turn coalesce into ten or four super-clusters. Pinpoint claim that, while PIN is a powerful general-purpose discriminator, Finpin is very much more powerful in relation to financial products; there is certainly evidence of this in particular cases. Finpin can be used in all the same ways as PIN itself.

vii) *Individual Analyses.* The trend of Pinpoint's development has been towards the provision of individually specific analyses for individual clients – with sector-specific analyses like Finpin being a sort of half-way house. Pinpoint claims to be unique in holding all 5,500 census variables on-line for all of the 130,000 EDs to which each applies; the company can thus build a new cluster system to conform to the needs of a particular client, using any collection of variables considered relevant; it can rank EDs on the basis of any one of the ten principal components derived by PIN (eg the Wealth component – a combination of census variables tending to indicate wealth) or the 20 derived by Finpin, or on the basis of a single census variable (e.g. percentage of children aged 0–15).

viii) *CENTRY.* This is a general purpose piece of software designed to ease the production of some of these individual analyses. It is in fact an area profiling system: it allows the user to define his own area, of any size or shape, and to obtain a report showing the occurrence of any combination of census variables – with comparisons either against the UK, or another defined area. Centry allows the user to work from a terminal in his office on-line to the Pinpoint hardware.

ix) *Retail Potential Reports.* Pinpoint uses Family Expenditure Survey (FES) data from the Department of Employment to estimate consumer spending by type of shop and type of goods/services. This estimate can be made for any defined area.

x) *Lupin.* This is a database consisting of the results of 60,000 telephone interviews to establish consumer shopping patterns. The survey covers 60 per cent of the country, taking 1 in 200 telephone subscribers in each area covered. Using this data, plus information about store locations and sizes, a variety of models can be built to illustrate shopping patterns and to predict the effects of openings/closures.

xi) *Mapping.* Pinpoint's greatest area of specialisation is in mapping; while all five systems have mapping capability, Pinpoint believes deeply in the virtues of expressing all manner of data on physical maps; it can produce these in the form of translucent overlays.

h) Mosaic. This system is an offering of CCN Systems Ltd, a subsidiary of Great Universal Stores (GUS). In origin CCN was a credit reference bureau for GUS, and this still underlies much of what they offer. Today, however, the company is a large supplier of services, particularly computer-based services, in direct marketing.

Mosaic has two fundamental differences from the other three systems considered in this paper. First, it is not based on enumeration districts, but on postcodes; instead of allocating postcodes to EDs and then clustering EDs with like characteristics, Mosaic ascribes ED census data to the postcodes that are held to lie in each ED, and then clusters the postcodes that have like characteristics. So far this sounds like a distinction without a difference – and so it would be but for the second factor: Mosaic incorporates into its clustering system information from non-census sources that is available at postcode, or at household (aggregated to postcode) level.

Thus, other systems have available judgement summons information; they can use this, for example, to screen out from a mailing list pre-selected by demographics, individuals with judgements against them. Mosaic, however, is unique in incorporating area data about judgement summonses into the classification system itself. This raises legal and ethical issues (on which CCN have wisely sought OFT advice). To screen out an individual person against whom a judgement has been entered, is unexceptionable. To choose not to send a mailing to an area in which there have been a disproportionate number of judgement summonses can scarcely be faulted – nobody is obliged to offer their goods on a universal basis. But to refuse to supply credit (or goods selling on credit) to an applicant on the grounds he/she lives in a high risk area must seem like unfair discrimination, and is probably illegal under the Consumer Credit Act. And this could be the result of using Mosaic, whose area classifications are based, in part, on such data. CCN's interpretation (following OFT advice) is that Mosaic classifications can be used to select prospects, with perfect propriety; they can only be used for credit screening in conjunction with other appropriate criteria (eg data from the applicant's form of application).

Mention of unfair discrimination prompts another thought: CCN have deliberately excluded from Mosaic all census variables dealing with racial origin; they are alone in this.

CCN initially chose 300 census variables from among the 4,000 available, and tested various combinations of these before arriving at a list of 38. This is the smallest number of census variables used by any of these systems; CCN stress the need to use only variables that have a high level of penetration among a large number of EDs.

Mosaic, then, uses 38 census variables, taken from EDs and ascribed to postcodes. It also aggregates at postcode level 16 other variables; these non-census items need some further consideration. Some information is gathered from the electoral register, which is inspected annually; other items come from the Lord Chancellor's list. Finally there is one source of information not available to CCN's competitors – the record of credit references sought by finance houses, credit card companies, and retail stores for whom CCN has acted as a credit reference agency.

We have seen that one of the problems with the census data is the way in which it ages. Mosaic attempts to deal with this problem by ascribing to the variables that go into its cluster analysis different weights. So, although the census data accounts for 38 out of 54 variables used, the overall weight ascribed to it in the clustering process is no more than 46 per cent, the remaining 16 variables being collectively weighted at 54 per cent. (Strictly speaking the electoral register weighting ought to be altered downwards each year, but CCN do not yet appear to be doing this; the interesting thing about the system is that it would be possible.) None of the non-census data is more than two years old at any time, and much of it is updated annually.

These 54 weighted variables are then used in a cluster analysis to cluster the 130,000 postcode areas into 58 Mosaic types, which in turn aggregate into 10 groups. It is noteworthy that the Mosaic types include a number of clusters identified as 'Post-1981 housing' – an identification made from the Royal Mail's Postal Address File (PAF); systems whose clusters are based on EDs cannot make this distinction. It is also interesting that many postcodes that are in the same ED fall into different Mosaic clusters: this ought to be an index of the extra discriminatory power of the non-census variables used by Mosaic. Of course, these non-census variables, and the weightings ascribed to them, will not necessarily be of equal relevance to all potential users.

The services offered by CCN in connection with Mosaic are:

i) *Postcoding.* CCN, like Pinpoint, is a Royal Mail approved supplier of computerised postcoding services; it can postcode client lists to Royal Mail approved standards.

ii)   *Prospect Profiling and Scoring.*   The systems that Mosaic offers for these purposes are not in principle different from those of their competitors. Any differences in practice will arise from the different construction of the demographic classification itself.

iii) *Mosaic Coding.*   As with other systems, Mosaic codes can be added to client files under the terms of a leasing agreement for the Mosaic directory. The initial coding work can be done at the same time as postcoding the file, if that function is also required.

iv)   *Market Monitor.*   This is a regular monthly service offered by CCN to clients with customer accounts. Each month the client sends in a tape of his accounts; CCN analyses these, by Mosaic type, and by a variety of geographic factors, and produces both a set of printed reports and a floppy disk. This disk can be used by the client on his own micro to produce, on screen or on paper, area maps of the data reported on.

v)   *CAIS.*   This stands for Credit Account Information Sharing. Some 60 mail order/retail/finance house clients of CCN provide a monthly tape of their account customers, and the performance of each; this information goes into a database where it is available only to other members of the club; the information can of course be profiled by Mosaic.

vi)   *Credit Applications.*   CCN vets applications for credit on behalf of clients against an electoral register database overlaid with the Lord Chancellor's list – and with details of other credit applications. The more clients use this system, the more powerful it becomes, and the fact of a credit application by an individual is itself a piece of data fed to the Mosaic classification of the area concerned, which, to complete the circle, is a factor in reviewing the application.

vii) *Nationwide Consumer File.*   This is our old friend the electoral register, held by CCN and updated annually. It is also overlaid with a regular record of new postal addresses from the PAF; it can be profiled by Mosaic, analysed by TV or ILR areas and by all the familiar geographic breakdowns.

j) **Superprofiles.**   This product belongs to Credit & Data Marketing Services Ltd, a subsidiary of Littlewoods, who bought it in 1987 from its original designers at OE McIntyre. This is the newest of the systems considered here, having been launched in 1986. It is also almost certainly the system which has benefited from the greatest quantity of academic research and testing – using facilities and staff at Newcastle and Liverpool Universities – to establish the optimal structure of census variables and ED clusters.

Initial selection of census variables was based on testing a wide variety of candidates against Littlewoods trading data, to see which were the best discriminators. This resulted in the selection of 55 variables (in fact not very different in numbers or composition from those used by other systems). The next step was to cluster the 130,000 EDs using these 55 variables. Every fifth number between 5 and 1,000 clusters was tried, to give the best compromise (although that implies a degree of subjective judgement) between concision and precision. Finally, the number of 150 clusters was chosen. This is more than double the number of clusters used by any other system; if matters had been left there, the result would have to appear unwieldy.

The next step consisted in ranking the 150 clusters (now simply iden-tified by a number from 1–150) on the basis of 10 further census variables not included in the original clustering. This ranking was intended to give an initial indication of wealth. Then a further 25 geographic variables (indi-cating region and broad employment type) were added for each ED and aggregated at a cluster level. These do not affect the already-determined clustering, but are used at the next stage.

Finally, market performance data derived from TGI was applied to the clusters in order to group them into 10 Lifestyles and 36 Target Markets. The Target Markets are ranked from 1–36 in order of affluence, and it is interesting that this measure of affluence, derived from TGI data, is dif-ferent from, while clearly still related to, the wealth ranking of clusters derived from census data. 36 Target Markets is a much more manageable number, and more closely related to the number of clusters used in other systems. But the important point to note is that the grouping of clusters into target markets was accomplished by use of current performance data: CDMS repeats this exercise with new data annually (the first grouping was done in January 1987). This means that, although the basic census data cannot change till 1993 – and the geographic data will not change anyway in the short to medium term – and although the clusters based on that census data cannot change, yet the Target Market and Lifestyle groupings can change annually. This is the CDMS answer to the problem of ageing census data – different from that of Mosaic, but a movement in the same direction.

The services offered by CDMS in relation to Superprofiles are:

i) *Directory Licences.* The Superprofile directory can be leased for a minimum period of three years, after which payments fall by 50%. After signing a lease, the client can apply Superprofile codes to his own list.

ii) *Rollcall.* This is the name given to the CDMS electoral register service, which offers essentially the same facilities as its competitors.

iii) *Tailor-made clusters.* CDMS will design a clustering system of anywhere between 5 and 1,000 ED clusters (based on the original 55 census variables) to suit the particular needs of any individual client.

iv) *Statsfile.* This is a system for performing customer penetration analysis. It will take data on client customers, and produce penetration reports by Superprofile cluster, Target Markets, and Lifestyles, or by any of the standard geographic expressions. The interesting aspect of this system is that it can be run, under licence, on the client's own micro; a floppy disk contains the Statsfile system, and there is a package to convert the client's data, as held on a main-frame, into input for a micro. This does in principle enable client marketing staff to use data much more creatively than is possible where every question has to be structured for answer at a remote centre. CDMS was the first producer of demographic systems to go down this path; its competitors have since followed.

v) *Profiling, etc.* CDMS offers the usual facilities for profiling client files, scoring, selection, retail site assessment, etc.

k) DEFINE. This system is the product of Infolink. This system, like MOSAIC, uses credit reference data to supplement census data. However, whereas MOSAIC uses credit reference data as part of the clustering process, DEFINE clusters first purely on census data, and then uses credit reference data to subdivide each of its 47 clusters into nine credit-related groups. This methodology has some similarity with the Superprofiles method of clustering on census data, and then adding TGI data to sub-divide its 150 clusters into 36 Target Markets. Since credit reference data is not static for the 10-year period between censuses, DEFINE, like both MOSAIC and Superprofiles, has found a way of offsetting, to a limited extent, the ageing problem inherent in the whole concept of demographics.

The main facilities offered by DEFINE are broadly similar in character to those of its competitors.

1) **Conclusions.**   Ultimately, there are only two questions that a marketing person wants to ask about such systems. Do all or any of them work, in the sense of assisting more profitable targeting of the marketing effort? And which one is the best?

The principle behind all of these systems – that demographics, as expressed in census data, can tell us something useful about markets – is undoubtedly sound. All of them have achieved profitable results for a number of clients – if this were not so, they would not still be in business. The systems as a whole are better at locating areas of poverty than of affluence; they are all better at relatively broad-brush descriptions of geographic areas (of a kind that can be invaluable in the retail trade) than at picking out individual persons for direct mail approaches (the purpose, ironically, for which they were designed). However, even at an individual level, they are all capable of providing a deeper insight into the demands of the market-place.

There can be no question of selecting a 'best buy', since the needs of every user are necessarily different. But I will venture some tentative generalisations. Acorn is much the oldest-established system, and CACI as a company has the longest operational experience in this field – although some of their competitors now have ex-CACI staff. Acorn is still the best-known and understood, and probably the most widely used system; if compatibility with what other parties are doing, or with their terminology, is a factor, one should seriously consider going no further. However, since the development of the original concept, CACI has not been the most innovative in the field.

Pinpoint has followed largely in Acorn's footsteps. It has done a service to the industry in pointing out some early sloppy habits that no one else much wanted to know about, but it is doubtful if this has allowed it to retain any marked competitive advantage. Its strength lies in two areas: anyone that sees significant advantage in a sophisticated mapping service should certainly explore Pinpoint's facilities; and the development of Finpin does look impressive for those selling financial services. Neither CACI nor Pinpoint has addressed the problems of systems deterioration as the census data ages: their other three competitors have, in slightly differing ways.

CCN would have to be a first stop for anyone with credit reference or associated problems – not just because the system is fundamentally good, but because of the volume of data supporting it. And MOSAIC, also underpinned by that volume of data supplementing the census information, has a broader basis of static data than any of its competitors. It is also the only system which can claim to be, without extra effort, improving rather than deteriorating over time, by virtue of constantly added data.

Superprofiles' approach to the ageing problem is extremely ingenious, but I doubt if it is, for the generality of users, as good an answer as MOSAIC's. Moreover, the large number of its clusters, and their smaller sizes, may make it particularly vulnerable to demographic changes. On the other hand, the weight of academic excellence that has gone into this system is impressive, and the facility to run analysis systems on the client's own micro was an early pioneering breakthrough.

DEFINE has also tackled the problem of ageing, and in some ways its methodology combines some of the best features of the MOSAIC and the Superprofiles systems.

Finally, where do we go next with demographic systems, now that the results of the 1991 census are finally coming to light? The overlaying of postcodes and enumeration districts, via map references, will certainly be less error-prone this time round than it was in the wake of the 1981 census – but the endemic problems of the operation will not go away, until a more rational system of drawing boundaries is introduced, if it ever is. All the systems that we have been discussing will be introducing, once the new data is available, new offerings, building on the experience of the last ten years. Those for whom demographic systems already work, can look forward to a substantial improvement, because both the data and the systems will improve in one giant step. Those for whom demographics have done nothing much in the past may not find that they do a lot even after 1993. But one thing is sure: anyone contemplating testing any of these systems should do so early, while the basic census data is still relatively reliable, and before the inevitable decay sets in.

3. PSYCHOGRAPHIC DATA

Whereas the use of demographic data in marketing has been growing in the UK ever since its introduction in the mid '70s, (and in the USA somewhat earlier), the use of psychographic, or lifestyle, data – at least in the sense of having such information available in the market-place – is a new phenomenon in this country, which made its first tentative appearance in 1983, and is only now getting under way, largely following in American footsteps.

The claim advanced by those who wish to sell a psychographic service to marketers is that very substantial numbers of people can be persuaded to provide comprehensive information about themselves, their households, their possessions, behaviour, and interests; further, that this data can be made to serve two purposes:

i)   It can provide, for any given trader, specific information about the kinds of people who buy his products, enabling him to tailor his advertising approach according to their characteristics.

ii) It can provide generalised information about a very large market-place, making possible extremely precise targeting of prospects based on self-submitted individual characteristics.

Our purpose here is to examine the present status of psychographic systems; to indicate what systems are on offer from whom; to discuss the similarities and differences of competing systems, and to give some evaluation of the claims made for the methodology as a marketing tool.

a) Demographics versus psychographics.   As we have seen, the use of demographic data was pioneered by the direct mail industry in the 1970s, with the object of finding a way to segment such huge, but undifferentiated, lists as the electoral register. But the only demographic data universally available (the census data) relates not to the individual persons, or households, that are the direct marketer's target, but to groups of households of an only roughly homogeneous kind. Moreover, the census data is an aggregated snapshot of the population at an increasingly remote point in time. For these reasons, demographics in direct marketing terms have had only a limited success; their true value probably lies in the geographic analysis of population groups for marketers whose prime interest is in groups rather than individuals – such as retailers.

Psychographics, by contrast, looks as though it may possess the capacity to revolutionise the direct marketing industry, and direct mail in particular, turning it belatedly, but for real, into that which it has always claimed to be – a highly selective and carefully targeted medium of communication between seller and buyer. Ironically, the techniques involved were not developed in the first instance either by or for the existing direct mail industry, but for manufacturers of consumer goods who were increasingly finding the conventional advertising and market research media either inadequate, or poor value for money.

The use of demographics and psychographics illustrates, better than anything else, the current convergence of marketing techniques. Each has something to offer to a variety of users, who would historically have regarded themselves as belonging to very different disciplines. Psychographics – that is to say the building and use of databases consisting of information about individual consumers' lifestyles – has a contribution to make in each of the three classic areas of marketing:

Market Research
Advertising
Selling

After a brief consideration of the general methodology of psychographic services, we will look at each of these areas.

b) **Methodology.** There were originally three sets of psychographic offerings in the UK market-place. Two now remain, both at quite an early stage of development. The original three were:

DataBank, originally established by ConsumerQuest and later marketed by The List Shop. This company still owns DataBank, but is no longer trading. No new names have been added to this database since 1987;

residual marketing of what is now an elderly, and declining, list is in the hands of Cheryl Nathan List Broking.

Behaviourbank, the property of Computer Marketing Technologies (CMT).

The Lifestyle Selector, owned, operated and marketed by National Demographics and Lifestyles (NDL).

All three operations collect(ed), by means of questionnaires distributed to consumer households, a wide range of information about individual consumers, which is then stored on a database. The method of distributing questionnaires varies from one company to another – and this is likely to be significant for particular users. All three operate a system whereby particular questions in the survey – or, in one case, the entire questionnaire – can be sponsored by individual companies. The returned questionnaires will be handled by the operating company, and the information on each will be data-captured. Sponsoring companies will receive full reports on the survey results in a pre-agreed format. Certain information (for example, anything that is brand-specific) will be regarded as confidential to the sponsoring company, which may, in addition, have certain continuing rights in further use of the data. Other data, including names and addresses, will become part of the general database, which may be used to provide names on a highly selective basis for direct mail users. Other, more sophisticated uses are in principle obtainable, and will without doubt become available as the market learns how to demand them; at the moment this particular marketplace is still rudimentary.

From the point of view of the companies operating these services, this methodology is highly satisfactory: Companies A, B, and C each pay a fee to cover the distribution of questions, and related services; as a by-product the operating company obtains voluminous information which can be sold – again with added-value services – to other clients X, Y, and Z. What the client can obtain, we will now consider.

c) **Market research.** The manufacturer of consumer goods who wants to discover more about the nature of the end-users of his products – perhaps in order to determine whether his choice (or his agency's choice) of advertising media is optimal – faces a problem: almost certainly he has no record of who these end users are, and no established means of communication with them. Gradually this situation is changing: it is now common form for motor manufacturers, for instance, to obtain from their dealers the names and addresses of customers, together with basic details of each purchase, which can be built into a database, enabling the manufacturer to communicate with his customers directly, rather than through blanket advertising media. Such a database, however, is unlikely to contain significant information about individual lifestyles, or to be of much value from a market research point of view.

The traditional solution to this problem is therefore to commission a market research company to undertake a survey. The value of even the most basic database, in this context, is that it provides a sampling universe for the market researcher. With or without this assistance, he will then, probably in a series of face-to-face interviews, record the lifestyles of a sample of buyers, extrapolate to cover the universe, and note the differences in his findings from what is known about the population at large.

The problem with conventional market research is three-fold. First, even at a modest level – the minimum required for the desired degree of statistical significance – it is expensive; extended to any substantial scale it becomes extremely expensive, with costs being closely related to numbers of persons surveyed. Second, the statistical tabulations produced from this kind of research are its sole output: the rules of the Market Research Society positively forbid the attribution of names to research data. Third, the methodology is somewhat inflexible, and requires 20/20 vision at the time of designing the questionnaire: it really isn't practicable to look at the response, and discover, at that point, some interesting further question that one would like to explore with certain respondents.

The strengths of the psychographic approach are the reverse of these weaknesses. First, the methodology is cheap: the design, printing and distribution of questionnaires, the data capture of responses, and the analysis of results, should give a cost measured in pence per respondent. Second, the chief by-product of the whole process is a potentially valuable list of self-submitted names and addresses, with a wide range of information about each. Third, because this list of names is available, any kind of follow-up suggested by the results of the original questionnaire is simple.

But there is one major drawback. The essence of conventional market research lies in obtaining response from a representative sample of the universe that one is trying to profile. Thus, one might go to a representative sample of the total population in order to discover what proportion of UK adults regularly drive a motor car; one would pick a representative sample of Porsche buyers in order to determine the age breakdown of all Porsche buyers. And so on. The trouble with lifestyle databases is that they seldom – never in the case of the systems examined in this paper – constitute a representative sample of anything definable; it is therefore not possible to extrapolate from what a lifestyle study shows to a universal statement. The very fact that the information on a lifestyle database is volunteered by the persons to whom it refers – an enormous strength in a direct marketing context – means that it contains a self-selected, and therefore non-representative, sample.

Tony Coad, managing director of NDL, tells the story of a US company selling portable barbecue sets; they directed their advertising at outdoor types liable to take off on hunting expeditions – until a lifestyle survey of their buyers suggested that their product appeal was dominantly to yuppies in metropolitan apartment blocks, on whose verandahs the barbecues fitted conveniently. A nice illustration; what we are not told – because nobody knows – is the precise proportion of barbecue buyers that fitted either profile. And nobody knows because the individuals surveyed were not a representative sample of all buyers.

Of course, this may not matter greatly: it is perfectly possible to obtain a worthwhile insight into one's market without having to quantify it to three places of decimals. We are, after all, in business to record profits, not statistics. And the larger the proportion that our sample forms of the total, the less its technically non-representative nature will matter. So, if we have access to a lifestyle database on which are recorded 30 per cent of this year's customers for a given item, we will give more credence to what such a source appears to tell us about our market than we would if the same records constituted only 3 per cent of the total. It is important to recognise the theoretical limitations of what this kind of data can tell us; it is not necessarily important to invoke the last degree of precision for our calculations.

Finally, conventional market research and research via a lifestyle database are not necessarily competitive approaches. One of the hardest problems in market research is knowing before the event what questions one wants to ask. Because the lifestyle questionnaire is a cheap way of obtaining large quantities of data, it may make sense to use it as a sort of saturation coverage, from the results of which one can construct a small-scale, more precise piece of conventional research. Such an approach will both make it easier to frame one's ultimate questions better, and to economise on overall research costs.

d) Advertising. The advertising function can make use of a lifestyle database in three main ways. First, as we have seen while discussing market research, it is possible to create a profile of the responding customers on such a database in order to determine whether existing advertising policy is consistent with what the lifestyle information reveals. Second, one can use a lifestyle database to select groups of individuals to whom to address a direct advertising message considered appropriate to their presumed needs or interests. Thirdly, one can vary the terms in which that message is presented to suit the particular circumstances of individual members of the selected groups.

e) Selling. The use of lifestyle databases in selling implies, of course, selling by direct mail. Direct mail has always claimed to be the medium, *par excellence*, which enables the user to target his sales efforts to specific individuals more likely than the undifferentiated mass to be interested in his offer. In the context of a user who has for years past been cultivating a database of his own customers, with records of their purchases, payment methods, changes of address, and so on, this claim has merit. Just as it is highly questionable whether demographic information can do very much to enhance the responsiveness of a database that already contains substantial purchase information, so it must also be doubted whether lifestyle information about customers' possessions, habits, and tastes can effect great improvements in a system already acquainted with their purchases. But where a sales effort is being directed not at past customers for whom considerable histories exist, but at cold prospects, acquired from the electoral register, or from a list broker, the situation is altogether different. Such campaigns are no more 'targeted' than a direct response advertisement in a national newspaper – perhaps less so. Segmenting the potential mass audience by reference to demographic characteristics – a practice that has become widespread over the last ten years – can certainly help, but to a rather limited extent. But to be able to select prospects from a database of persons known to have responded to a questionnaire through the mail, and known to be willing to receive advertising material by post; to be able furthermore to segment this audience by reference to its self-submitted characteristics – that is an altogether different matter, going a very long way to justify the contention that direct mail is a precise instrument.

What is needed now in the lifestyle, or psychographic, field, is the same level of professional expertise in modelling, scoring, regression analysis and such techniques, as already exists in large users of established customer lists (such as the Consumers' Association, or Reader's Digest) and, indeed, in the companies offering demographic services. It is ironic that the most sophisticated statistical techniques should be daily used to provide demographically profiled selections from the electoral register – rather akin to using solid gold cutlery to eat chip butties – while the chief demand to date on psychographic databases has been for lists of households with gardens, or of people with an interest in DIY – analogous to drinking Gevrey Chambertin out of polystyrene cups.

There is no problem for companies in the psychographic field in acquiring such skills: in some cases they are already in place. So far the demand for their exercise has been slow to surface. No doubt this will change quite quickly.

f) **Critical mass.** Part of the reason for this present lack of sophistication lies in the relatively small size of the lifestyle databases now available. Although the quantity of information available on any one name is large, and thus very complex selections are possible, this may not make too much sense on a list of, say, 250,000 households. This raises the whole question of what size might ultimately be achieved by such a database.

If we regard the useful life of a single, non-updated, database entry as being between two and three years, then the answer to this question is going to depend on the number of questionnaires that a company can distribute in this period, and on the response rate that it can expect. This in turn will be affected by the different methods of distribution used by current practitioners, and on the incentives offered to consumers to respond. As we shall see, different practitioners have different expectations. My own view would be that a lifestyle database of less than 2 million households (which is close to 10 per cent of the population) is not likely to be viable long term. On the other hand there seems little reason to suppose that a database of at least this size cannot be created and sustained without undue effort.

g) DataBank. DataBank was the property of ConsumerQuest, a company set up in 1983 to operate in what was then the virgin field, in the UK, of psychographic, or lifestyle, marketing. Questionnaires were sent out under the ConsumerQuest name, and in 1985 names were offered from the database thus compiled. ConsumerQuest itself is no longer trading; the understanding in the trade is that it ran out of money in early 1987, and its erstwhile directors have departed hither and yon.

The original ConsumerQuest questionnaire was distributed mainly through the Home Delivery Service (HDS) of the Royal Mail – ie an unaddressed blanket coverage of specific areas. Acorn classifications of the electoral register were used to exclude the areas of greatest poverty which were thought to be of least interest. Response to the questionnaire varied from 1 per cent (in a number of urban areas) to 6 per cent (in some rural areas), giving a total database, compiled in 1985–86, of some 250,000 households, or 320,000 names. The questions covered in the questionnaire related to:

Household composition
Age
Occupation
Motoring Habits
Travel
Hobbies
Financial Affairs

ConsumerQuest's early version of the questionnaire attracted a certain amount of public criticism for seeming to be other than what it was; this was quickly rectified, and those completing the questionnaire were also asked to indicate whether or not they were willing to receive direct mail advertising for items that matched their expressed interests.

ConsumerQuest offered entry to a free prize draw as an incentive for filling in the questionnaire – although this was presented in a fairly low-key manner. Responses to the questionnaire were returned through the mail.

With the exception of one question on motor cars, none of the questions asked were brand-specific; however, individual companies were invited to sponsor, exclusively or on a shared basis, individual questions. They then received exclusive (or shared) rights for 90 days in the results of these questions for direct mail purposes. Not all of the information collected on the questionnaire forms was retained in the database. The reason given was that some of this information is short-term by definition – eg the answer to the question 'If you were thinking of buying a new vehicle within the next six months, which brand would you consider?'

DataBank is now almost entirely of historical interest; the list is not being refreshed by new surveys, and usage is small. Most of what the company set out to do, and some of the staff who set out to do it, now rest with Behaviourbank.

h) **Behaviourbank**. This is the name of a psychographic database owned by Computer Marketing Technologies (CMT). This company was set up in the USA in 1980, and has been conducting questionnaire surveys there under the name Select & Save. The company is represented in this country by CMT (UK), which handles the data relating to fmcg (fast moving consumer goods) products, and Bricoda, which deals with the non-fmcg side of the business, with list rentals, and with the issuing of surveys, similar to the DataBank survey, under the banner of the National Shoppers' Survey.

Behaviourbank's effort is directed mostly at fmcg companies. The aim is to find sponsors for the questions to be included in a questionnaire which will be distributed over a six-month period. At the end of that time the questionnaire – and possibly the sponsors – will change. The sponsor will receive full statistical reports, both on his sponsored question and on the non-branded lifestyle questions; he will also qualify for three free uses of the names of responders to this questionnaire; thereafter further use will be at the reduced rate of £40/thousand. He will pay £250 per question sponsored, per thousand questionnaires distributed, with a minimum order

value of £150,000; this covers printing and distribution of questionnaires, data-capture of response, statistical analysis, printing of reports.
Information collected by Behaviourbank covers:

Credit Cards	Home Ownership
Travel	Type of House
Investments/Insurance	Length of Occupancy
Health Interests	Marital Status
Sports Interests	Adult and Child Ages
Outdoors Interests	Grandchildren
Social/Charity Interests	Income
Collecting Interests	Occupation
Food/Wine Interests	Working Women
Electrical Products	Cars

The incentive for the consumer to fill in the questionnaire is the promise of a free pack of discount vouchers on branded groceries and household goods; these are personalised, laser-printed, and despatched as part of the response fulfilment process. However, the manufacturers whose coupons are included in the packs to be despatched can call for the value of each coupon, and the message on it, to be varied according to the nature of the answers given in the questionnaire. Behaviourbank also sells space in the fulfilment envelope for further brochures etc; these too can be included or omitted on the basis of response. In this way, manufacturers can distribute their coupons much more precisely than is possible at point of sale – concentrating on the buyers of competing brands in order to persuade them to switch, rather than on their own established customers. Moreover, the activity in this field of any one manufacturer is invisible – or at the least unquantifiable – to his competitors. It is alleged that the redemption rate of coupons distributed in this way is 20 times higher (30–50 per cent) than the norm for point-of-sale coupons. (NB Fulfilment costs are not included in the charges quoted above, and will vary according to volume of printing and complexity.)

Methods of distribution for the questionnaire vary; some household delivery is done, but the bulk is via loose inserts in magazines and newspapers. Claimed response rate in the USA is 10 per cent (the American database has 7 million names); reliable rates are not yet available for this country, but the first pilot questionnaire, in early 1987, pulled 13%.

Data capture is performed overseas (in Jamaica and Sri Lanka). Business names are rented at £70 per thousand, and others at £60, plus, in each case, £5–7 for selections.

j) The Lifestyle Selector.   This is the name given by NDL International Ltd. to its database. NDL – or National Demographics & Lifestyles Inc – originated in the USA. NDL in this country is an affiliate of the American company, and has substantial offices and staff in central London. Its approach is significantly different, both in objective and in methodology, from that of the other two players examined above.

NDL designs a separate questionnaire for each manufacturer-client. The client thus 'sponsors' an entire questionnaire, and this is distributed by being included in his packed products at point of manufacture. It follows that NDL's initial target clients tend to be manufacturers of consumer durables. The client pays a flat-rate fee, and for this, NDL will help him to design a questionnaire (which the client will produce and insert in packs at his own cost), data-capture the response, analyse and report on the results, and hand over a tape of names and addresses with product-specific data. This agreement lasts for one year; reports are provided on the first 4,000 responses, plus three further quarterly reports. Thereafter the agreement can be continued annually for a further fee; the sum is independent of the number of questionnaires distributed.

Although questionnaires are individually tailored, the normal format consists of questions covering such subjects as:

Date of Purchase	Sex
Product	Date of Birth
Price	Marital Status
Place Purchased	Occupation
Reason for Purchase	Ages of Children
Source of Information	Family Income
Important Product Qualities	Credit Cards
Use of Product	Housing
Related Product Interests/	Car
Activities	

Product-specific data from these questionnaires belongs solely to the client; non-specific data belongs to NDL, and is included on the database. Names from this database are available for rental, and the company stresses that any combination of selections is acceptable to the system.

At the time of writing NDL has 67 clients in the UK. Response rates are reported as being even higher than in the USA, averaging 20–25 per cent, but with some running as high as 50 per cent. However, NDL has insisted from the start that every questionnaire must contain a clear opportunity for the consumer to indicate that he does *not* wish to receive promotion; the company claims that 30 per cent of responders avail themselves of this opportunity. (The company's whole mode of operation has come under intense scrutiny from the Data Protection Registrar in the late 1980s; its current procedures would appear to have satisfied this severe critic.) This clearly reduces the net response rate, so far as further use of the names is concerned – but it also does indicate that those net names are genuinely prepared to receive further promotion material. During late 1988, responses from all current efforts were coming in at the rate of 35,000 per week, and the database had reached some 1.6 million names, the ultimate aim being 8 million households. Records are discarded after two years if no further movement takes place.

NDL also offers to rent to its clients PCs complete with software and disks to enable them to run their own product-related data – at a cost of £5,000 pa plus £1,000 per PC. NDL's data capture is performed in Barbados; it uses the main-frame of the American company in Denver for its database, but also has a substantial computer installation in London.

NDL's publicity literature makes much more reference than does that of its competitors to the possibilities of sophisticated customer targeting that such a database makes possible, instead of thinking in terms of discrete 'lists'. The company does possess the skilled staff to implement advanced schemes of profiling, modelling, and scoring for customers, and if the database grows to even half the size projected, such facilities will be of great value. A client who has used an NDL questionnaire will then be able to build a profile of his own customers from the responses, and to select from the other names on the database those that match this profile to a given degree of accuracy.

NDL is also offering a system called the Lifestyle Network. This is based on the electoral register, overlaid with area data from the Lifestyle Selector and from Infolink's DEFINE; it bears, in fact, a certain resemblance to the kind of demographic systems we have discussed above.

k) Conclusion. Psychographic, or lifestyle, marketing is still in its infancy in this country; it is fairly new in the United States as well, but has there accomplished enough to demonstrate its real potential. What has been done in the UK so far does at least suggest that there is every indication the UK market is at least as responsive to the concept as is the US market.

The first indigenous attempt in the UK, undertaken by ConsumerQuest, does not appear to have flourished. Although a small database was created, the company lost its opportunity to carve out a position for itself ahead of the competition (as, for instance, Acorn did in the demographic field).

The two remaining contenders – although they are not in very direct competition – are both drawing on American resources in terms of experience. Behaviourbank has headed straight for a particular niche in the market, trying to muscle in on the coupon incentive business and offering a powerful new weapon to fmcg brand managers – at least until everyone is using their methodology and we are all back at square one. Meanwhile, this does look like an exciting new tool. Whether the database that will result from this activity will have predictive power for the general user is perhaps less certain: I would expect its profile to be somewhat down-market.

The List Selector has much the most elegant solution for distributing questionnaires. Moreover, the chosen method of distribution will tend to create a relatively up-market result. I do not believe it probable that any lifestyle list can be made, in the UK, to grow to a size of 8 million households, but even a third of that (which I do believe can be exceeded within the two-year useful lifespan of a name) would make a superb database – *provided that* adequate customer education is available in the arts of name selection and multi-variate analysis.

It has seemed worth while to deal at some length with specialised demographic and psychographic systems, partly because, while widely talked about, they, and the differences between the various systems on offer, are not well understood, and partly because they do illustrate a number of interesting facets of the database problem, namely:

a) how to apply publicly available census data to individual records of customers or prospects, based on their geographic locations;

b) how to acquire, or deduce, a limited amount of information about individual households from publicly available records such as the electoral register, or the Lord Chancellor's list of county court judgements, etc;

c) how to obtain personal, or lifestyle, information from at least a proportion of one's potential audience by questionnaire;

d) in general, how to convert a mere list of names and addresses into something more valuable.

But we should end this section by coming back to where we started the whole chapter – with the collection of sales-related customer data. Demographic and psychographic data can make a welcome additional slab of information for a customer database; equally, when we are looking at prospects rather than customers, and therefore necessarily at people about whom we have very little information to begin with, then the acquisition of demographic and psychographic data can make a very great difference to the value of our database. But far and away the most important and valuable information any trader has about any consumers is information about his own company's dealings with them. It is towards the capture of that information above all that every effort should first be devoted; when that has been done, and a strategy has been worked out, and proved in practice, for the use of that data, then the bells and whistles that extraneous information represents can be added at leisure.

4. BUSINESS-RELATED DATA

It is a perennial problem in discussing databases – or direct marketing – that we must consider two groups of users of the techniques in question: those whose marketing effort is directed towards consumers, and those who are addressing themselves primarily to other business people. Chapter 3 on Database Applications used examples from both camps. In this chapter, some of what we have had to say so far has had greater relevance to consumer than to business marketing; some has had little or no point for the latter category, and in some places considerations relevant to business marketing have been left out altogether. We will try in this short section to fill in some of the gaps.

a) Data protection. Those whose databases hold information primarily on business customers rather than private persons are not necessarily exempt thereby from the Data Protection Act – although by no means all the possible issues are totally clear. If, for example, one holds on a computer the name and address of Marks and Spencer plc, together with details of that company's dealings with one's own business, then, even though in other contexts Marks and Spencer plc is a legal person, this information is not personal data within the meaning of the Act – which is concerned solely with living individuals. The same position would probably apply even if Mr Marks and Mr Spencer were both alive and conducting the affairs of their emporia – since the entity 'Marks and Spencer plc' is distinct from Messrs Marks and Spencer either singly or jointly. If, however, your data about Marks and Spencer includes the information that Lord Sieff is its Chairman, then it would appear incontrovertible that this is personal data, within the meaning of the Act, about Lord Sieff. Again, if your database held the information that Robin Fairlie, an unincorporated individual, was running a business from 15 Vincent Terrace, London N1 8HJ (whether or not that was also his private address) it would be difficult to maintain that this was other than personal data. As always with the Data Protection Act, the answer has to be: if in any kind of doubt, register. It can do no harm; the cost is marginal, and probably less than scrubbing around trying to find an exemption or other way out.

b) Duplication. Everything said above under this heading applies to business addresses as it does to consumer addresses. But the problems in the former case go further. First, business addresses are typically longer and more cumbersome than consumer addresses:

John Smith Esq,
Managing Director,
J Bloggs & Co. Ltd,
Bloggspalace,
1984 Animal Farm Road
George Orwell Industrial Estate,
Wigan Pier,
WIGAN,
Lancs WI17 2FA

gives a not uncommon flavour. Such addresses represent a real challenge to computer programmes to analyse, to verify against the PAF, to correct where necessary, and to postcode where this has not been done. Lots of bureaux in the market-place today are offering postcoding and address correction facilities. Almost all of them will admit, when pressed, that these computerised facilities operate much less effectively for business than for consumer addresses. This problem is dealt with more fully in Chapter 5, Section 4 – Postage.

Second, the owner of a business database must address, and answer, a fundamental question about the data he holds: is he primarily interested in the individual persons in his database, or in the holders of particular job-titles, or simply in targeting particular companies, or indeed trades. This will influence his attitude towards updating his information. Updating a business database poses more numerous, and more difficult, problems than are usually encountered with a consumer database: these will be discussed further in the next Chapter, Section 1, paragraph c).

c) **Demographic and psychographic data.** In some cases census-derived demographic data will be very important to a business database. Where, for example, the records on the database relate to retail shops, then the demographic profile of the surrounding area is highly relevant. Indeed, in such a case one may well – depending on the nature of the shops con-cerned – wish to amalgamate census data from a number of enumeration districts within a given radius, to give an overall profile of an outlet's market-place. *Individual* demographic or psychographic data will also be valuable in such cases, when it can be expressed in statistical form: eg that of the 1,763 persons for whom we have information in such and such an area, 35 per cent have expressed a burning interest in archery. Data manipulations of this kind are the bread and butter of the types of database bureaux we have discussed above.

5

Data Handling

1. LIST HYGIENE

I was first exposed to this piece of terminology in a transatlantic telephone call with a client: it seems a useful heading under which to sweep up a number of considerations. The problem of duplication, dealt with in Chapter 4, is of course one aspect of list hygiene. Other examples include changes of address, gone aways, deceased, and all the other changes relating to the whereabouts of his prospects that may, or may not, be notified to a list or database owner.

Collecting information for a database is one thing; keeping it up to date is altogether another. It will not have escaped notice of anyone reading the provisions of the Data Protection Act in the previous chapter, that the fifth principle in the Act provides that personal data should be kept up to date. To the harassed businessman, who desires nothing more than to keep *all* his data up to date, but is frequently puzzled how to find appropriate means towards this end, it may seem that an Act of Parliament is a curious place to find such a pious statement of the obvious. Act or no Act, it is an inescapable fact that personal data loses accuracy over time – indeed minute by minute, thus following the universal law of entropy, that everything decays. So there is no point in setting out to build a database unless thought has first been given to how it is to be maintained and updated.

The first thing that anyone renting a list of names and addresses, with or without associated information, should seek to know is: when the data was collected, and what is done, with what periodicity, to maintain it in an accurate condition. Of course, some of the information on a database is not subject to updating, or change, in this way: once-for-all information about historical fact, if properly verified at time of collection, will scarcely require updating. Which is why a database will never record, directly, a person's age, but always their date of birth. Similarly with product purchases, or other events that happen at a moment in time – if true once, they continue to be true. Data, however, about a continuing state of affairs rather than a precise occurrence is another matter, and nowhere can this be more clearly illustrated than in reference to the name and address itself. We will consider the problems separately for consumer and business addresses.

a) Consumer addresses. Approximately 12 per cent of the population moves house every year. Or, to put it another way, the average person moves home once in every eight years. This gives a simple indication of the speed with which a consumer database, if not properly maintained, goes out of date in respect of its most fundamental piece of data, without which the rest is of questionable value – who lives where. If one rents a list of names and addresses that has been compiled over a five-year period, one knows (or should know) that something like 60 per cent of the persons on the oldest part of the list no longer live at the address on record – unless there has been a regular process of maintenance to offset this factor.

List maintenance takes a variety of forms, and some of these are more valuable than others. A publisher, for example, whose database is composed of subscribers to one or more learned periodicals, may reasonably feel that his customers will do much of his list maintenance work for him. He will be well advised to print a reminder on the backs of his magazine wrappers for subscribers to fill in and return if they are about to move, or have just moved. But mostly his data subjects will *wish* to hear regularly from him with the periodicals for which they have paid, and can therefore be trusted to notify changes of address fairly quickly. This in turn means that any user who rents a list of periodical subscribers has reasonable security (depending to some extent on the frequency of publication) that the addresses concerned will not be too wildly astray: there is a built-in feedback mechanism.

(Note, however, that this is *not* true of readers of controlled-circulation magazines, who do not pay for their copies.)

People who are members of a club, or similar organisation, are less reliable. By and large they are not obtaining a perceived benefit *through the mail* from the organisation to which they belong (and even if the organisation produces a periodical, this is probably not the subscriber's prime interest in joining). Such people have, therefore rather less incentive to notify the organisation of a move – at least until the time comes to renew their subscriptions. The addresses on such club databases are therefore about as good as their last renewal dates: if renewal is annual, and individual renewals are spread randomly through the year, then one could reasonably expect anything up to 6 per cent of addresses to be invalid at any one time – but not more.

Lists of past buyers, or guarantee card holders, or enquirers, occupy an even shadier area. In some cases there may have been no occasion for communication to or from the individuals concerned since their names were collected – in which case the list becomes pretty valueless after a couple of years at the outside. But it may be that these past buyers have been mailed regularly with further offers, or information. Those that have responded – depending on recency of response – are clearly more likely to be still contactable.

But a database which is being mailed regularly benefits not only from being able to update the addresses of respondents; it is also the case that a proportion of those mailing pieces that fail to reach their addressees will be returned marked 'Gone Away': this is, of course, a valuable piece of information, since even though one may not know where the addressee has gone to, at least one knows not to expect him at his old address, and one can avoid the cost of uselessly writing to him there.

The issue of Gone Aways is more complex than it might at first appear. There are a number of points worth making:

i)   Every mailing piece addressed from a permanent list or database should carry a return address on the reverse, so that rejected mail can be returned easily.
ii)   All Gone Aways should be recorded on the database.
iii) List owners who are renting their lists to third parties should be

prepared to pay the renter a small sum for each Gone Away returned to them: not only does this recompense the renter for some of the money he has wasted, it also assists the owner in keeping his list clean *and* improves the credibility of his list in the eyes on the next prospective renter.

iv) However, not all mail that fails to reach the addressee will be returned: many householders, receiving what is clearly a direct mail envelope addressed to the previous occupier, will throw it away; even if he does forward it the first time, he will not go on doing so indefinitely if the addressee, having received the first forwarded piece, does not then notify the list owner of his removal.

v) Where a Gone Away *is* notified, the database owner may find it worthwhile to send a special letter (in a plain envelope, marked Please Forward, and *without* a return address) to the old address, enquiring of the addressee's whereabouts; this may be forwarded and elicit a response.

What, then, about databases where the persons listed are not receiving goods through the mail, are not subscribers to a club or service, and are not being regularly mailed? A partial example, at least, of such a situation would be one of the lifestyle databases described in the previous chapter: the entries are up to date at the time the questionnaire responses arrive, and deteriorate thereafter. It is of course true that the names from these databases are mailed, as a result of list rental activity, and no doubt the database owners will make appropriate arrangements with the mailers for the return of gone away information. But such databases are mailed piecemeal – some elements very frequently, others hardly at all. One possible answer to this dilemma is to have one's database checked periodically (ideally annually) against the electoral register. Most companies that offer to rent selections from the electoral register are capable of offering this service too, and this does at least tell one, each spring, who *was* living where as at the previous October. What it does not do is to indicate where any previous occupier may have moved to; as a result there is no way for the database to know that the Mr J Smith on whom it possesses ample information, but who no longer lives at a Acacia Avenue, Bedford, is the same person as the Mr J Smith now revealed by the electoral register as having recently taken up residence at 16 Laburnum Grove, Aberdeen. In consequence, a database whose only means of maintaining addresses is an annual electoral register check, is continually losing data about persons who move. Even if the individuals concerned are subsequently picked up again, their past history will have been lost.

As with gone aways, having once learned from the electoral register that an individual has moved, one can write to him or her at the old address with a request for forwarding; no doubt this will produce some results, some of the time. The only other hope on the horizon is that the Post Office, which has been considering this issue for some years, may eventually be prepared to play a part by producing lists that link individuals moving house from old address to new.

b) European addresses.   As the Single European Market moves closer to becoming a reality, it is increasingly necessary for all sorts of businesses to reflect upon the effect that this will have on them. In a direct mail context, there are British companies wishing to sell their goods or services on the Continent; there are foreign companies (often American) wishing to use the UK as a base for pan-European sales; and there are British service companies – advertising agencies, computer bureaux, list brokers, mailing houses – eager to offer services to the previous two categories.

The UK has for some years now been the European leader in database work, and in particular in the computerised handling of names and addresses. This partly reflects the early lead of the UK Post Office in postcoding, and partly reflects the intrinsic complexity of UK addresses compared with most Continental addresses: this complexity demanded the early development of a high level of skill in address work. To turn this skill to the handling of Continental addresses is not in principle difficult. However, although beginnings have been made by one or two bureaux, which do hold and maintain pan-European databases, these beginnings are still fairly crude, and it is necessary to recognise the many differences that exist in Continental address structures as a prerequisite to dealing with list hygiene questions for a European database.

This is not the place to deal exhaustively with this subject, but let me offer one or two examples, some obvious, some less so:

i) In order to be able to handle a name and address properly, a computer system must be capable of recognising the component parts of the address. It must be able to distinguish titles, initials, forenames, surnames, honorifics, house numbers, street designations, town names, post codes, etc. This is a task infinitely harder for a computer, which can't read words 'in context' (indeed can't *read* words at all) than it is for a human being. Most computer systems cope by building tables – of titles, forenames, honorifics, street designations, town names, etc, and looking up specific parts of the address in the appropriate table. Clearly, Continental tables, while similar in principle, will have totally different contents – indeed most of them will be different for each country.

ii) In many (but not all) Continental countries it is normal for the house number to follow the street name, rather than precede it.

iii) In most Continental countries it is correct for the postcode to precede the town name rather than follow it.

iv) In most European countries a surname will be the last continuous batch of letters at the end of the first line,* after having disposed of any honorifics (such as MP, CBE, etc). However, In Spain it is common form for a person to retain the patronymics of both father and mother: hence the desire of Senorita Sanchez, famous Spanish tennis player, to be known as Arantxa Sanchez Vicario. The system must be able to recognise that the lady's surname, in this case, is in fact the last *two* words.

v) If the advertiser wishes to mail his piece outside of the country in which it is to be delivered, then the country name must, of course, appear at the end of the address. However, if the mail is to be posted in the country of destination (a possibility we comment on further under Postage in Section 4, paragraph c)) then the country name should not appear. Indeed, in this case, other criteria need to be borne in mind: town names should be spelled in the local manner: Munchen, not Munich – and it should have an umlaut over the 'u'.

---

* Consumer addresses only: for the different considerations applying to business addresses, see the next section.

To summarise: the UK is better placed than any other country to handle pan-European addresses and database systems – but even here the art isn't nearly as far advanced as it needs to become within a short space of time. For those who are in the direct marketing service business, there is a huge market in America: American handling of European addresses is atrocious, and their need for a properly equipped European base is growing rapidly.

At the time of writing, the Royal Mail is attempting, with help from members of the UK Direct Marketing Association, to set up a project known as Gateway Europe, to sell UK expertise in direct marketing service operations to American (and later, if this is successful, to other overseas) companies. The Dutch PTT, as ever quick off the mark, already has an office in the USA for just this type of purpose.

c) Business addresses.   As in a number of other areas, the problems of name and address maintenance are somewhat different, and in some respects more difficult, when one is dealing with businesses rather than consumers. That consumers change address every eight years on average (or did prior to the fall in house prices in the early 1990s), creates problems; these are as nothing compared with the difficulties posed for business databases where any or all of the following can occur:

A business changes its address.

A named executive moves company and is replaced.

A named executive changes his or her job within the company, and is replaced in his or her former job.

A named executive changes his or her job title, and/or his or her reporting structure, but not his or her function.

A company change of address is probably less frequent than a consumer change of address, and no more problematical. But keeping a check on who, within which company, is doing which job (and, even worse, on what are the decision-making functions, in practice, of different jobs/job titles/ individuals) can be a nightmare. For this reason, much business-to-business direct mail is addressed to a job title rather than to a person. There is available in the market place a much wider variety of well-defined business lists than there is of consumer lists: if you are a manufacturer of widgets, it is not unreasonable to suppose that you can identify, and reach with fair precision, every company in the country that is an actual, or potential, user of widgets – whether such companies be defined by standard industrial classification (SIC), by area, by turnover, by number of employees, by capital employed, by profitability, or by some combination of these factors. In some cases list brokers will offer to rent such business lists complete with the names of each company's chief executive, or whatever. But if you want to mail named financial directors, or sales managers, that is likely to call for (expensive) research – probably by telephone. And keeping that sort of information up to date once you have it is difficult – unless you have a sales force that is in regular touch with the companies concerned, or unless your personalised communications through the mail are such as to give addressees an incentive to inform you of changes – for example, if you are supplying periodicals. Otherwise, it may be back to the old – and unsatisfactory – device of the annual questionnaire.

2. DATA PROTECTION

We dealt with one aspect of the data protection issue in the previous chapter, where it was pointed out that to hold data about an identifiable individual on a computer without registering with the Data Protection Registrar is a criminal offence; this makes it mandatory to complete registration formalities before starting to collect the data. Even after this has been done, and even where the database is operated in a manner consistent with the Data Protection Act, there are still ongoing issues not covered by the Act, which, broadly speaking, relate to data protection. Thus, the Advertising Association's Code of Practice, referred to above, on data protection, states (Part III, paragraph 5.2):

> Even though the Act does not state that data subjects have a right to have their names excluded from mailing lists, the Council of Europe's Recommendation on Data Protection and Direct Marketing proposes that such a facility should be made available. Accordingly, data users to which this Code applies must comply with the requirements of the Code of Practice of the Mailing Preference Service, and should, wherever possible, use the recommended method of not erasing the name, but of retaining it on file with a suppression marker.

What this means, is that all database owners who are using their databases for consumer mailings have an obligation to use the MPS files in order to mark on their databases the names of any persons that have indicated to MPS that they do not wish to receive direct mail promotions. MPS is a creation of the industry itself, and obedience to its rules is not a legal obligation, but it is sound common sense. Much irritation continues to be expressed in the newspapers by people who receive what they regard as unreasonable quantities of direct mail advertising. A lot of this irritation is factitious (newspapers have their own strictly commercial reasons for disliking direct mail, and I suspect some editors are not, when copy is short, above penning the odd letter of this kind themselves, to themselves) but the cry that unsolicited mail constitutes an invasion of privacy, however pompous, silly, and over-the-top it may sound, does find an echo with the public, and could result in further legislative interference in commercial life – unless those involved in advertising by mail can demonstrate a serious and effective commitment to sensitive handling of public complaints about the medium. MPS is an attempt to demonstrate such commitment, and as such it should be supported, if only because the most likely alternative will be very much worse.

MPS, in its early days, was funded by a small number of enlightened companies who were 'subscribers' to the service, and put up the funds necessary to run it. It is now funded (like the direct marketing part of the British Code of Advertising Practice, looked after by the Advertising Standards Authority) by the Mailing Standards Levy. This levy is raised (except where different arrangements have been made) by the Royal Mail as a levy of 0.5 per cent on the postage value of Mailsort invoices. The money so raised is paid to the Advertising Standards Board of Finance, which controls its expenditure by the ASA and MPS.

3. PERSONALISATION

In the early days of direct mail, virtually all mailing pieces were directed to their destinations by a name and address label, either stuck to the outside of the envelope or applied to some part of the mailing in such a position as to show through a window in the envelope; the letter inside would then start 'Dear Sir/Madam' or perhaps 'Dear Customer' or 'Dear Reader'. With the advent of clever computers, and even cleverer programmers, it became possible to contemplate producing letters which started 'Dear Mr Jones', or whatever; testing showed that such 'personalised' addressing produced significantly better response. Today it is a virtually universal characteristic of computerised mailing systems that they offer the facility to personalise letters – not only by adding a correct salutation, but by varying any part or parts of the text of the letter as may be required, by reference to the individual data found within the subject record. The advent of laser printers has greatly assisted this process, in consequence of their immense speed (compared to the old line printers) and enormous flexibility (eg ability to cope with varied type fonts and sizes, and to print sideways, upside-down, etc).

Take, for example, the case of an insurance company wishing to offer a life policy to a number of existing policy-holders who have house-and-contents cover only. A few years ago, prospects of this kind would have received a fairly bland letter – with a personal salutation to be sure – but otherwise undifferentiated between one person and another. And a leaflet would have been enclosed with separate male and female age tables which the punter would have had to examine in order to see what his or her monthly premium would be. Today age tables are all but redundant; indeed each letter can be tailored to the individual's circumstances, and can say, for example:

> In return for this security, your monthly premium – provided you start *this month* while still aged 39 – is only £x per £1,000 of cover. So, for example, provided you act NOW you can buy £100,000 of life cover for a payment of only £y per month. (Of course, if you delay till next month, the same level of cover will cost you an increased premium of £z per month.)

As with everything else, there is a price to be paid for personalisation. If you spell a person's name wrongly on an impersonal address label, he may be irritated, but this is unlikely to affect his judgement of your message. But if your letter addresses him as 'Dear Mr Fairy' instead of 'Dear Mr Fairlie', your chances of business from this individual are certainly less than if you had addressed him as 'Dear Customer'. While if you have referred to his age as 27, when he is in fact 54, then your pitch is hopeless.

There is, of course no way of securing complete accuracy of data. But there are rules which, if they are observed, will minimise risks:

a) No data should ever be permitted into a database unchecked. In the early days of computers it was always regarded as axiomatic that all data was double-keyed: one clerk punched data onto a punched card, and a second verified what was punched by re-keying from the original document. In these present days of direct entry from keyboard to computer, this process of verification is all too often ignored: the quality of much data going into computers today is substantially lower than it was twenty or thirty years ago. Sometimes the system itself can check: as we have seen already, addresses can be checked, and even corrected, by reference to the Postal Address File. Names for given addresses can be checked against the electoral register (if the system has access to it). And so on – but a check of some kind there must be.

b) Systems themselves must be tested and checked. It is quite easy to program a system that will take:

> A. Jones Esq.,
> 3 Acacia Avenue,
> Malden,
> Surrey.

and produce the salutation 'Dear Mr Jones'. But what is the system to do when presented with:

> Admiral Sir Roderick ffotherington-Jones Bart, KCB

You might be happy if it printed 'Dear Admiral' or 'Dear Sir Roderick', or even 'Dear Sir'. But less happy if it came up with 'Dear Mr KCB' or 'Dear Mr Bart', or 'Dear Admiral Bart', or even 'Dear Mr Admiral' – analogies to all of which I have seen in my time. In practice, of course, no system can be expected to cope optimally with all possible variants (especially of our Pickwickian British modes of address): the good system is one that will handle correctly 99.9 per cent of cases, but will recognise the other 0.1 per cent where it is out of its depth, and thereupon will fall back on 'Dear Customer', or some other pre-provided catch-all. This principle runs all through the personalisation business: programs have to have a fall-back position for use in any case where the required bit of personal data isn't there, or can't be recognised or analysed by the rules available. It is in the ignoring of this principle that some of the funnier foul-ups – inevitably reproduced in the Press – occur.

c) Apart from names and addresses, most data in a marketing database is fixed – in the sense that if it is correct at the time of input, subsequent events are not going to alter it. There are, of course, exceptions, which can usually be handled quite simply if thought about in time. (This is, of course, why computer systems never record a person's age – only his date of birth.)

But, although data about past events is normally fixed, information about present events is not – and both demographic and psychographic data fall into this category to varying degrees. Demographic data derived from the electoral register – such as size and composition of household – will date unless checked at intervals against the new register (which is itself published some five months after its data is collected). Data derived from the census can only be checked every ten years, and is only published some two years after its original collection. But by far the most difficult problem relates to lifestyle information supplied in response to questionnaires by consumers themselves: clearly, the longer the time-lapse since this information was supplied, the less reliable it is. The ideal answer might be to repeat the same questionnaire to the same consumers annually: one company holding a rather specialised database does just this. Ibis maintains a database of academic staff at universities worldwide; annually the company writes to each person listed in each university calendar with a questionnaire about their academic subject areas, and receives a very high rate of response. The case is no doubt unusual, because the individual concerned stands to benefit from responding: the promise made by Ibis is that, when academic publishers mail book promotions through the Ibis database, those persons with recorded interests appropriate to each book will be selected, and those without, will not. In the absence of a similar incentive, it is not clear what level of response to a regular questionnaire could be achieved – of course direct incentives of a more commercial kind are not ruled out, as with the original collection of data. Repeat questionnaires also have the obvious advantage of ver-ifying addresses, at least for responders. But the total cost of the exercise is fairly high, say 20 pence per person addressed, or 25 pence per response, given an 80 per cent response rate. How important it is to update demographic and lifestyle data – or how much cost it is worth incurring in the process – will in each case depend upon the uses to which the data is being put, and to the extent of personalisation in the data user's dealings with individuals on the database.

4. POSTAGE

Something should be said on this subject for the benefit of those who will be addressing mailings to prospects on their database, because the need to maximise cost-effectiveness in this area may dictate decisions regarding database design. To post a thousand promotion pieces by second-class mail at the basic 60-gram rate, cost (in 1992) £180. This is a very large pro-portion of the total cost of perhaps £450 which each thousand mailing to a consumer list might be expected to incur. (Nevertheless, it is the relative stability of postal prices in the 1980s which has been the largest single factor in the increasing cost-effectiveness of direct mail – in contrast to its main media competitors, whose costs have grown much faster – and, in consequence, for the rapid growth in direct mail activity.)

Moreover, for many years past the Post office has been prepared to offer a substantial discount, or rebate, from public tariff to bulk mailers (which basically means those with single postings in excess of 4,000 items) who meet certain terms and conditions. Various schemes of this kind were introduced over the years in a rather piecemeal fashion; in 1987 the Post Office announced its intention to rationalise these schemes under the generic title of Mailsort. A broad description of this service follows.

a) **Mailsort.** The Mailsort service comes in three different varieties: Mailsort 1, Mailsort 2, and Mailsort 3. These services, together with Presstream 1 and Presstream 2 (which are designed for the bulk postage of magazines), are run under the banner of Royal Mail Streamline. Choosing which service to use depends upon optimising three linked factors:

Speed of delivery required
Cost of postage
Pre-posting sortation undertaken

Mailsort 1 offers the same level of service as the first-class letter post, with a discount from first-class prices that improves as volume rises; in return the user must meet certain sortation and presentational requirements which reduce the workload of the Royal Mail. Mailsort 2 operates on the same principle, except that the service offered is that of the second-class letter post, and the discount is from second-class prices. Mailsort 3 also works from the baseline of second-class letter-post prices, but the service offered in this case is delivery within seven working days. The percentage discounts available vary for each of the three services, and within each service will vary again according to the level of sortation achieved. In the case of all three services, some level of sortation must be undertaken before handing the mail over to the Royal Mail; basically, the lower the net price that you wish to pay for a given level of service, the more stringent are the sortation requirements. All sortation for Mailsort is based upon postcodes.

Perhaps the most interesting departure from previous Post Office practice is the introduction under Mailsort of a sliding scale of charges for increasing weight of items over 60 grams, rather than the traditional 'stepped' scale, as currently used in the public tariff. The effect of this new departure, illustrated in the diagram opposite, is to give a substantial saving – even before applying the Mailsort discount – to mailers of letter-post items weighing anything over 60 grams. As can be seen, the saving widens as the item-weight increases.

To take an example, a piece weighing 61 grams would cost, under second-class public tariff, 28 pence; under Mailsort 2 or 3 it would cost 18.2 pence – less whatever discount was allowable for sortation undertaken. At 601 grams the difference is between 135 pence at public tariff, and 106.2 pence before discount under Mailsort. The overall effect is that, under Mailsort 2 or 3, one is paying an extra 0.163 pence for each gram over 60. A ready reckoner for this straight-line pricing system (and a separate one for Presstream) is available from Royal Mail Streamline.

The formula for calculating the correct Mailsort price (pre-discount) is as follows for Mailsort 1: [(Weight of item in grams − 60) x 0.208] + 24

Mailsort features a simple, straight-line pricing calculation for weights up to 1kg

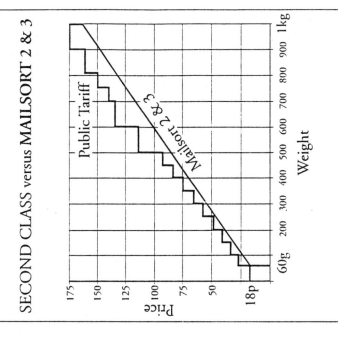

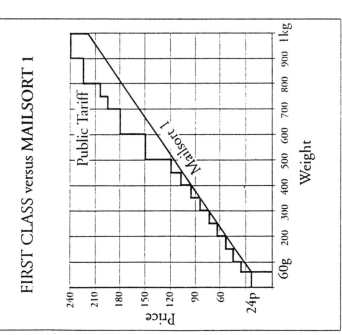

pence. Thus, a 75 gram piece would cost [(75 – 60) x 0.208] + 24 = 27.1 pence. And for Mailsort 2 and 3, [(Weight of item in grams – 60) x 0.163] + 18 pence. Thus, a 300 gram item would cost [(300 – 60) x 0.163] + 18 = 57.1 pence.

The discount available from the straight-line Mailsort tariff varies according to the level of sortation achieved, with a top rate of 32%. To earn these discounts, the mailer must meet a number of conditions, of which the most important are:

i) Mail must be sorted according to a sortation plan based on the post-code.

ii) At least 90% of all items in the posting must be fully, and accurately, postcoded.

I have not attempted to deal here with all the details of Mailsort: this is not a how-to-do-it book, and further details can be had from your postal sales representative.*

The important point for present purposes is that anyone seeking to collect information in a database and to use it for mailing purposes must take account, in the data collection, and in the database construction, of the requirements of the postal system – and therefore of the need for post-coding and for mail sortation.

b) Postcoding.   Since postcoding is going to be an essential feature of any database which is to be a source of bulk mailings – quite apart from its other marketing advantages that we have examined in Chapter 4, Section 1, paragraph b) – it is relevant to consider here the alternative possible approaches to postcoding for a database owner. There are two aspects of postcoding to be considered: how to add postcodes to an existing large collection of names and addresses, and how to ensure that new addresses, as they are added to the database day by day, carry correct postcodes with them.

By far the simplest answer to the first problem is to use a computer

---

* Additionally, copies of the *Mailsort User's Guide*, edited by the present author, are available from Royal Mail Streamline on request to the Streamline Marketing Department, Beaumont House, Sandy Lane West, Oxford OX4 5ZZ. Tel: (0865) 780310.

bureau. A number of computer bureaux now have programming systems capable of taking bulk addresses in a wide variety of formats, analysing them, looking them up in the Postal Address File (PAF), correcting some types of error, and allocating the correct postcode. Unanalysable or ambiguous addresses are, of course, rejected for clerical scrutiny.

Nor is it necessary – at least for consumer address files – to conduct an exhaustive survey of which bureau has the best system, or offers the best value for money. The Royal Mail, which has an obvious vested interest in maximising the use of postcodes, has given its seal of approval to post-coding systems run by a number of computer bureaux.* (Indeed, a few years ago the Post Office actually ran a scheme under which it was prepared to meet the computer bureau costs of any company using one of these Post Office-approved systems to postcode a file in excess of 20,000 addresses. This scheme is believed now to have been terminated – but if there is still anyone out there with large unpostcoded databases, it would be worth enquiring whether the Royal Mail is still willing to extend financial help.

What remains to be determined is how to handle the residue of rejected addresses that the computer system cannot deal with. In the case of consumer addresses, any of the Royal Mail-approved systems should be readily able to postcode accurately upwards of 80 per cent of the addresses submitted to it. (The actual percentage achieved is much more likely to be a reflection of the condition of the original data than of the competence of the particular system.)

In the case of business addresses, whose format is more variable and more complex, it may well prove beyond the capacity of many postcoding systems of a general nature to postcode more than 60 per cent, and those with complex business databases may well find that it pays to look for a bureau that specialises in, and has a good record of, dealing with such cases, since systems developed primarily for consumer addresses are likely to perform rather poorly on business files.

Even in the consumer case, this still leaves a substantial proportion of addresses that the computer system can't handle; there remain three possible courses of action:

---

* A list of these firms is available from Royal Mail Streamline.

Put them away on file unpostcoded;

Throw them away;

Take clerical action to postcode, and re-insert on file.

The first alternative is feasible only so long as the proportion of unpostcoded addresses then appearing in bulk mailings from the database does not infringe Mailsort requirements. Even then, it seems to me an undesirable option, leading, as it does, to an untidy and undisciplined database which fails to take full advantage of all its potential assets. (In particular, unpostcoded addresses are a fruitful source of untraceable duplications at a later stage.)

Manual postcoding is expensive. Each address has to be looked up in the Post Office's Blue Books (the printed equivalent of the PAF) and the very fact that the computer has failed to recognise them means that a high proportion of them will be pretty troublesome to a human operative as well. Some will certainly be untraceable by anyone less skilled than the local postman – and sometimes by him too. The cost of this exercise must be borne by the database owner. Nevertheless, the sensible course with computer-rejected addresses will usually be a mixture of the second and third options: manual look-up of all, with a judicious discard of those that are time-consuming beyond a certain agreed point.

Adoption of such a policy means that one's choice of bureau, from among those certified by the Royal Mail, should be governed by consideration of the price and quality of its services in relation also to manual postcoding of the expected computer residues. Clearly it is desirable to use a bureau that will perform the total exercise involving both computer and manual phases, presenting its client at the end with a clean and comprehensive result.

Solution of the second problem – how to cope with ensuring the accurate postcoding of day-by-day additions to the database – is liable to be more problematical. If the database owner intends to have his database built and maintained by a bureau, then matters are reasonably simple: one chooses a bureau that is possessed of appropriate postcoding software, and specifies that, in addition to the one-off postcoding of the existing collection of addresses, the system must contain the facility to postcode each incoming new address prior to adding it to the database.

But database owners who propose to run their own databases in house on their own computers must do one of two things. Either they must build their own 'front-end' postcoding system to analyse and postcode new incoming addresses; this will include purchasing from the Royal Mail a copy of the PAF (and an updating service for the same). Alternatively, they must seek to find a bureau which can supply a software postcoding package that they can incorporate into their own systems. The former course is a very considerable systems undertaking, which involves reinventing not just the wheel, but the internal combustion engine as well. The latter is preferable, but the range of choice is not wide.

For those who are possessed of a small database, to which there is not a large quantity of daily new input, there is another possibility. The PAF is available on CD-ROM (standing for Computer Disk, Read Only Memory).* A PAF in this format can be loaded on a CD-ROM reader attached to a microcomputer (if the database concerned is on a micro) and used by the operator as a sort of sophisticated microfiche reader, to call specific addresses to the screen, from which the associated postcodes can be read off, and entered on the keyboard. The PAF in this form is a great deal cheaper than the version for use on a main-frame; on the other hand the CD-ROM version is slow in use.

c) **European postage.**   With the Single Market almost upon us, and with the growing number of businesses, both British and foreign, wanting to use the UK as a base for marketing throughout the EC – and perhaps even wider afield – it seems desirable to say something about the European postage scene.

At the time of writing, the European Commission in Brussels has just published a Green Paper on postal affairs. Its principal objective is to create a 'level playing field' throughout the Community, so that every citizen, and business person, can enjoy an equally high standard of postal service at an affordable price. The obvious answer would be to create a European Post Office. This is impossible, since there is no one to whom it could report. So

---

* Available from Silver Platter Information Ltd., who produce the PAF/ROM, and also from Computer Factors Ltd of Coventry, who market it, particularly in conjunction with their database system Mailbrain.

we are left with national post offices – some quite efficient (the UK and Holland), some expensive and very heavily loss-making (Germany) and some utterly incompetent (Italy).

Achieving the Commission's ideals in regard to European postage will take a very long time. However, one thing will change quite quickly: it will be possible for businesses in one country to insert their mail directly into the postal system of another country in which that mail is to be delivered, and to enjoy (if that is the right word) all the conditions open to domestic mail users in that country. This means, to take one example, that if the French continue to grant large subsidies on the postage costs of French magazines, it will be open to any magazine publisher with journals to be delivered to French addresses, to truck his journals to France, insert them into the French postal system, and claim the self-same subsidy that a French publisher obtains.

Even in postal areas where there are no subsidies (and subsidies are the exception) it will frequently be cheaper for a mailer in the UK to truck his German mail into Germany, and his Spanish mail into Spain, and to insert it into the domestic mailing systems in these countries at the local equivalent of the Mailsort postage rate – rather than to put that mail into the hands of Royal Mail International. Those who have postal business to conduct on a European basis will have to be fast on their feet to keep pace with the changing postal scene in Europe over the next few years.

6

Data Selection: Regression

1. CONSUMER LISTS

In the days, still not so far distant, when data of any kind about individual consumers was scanty, and hard to come by, the business of despatching a direct mail promotion involved searching out such lists of names and addresses as could be found to which were attached some characteristic which could be held relevant to the matter in hand. This business of marrying lists of names, via some one characteristic to marketing campaigns, is still the staple of the list-broking trade. So, one can rent a list of members of the British Film Institute, a list of commodity investors, of purchasers of thermal underwear, or buyers of specialised chrysanthemums. Nothing save this one characteristic is known of the people making up those lists – other than their names and addresses.

Most of the time making decisions to mail to anyone other than one's own past customers used to be a matter of hit or miss – or at least of trial and error: if you were in fact successful in selling micro computers to buyers of thermal underwear, it was much more likely to be because the list was well-maintained, up-to-date, not over-exploited, and composed of persons already accustomed to buying through the mail, than because of any product affinity.

A direct mail company with its own list of past customers was in a similar if somewhat better position: customers who had bought one thing from the company were probably quite good prospects for another thing – and better still if the 'things' bore some relationship to each other. As the amount of data on customer lists (one can scarcely call them databases at this stage) started to grow, so companies started to distinguish between past customers – on the basis of time elapsed since last purchase, or type of goods bought, or speed of payment, or some such. The distinctions were 'broad-brush' and based on common sense, or at any rate on observation. It might come as a surprise, for example (at least to a non-gardener like myself), to discover that buyers of a truly encyclopaedic gardening book, far from being poor prospects for yet another gardening book, were actually superb prospects. Gardening enthusiasts, it appears, actually *collect* gardening books, as insatiably as lepidopterists collect butterflies. And the same is true, only more so, of cookery books. But, surprising or not, the phenomenon was readily observable and, being observed, easy to adjust to.

As the amount of data available on customer lists grew, so the problem of classifying groups or individuals according to their probable propensity to respond to this or that offer became more complex, and through the 1960s and 70s organisations like Consumers' Association, the Automobile Association, and Reader's Digest, with huge mailing programmes and ever-increasing banks of information, were forced into developing fully functioning databases. Even then although the software available for selecting names and addresses on the basis of extremely complex algorithms was sophisticated, the actual methods for determining what the algorithms should be hadn't advanced at all: it was still a matter of common sense, or guesswork, or trial and error.

The first breakthrough came in the early 70s, with the availability of census data from the 1971 census on magnetic tape. For many years past Reader's Digest had been using the electoral register (in printed form) as a source of names to whom it could offer magazine subscriptions. In fact the electoral register was the only source of names large enough to supply the Digest's immense mailing campaigns (which had to sustain a magazine circulation at that time of one and a quarter million UK subscribers). With this background, the Digest was the first company to undertake the expense of converting the electoral register itself to magnetic tape. But how to determine whether any given addresses or groups of addresses from the register were better or worse prospects than any others, was still largely a mystery.

The census data, it was felt, might provide the key. But how to use this amorphous mass of information? Some of it was probably relevant, and some possibly so – for example, the information that such and such an area had a 30 per cent higher proportion of children than the national average, or a large concentration of houses with two bathrooms. But relevant in what ways? Was the Digest dominantly read by persons with children, or by persons with two bathrooms, or both? And what about the information on persons travelling to work by motor bike – was that, too, significant? And if one's instinct was to say No – how could one be sure? Harder still, might it not be the case that *combinations* of particular data items would be found much more significant than each item singly might lead one to suppose?

The answer was to be found in a collection of mathematical techniques that the industry, incorrectly but conveniently, has come to lump together under the general heading of regression analysis. Since this book is not a mathematical treatise, and hopefully will be read with profit by many who might flinch at a mathematical symbol, we will follow common industry practice and refer hereafter to regression analysis *tout court*, without being particular as to whether we are dealing with what the mathematician would recognise as a multiple regression process, or discriminant analysis, or principal components analysis, or any one of a number of other specific mathematical techniques.

The problem can be stated in this way: we have a group of people – potentially the whole adult population – about which we have a wealth of statistical information. We want to use this information (if we can) in order to predict, for each of these people, their relative propensity to behave in a particular way – in this case to respond to a particular mailing.

And the methodology can be described in some such way as this. First, we take a representative random sample of our universe – and it *does* have to be representative, or the whole exercise is invalidated. Then, we expose this sample to the same mailing as that we are enquiring about. (The size of the mailing should be such as to bring in not less than 500 responses.*) Mark the record of each respondent. Then submit this 'model', consisting of all

---

* For a much fuller discussion on the mathematics of random sampling, see The Royal Mail's *Direct Mail Handbook*, published by Exley (2nd edition, 1989), Chapter 4, by the present author.

the sample records, together with the statistical information available on each, to a regression programme. This will analyse the characteristics (in this example our statistical census data) associated with each respondent in the model in order to deduce what combination of characteristics best distinguishes between respondents and non-respondents.

The result of this process will be to produce a formula which can be expressed along these lines:

$$\text{Propensity to respond} = a.x + y^b - \frac{z}{c}$$

(or some such) where x, y, and z represent numerically stated characteristics of the record (in this case census variables), and a, b, and c are constants assigned by the regression programme.

The next step is to put the whole universe which the model represents through a further programme which will evaluate each individual record against the computer formula, in order to determine each person's relative propensity to respond. This propensity – or 'score' as we may now call it – is simply expressed as a number: the higher the number, the greater the propensity. Finally, the computer will produce a statement of the score distribution of our universe, showing what percentage of the total has a score of x, x+1, x+2, etc, together with a statement (known as a gains chart) of the average percentage response to be expected from the highest-scoring 10 per cent of the list, the next 10 per cent, and so on. This enables one to select and mail only those parts of the list that are predicted to respond at or above a given level.

So much for the theory. In practice some short-cuts are required. No one, for example, would attempt to use all 4,500 census variables in a regression analysis of this kind: even to record such a mass of information against all 24 million households in the country would result in an absurdly large file, and clearly many of the variables are redundant (through irrelevancy, or duplication of effect) for marketing purposes. Moreover, a full regression analysis employing this number of variables would occupy an inordinate amount of computer time. Even where each extra variable adds something to the accuracy of the result, the law of diminishing returns is inexorable, and after a while 'improvements' become minimal, and not worth the increasingly high cost.

We have already seen* that the major bureaux handling demographic data use between 38 and 104 census variables for the purpose of grouping census enumeration districts into homogeneous 'clusters', and a similar 'boiling down' of census data – again using mathematical techniques – is a prerequisite of any use of such data for regression purposes.

In effect, of course, the demographic type (as described by Acorn or one of its competitors) into which a given household falls already represents a generalised distillation of the census variables; many advertisers are content to determine (by analysis of a sample mailing) that response to their effort comes predominantly from certain Acorn types, and thus to ensure that further mailings are directed to those types. Or, of course, the Acorn type itself can become one variable, along with purchase behaviour and lifestyle data, to a regression process as described above.

Some advertisers are frustrated by the lengthy process of performing a sample mailing, waiting for, and then analysing, the results. From this has grown the practice of analysing the demographic characteristics of existing customers on one's database, and selecting as new prospects those with similar characteristics. This is a highly dangerous practice, amounting to a form of in-breeding. If, by way of example, your present database contains a very high proportion of people living in Acorn Neighbourhood 15 (Council Estates, Well-Off Older Workers), is this really because this is the type of audience that is attracted by your offer, or is it because your earlier advertising has been particularly concentrated – perhaps by mere accident – on this type of person, possibly through selective use of Press media, or through geographic concentration, or whatever?

A real-life example may serve to make the point. A magazine publisher, selling subscriptions to his general-interest title, was very concerned to discover that his subscribers were heavily weighted to the over-35s. Did this mean that his editorial material didn't have sufficient appeal to younger people? Was he not in serious danger of losing circulation as his existing subscribers grew older and died off? Or would those now younger than 35 take to his product in greater numbers as they in turn reached the magic age? And if so, why – what was the trigger? The answer was laughably simple: the publisher was recruiting new subscribers by mailing offers to

---

* See Chapter 4, Section 2.

heads of households from the electoral register; not surprisingly young adults were grossly under-represented in his advertising campaign, and hence among his subscribers. The age profile of the subscribers on his database had nothing – or at least nothing ascertainable – to do with the nature of his editorial material, or the appeal of his offer, but everything to do with the built-in bias in his previous advertising universe.

Regression analysis in a marketing context began, then, as a way of discriminating better from worse prospects on a very large list (the electoral register) by reference to very large volumes of data (census variables, or at least a selection of them). The techniques are, however, generalised, and can be used on any list of any size where the individual records have any number of variable characteristics. Basically the regression process is simply a way of constructing, from a quantity of variables, an algorithm for selecting those individuals most likely to behave in a certain way. The process is fairly cumbersome, and, if done properly, may require a lot of elapsed time. But the improvement that it makes to response, compared with 'common-sense' methods of constructing algorithms, will increase rapidly with the number of variables to be considered. If there are only half a dozen variables, each with a small range of values, for each individual record on the database, then it isn't difficult, by intuition or experience – or after a cursory glance at the results of a sample mailing – to construct a near-optimum formula for selecting the worth-while prospects. But where we run into dozens, or scores, of variables, each with a potentially wide range of values, regression (otherwise referred to, with less offence to mathematical niceties, as modelling and scoring – a term which is not committed to any particular collection of mathematical techniques) becomes an essential tool.

Finally, we can complete our picture of a marketing database. As indicated in the earlier database diagram on Page 65, a database as I have defined it consists of data, computer hardware, and computer software. The data may include some or all of:

Information derived from sales or enquiries
   (including names and addresses)
Demographic data
Lifestyle data

The software must allow for address handling (including postcoding and postal sortation), for profiling and reporting on the information contents of the database, and for selection of records from it. This selection in turn should be capable of being activated either by an algorithm based upon record contents, or via a modelling and scoring exercise. And the whole might be diagrammatically represented thus:

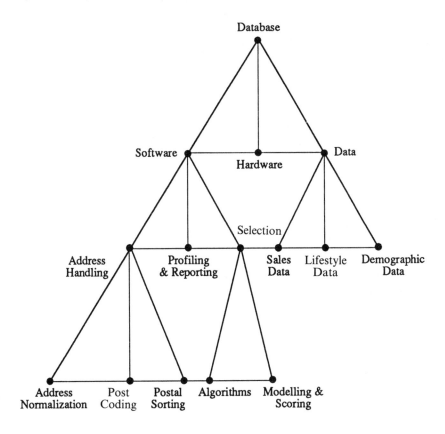

2. BUSINESS LISTS

The problems of selection for mailings to businesses whose records are held on a business database are substantially different in practice – even though much the same theoretical considerations apply – from those of consumer databases. Looking again at the diagram above, of the five main triangles appearing there, two will require modification if the diagram is to describe a business-to-business marketing database. Starting first with the Data triangle, clearly lifestyle and demographic data are not relevant to the description of a company. The sort of data we might hold in a business database could be represented thus:

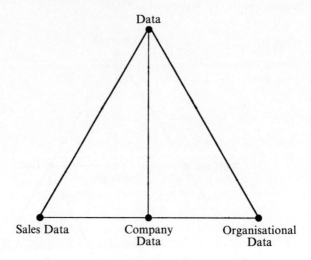

The sales data, as in a consumer database, would deal with the advertiser's two-way relationship with the prospect. Company data would typically include such items as:

Standard Industrial Classification (SIC)
Number of Employees
Size of Premises
Type of Premises (eg Head Office, Branch, Factory)
Turnover
Advertising Expenditure, etc.

Organisational data might include names and job titles of individual executives, perhaps with functional descriptions and an indication of reporting structure.

Secondly, the Selection triangle in a business database representation would effectively disappear. Selection criteria for business-to-business mailings are normally fairly simple and, with rare exceptions, will not call for such advanced techniques as regression analysis: a fairly simple algorithm will do the job perfectly well. The prime problem with business direct mail is not one of knowing to which prospect companies a given approach should be made, but rather one of understanding, within each prospect company, the decision-making processes – a task rendered much harder by the fact that these same processes can change overnight with a change of personnel – without, necessarily, any visible change in structure taking place. In the case of a consumer database, data collection and data maintenance, while rarely simple, can usually be reduced to a routine; in business databases they are an art form. By contrast, selection processes for consumer mailings demand constantly renewed ingenuity, and inventiveness at a high technical level; in the case of business mailings, such is rarely the case.

7

Planning a Database

1. INTRODUCTION

Let me try to summarise to this point. The increasing affluence of today's consumer society has created a market-place that is rapidly fragmenting in such a way as to render older mass-marketing techniques increasingly expensive. The effort in consumer marketing to distinguish one's *real* prospects from the undifferentiated mass is increasingly important. In the first instance this has resulted in a realisation that those persons who have already differentiated themselves by becoming customers have, in so doing, provided a wealth of valuable information, which must be retained – and maintained. These past customers are not only the best possible prospects in themselves; analysis of their behaviour can provide invaluable insights into the direction to be taken by one's marketing to new prospects.

Nor are those whose marketing efforts are directed towards other businesses exempt from these trends. As businesses increasingly specialise – or form specialist divisions – to cater for the fragmenting market, so their own needs and interests reflect the specialisation of the consumer market they are trying to serve; the marketing effort of their suppliers needs to take account of this.

The extent to which businesses in the past have ignored information laid before them by their customers – utilising only what was required for the delivery of goods, or the creation of an accounts receivable, and discarding it when these necessary functions were performed – is truly astonishing. But that time is now passing. In order to be able to collect, retain, maintain, and use information about past customers, companies require access to database techniques. And in order to be able to pinpoint new markets with the greatest possible degree of precision, the same is true. And direct mail in turn is either the major means, or at the least a valuable secondary means, through which an investment in database can be rendered profitable – and indeed through which the database can be maintained. How then should a marketing director plan his company's approach to database marketing and direct mail?

2. STRATEGIC PLANNING

The first step in building a database – as in any other long-term business project – is to produce a strategic plan, that begins with a consideration of objectives – in this case the overall marketing objectives of the business, followed by a definition of the audience to be reached in pursuit of those objectives. The next step is to ask what purpose(s) in relation to those objectives the putative database is intended to serve; the plan will then go on to consider:

Data Availability and Sources
Hardware and Software Needs
Database Structure
Data Capture
Data Verification and Enhancement
Database Design
Data Maintenance
Data Analysis/Selection/Reporting

Similarly, a direct mail campaign must derive from the company's overall marketing objectives and the nature of the audience it is addressing. Consideration of these factors will make possible a statement of direct mail objectives, both overall and for a particular campaign, followed by:

Definition of the Market
Creation of Promotion Material

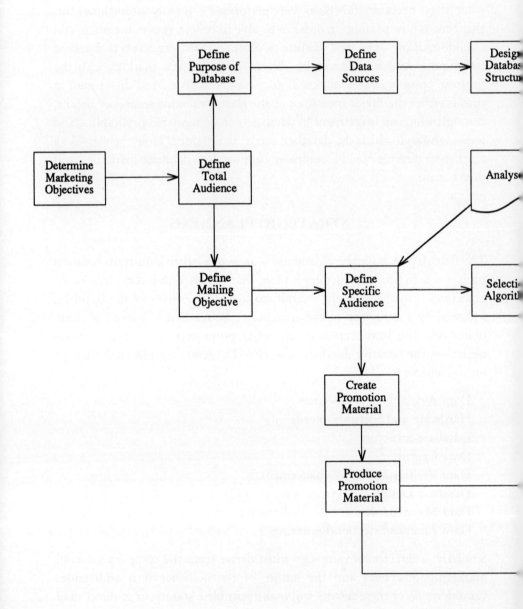

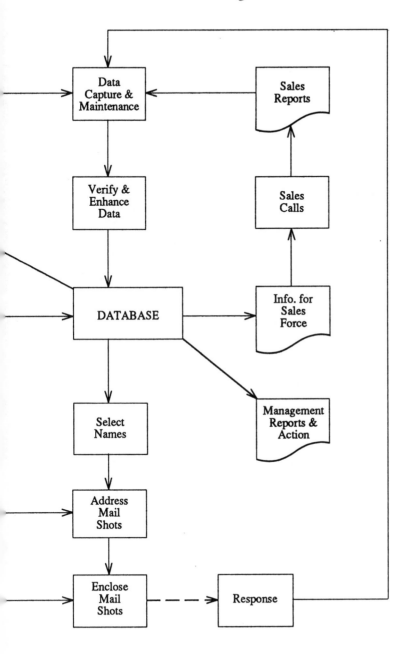

Production of Promotion Material
Creation of a Selection Algorithm
Selection of Names
Addressing
Enclosing and Despatch
Response Handling

These strategic overviews can be represented diagramatically, in a way that also shows the connections between the two types of activity, as indicated in the diagram on pages 170–71.

This diagram shows a central database which initially is fed with accumulated data from sources both inside and outside the company. Maintenance of the data is ensured by two separate feedback systems – the provision of database information and analyses to a sales force, which responds with details of its customer-related activities; and the handling of response to direct mail material addressed to persons on the database. Clearly, not all database applications will possess all the functions here shown; the important point is that some kind of maintenance mechanism, performed here by these two feedback loops, is essential.

3. HARDWARE

Having defined a database at an earlier stage in this book as comprising hardware, software, and data, we have reached this point where a good deal has been said about the data, a little about the software required to handle it (and there is more to come on this subject in a moment) and virtually nothing about the hardware.

This isn't a book about computers, so we will not spend too long on the subject, or become technical. But it does seem desirable to address briefly the question, which arises time and again when considering the construction of a database: what kind of, or how much, computer capacity is needed to support a marketing database? In this form, of course, the question sounds like asking how long is a piece of string; nevertheless some guidelines can be given which may assist in providing answers for particular cases, even though there is no generalised formula to fit all needs.

The question most commonly asked in this area is how much hardware capacity is required to run a database, or perhaps, more specifically, can one run a database on a micro computer. I will address the first question, in the hope that in answering it, so far as that is possible, light may be shed on the second question also.

First, then, let us examine the constraints that operate, under each of the following headings:

Storage
Processing Speed
Multi-User Facilities
Print Capacity
Communications

a) Storage. Any serious database application involving more than a few hundred records will require hard disk memory: there is no future in trying to run a database of any significant size on floppy disks. If we consider records consisting only of names and addresses, it should be possible to store up to 4,000 records per megabyte (one million bytes) of disk space. This figure should be reduced for business addresses, which are typically longer than consumer addresses, and in any event assumes that the software in use permits variable-length records, and variable-length fields within records: if this is not the case, there will be large quantities of wasted space caused by catering for maximum-sized records, and fields within records.

For a consumer marketing database with name and address plus other data, one would typically be down to 2,000 records per megabyte – but even this figure assumes no waste space; it is also desirable that the software used be able to pack and unpack data in binary form where this is logically feasible.

Current hard disk storage on micros can be taken up to 175 megabytes – which is probably a greater capacity than one would wish to use for a micro-based database, on account of other constraints. If the maximum sensible size for a database on a micro is felt to be not much more than 200,000 records, this would require disk capacity of 100 megabytes – or more if the records are particularly long. On mini, or main-frame, computers, where the other constraints (which we discuss below) are less pressing, and where the amount of memory available seems almost unlimited, the size of database that can be handled is scarcely a problem, so far as mere memory capacity is concerned. Even on a micro, given the amount of storage now available, plus the probable further extension of this in the near future, it is much more likely to be other factors that impose limitations: a substantial further leap in the processing power of even today's micros will be required before their full potential memory capacity can be used. (However, it is important to discover whether the software to be used – in particular the Database Management System (see Section 4) imposes severer limitations than does the hardware on the size of the database, or of individual files within it.)

b) **Processing speed.**   There are two aspects to this: the speed with which an individual record can be called to the computer's screen, and the speed with which sequential records can be processed – eg in the course of a selection run.

i)   It is desirable that any required record reach the screen in a time not exceeding 2 seconds. (That may sound very fast, but in fact for an operator sitting at a keyboard, delays that sound quite trivial can be devastating in their effect on productivity.) Current-technology micros can achieve this on databases under 200,000 records – although the extent of multi-user processing (see below) is a potentially limiting factor very hard to assess.

ii) Great strides have been made recently in micro processing speeds; with the latest technology equipment it should be possible to handle in excess of 100,000 records per hour – five or six times as many as could have been achieved just a few years ago. This does, however, assume the use of software capable of fairly sophisticated data structure – in particular the separation of static data such as name and address from key selective data, together with appropriate cross-indexing. This still means that to select from a database of 200,000 records will take two hours on a micro. I would regard that as a sensible limit.

c) **Multi-user facilities.**   2–5 user systems (that is, systems where 2–5 operators, each with a screen and keyboard, can use the same computer at once) are common nowadays even on micros. It isn't really possible to set a theoretical limit – one leading software house claims to be able to provide a

40-user micro system, should anyone want one. Clearly a lot depends on the level of activity by each user and, if activity is other than constant, the extent of 'bunching'; the greater the activity at any one time, the greater the probable consequence in slowed response time. Any user contemplating going to, or extending, multi-user facilities *must* begin by simulating worst-case conditions on an actual installation.

An alternative approach is to link two or more micros in a local area network, in which they share access to a single database. This makes sense where individual users required substantial processing capacity, but relatively infrequent access to the database.

d) **Printing capacity.**   The advent of desk-top sheet-fed laser printers has been a boon to micro users. These machines are quoted as being able to print up to 500 sheets per hour. However, they are essentially small office equipment, and not an adequate solution to volume printing – eg of names and addresses from a database. The only sensible answer here is still a line printer, or continuous stationery ink-jet or laser equipment; these cannot be driven by a micro as of now; this means that large-scale output has to be transferred in magnetic medium to a bureau with a main-frame or mini driving a suitable printer.

e) **Communications.**   Transferring data requires a suitable medium of transfer. Of course, data transfer by floppy disk is feasible; it will require access to a facility for transferring data from floppy to some main-frame medium such as 9-channel magnetic tape. More interesting is the recent advent of a conventional magnetic tape unit that can be linked direct to a micro: this makes bulk communication between micro and mini, or main-frame, a simple matter for the first time.

The concepts discussed above can in principle be handled on any IBM-compatible micro equipped with hard disk storage: the most basic level, in terms of cost, being an Amstrad 1512 at something over £1,000. Clearly there will be additional costs for printing facilities, communications, multi-user stations, etc, as required.

4. SOFTWARE

It is convenient to distinguish under this heading two different kinds of software: that which is completely generalised and application-independent, and that which is needed to perform the particular application of an individual user.

Under the first label we may distinguish first the computer's own operating system, which need not detain us here: on a micro, most of which are IBM-compatible, it will be a variation on IBM's DOS (Disk Operating System). There will also, for anyone wishing to run a database system, be some form of DBMS (Database Management System), comprising both the programme that allows one to structure a database in the computer's memory, and the language through which the user can access the database. The software that we have indicated thus far – the operating system, and the database management system, are items that no sensible user would wish to create for himself: this would be akin to reinventing not just the wheel but a substantial slice of the universe.

A number of database users have however started with a proprietary DBMS, incorporating an operating system, and then built their own particular application software to go with it. The alternative approaches to this course are:

a) Purchase from a software house a software package that, with a greater or lesser amount of customisation, and a greater or lesser degree of compromise over user requirements, can be adapted to do the job.

b) Go to a computer bureau with a specification for the building of a database system. The bureau will then have the same options of building a wholly particular system from scratch, or of adapting an existing package. The user will also have the choice of having the bureau run the system on its own hardware for a shorter or longer period, and of bringing it in house onto his own hardware earlier, later, or not at all.

c) As a subset of either of the above solutions, some software houses, and some computer bureaux, offer a 'turnkey' service: that is to say, they offer to provide to their client a total working system incorporating the hardware and the software to meet his needs, installed on his premises, and up and running, complete with training facilities for his staff.

Which of these options it is best to adopt will vary from case to case. The larger and more complex the database application, the less likely it is that the user can find a suitable package that will, even after customisation, meet his needs. If, in addition, the user already has a substantial computer installation, and a systems and programming staff, then he may feel that the best course is to develop his own system in house. This will depend, however, on the degree of priority which he can command within his in-house systems team: systems departments tend to have a long queue of jobs and over-stretched resources. Where this is the case, the bureau option may be quicker and involve fewer problems all round. The question of whether the system, once developed at a bureau, should run on the bureau's hardware or not will be a simple matter of weighing up in-house computer capacity and bureau cost. We will discuss in a later chapter the criteria that need to be considered in choosing a particular bureau.

For smaller and less complex databases it should be possible to find appropriate packages which, with some customisation, will fit the bill. There is not, at time of writing, a wide range of choice on the market, but there are a few good offerings. At the bottom end of the size/complexity scale, the question of where to run the database scarcely arises, since even if the necessary hardware has to be purchased from scratch, the costs are relatively trivial. (Printing is another matter: if bulk printing is required, and facilities are not available in house, then use of a nearby bureau for this limited function is likely to be the best answer.) Therefore, where we are talking about a database system to run on a micro, for example, then however the software is obtained – by in-house development, by purchase, or by development at bureau – the supposition must be that it will ulti-mately be run in house on the user's own micro.

5. ECONOMICS

The diagram in Section 2 above indicates the planning steps that are a necessary prerequisite to the creation of a marketing database, and to the despatch of a direct mail shot addressed to selected promotees from such a database. What it does not deal with is the cost-benefit question: how does a company determine in the first place that building a database will be beneficial – which means that it will improve the profits of the company.

Too many cost-benefit studies that are done to justify investment in business and industry are over-ambitious, and their conclusions thoroughly bogus. Much of the work done in this area is derived from American models, and is infected with the transatlantic assumption that no concept is worthwhile until a precise numerical value has been put to it – and conversely that any concept to which such a value has been put, has thereby acquired a sanctity of precision in which the dubious and wholly imprecise methodology by which that value was 'guesstimated' in the first place can be conveniently forgotten.

The approach of those who favour this model is to identify every foreseeable consequence, negative or positive (cost or benefit) of the course of action being examined, and to follow it through to its second or third order outcome, tagging each manifestation with a precise value. These values are then summated, and a series of impressive-looking calculations is produced to show the expected discounted cash-flow effect of any particular decision over a period of time, the return on capital employed, and the effect on a series of annual profit and loss figures.

The difficulty with this approach is that not all costs and benefits are equally forecastable; consequently, while some of the figures in the calculation will be accurate, others may be wide of the mark by several hundred per cent, and still others – even without allowing for incompetence on the part of the compiler – may be overlooked altogether.

Consider, for example, the case of the Royal Mail and the Postal Address File (PAF). This file, constructed and maintained by the Royal Mail, gives the postcode for every UK address; the Royal Mail sells the file under licence, and an updating service, to all-comers, and derives a substantial income from this source. This income helps to pay for the basic costs of maintaining the file – which, however, the Royal Mail would have to incur on its own account anyway. The direct marketing industry has always maintained that, since the PAF is used to correct users' address files, and to apply postcodes to them, and since such activity is in the Royal Mail's interest, the PAF should be available free.

Theoretically it should be possible to evaluate the net consequences of such a proposal. On the one hand, the Royal Mail would lose the revenue stream it now enjoys from this source: this is reasonably easy to project in a quantified form. On the other hand, a higher proportion of addresses would be postcoded; a lower proportion of mail would be incorrectly addressed;

there would be a lower incidence of duplication of mailing pieces (a short-term loss to the Royal Mail); ultimately the image of direct mail might improve, leading to better response rates, and therefore to greater use of the medium.

The benefits accruing to the Royal Mail from these considerations might far outweigh the costs, or might be comparatively negligible: the point is that they are very hard to assess. It is a characteristic failing of British management (and certainly not just in the Royal Mail) when faced with such a situation, to shrug the shoulders and make no numerical assessment; the characteristic American failing is to guess at some starting figures, and manipulate them to produce a scientific-looking answer that just happens to substantiate the author's initial prejudices.

In the case of most investment decisions – and certainly when we are considering database investment – the costs are more readily quantifiable, in fairly precise terms, than the benefits. This fact provides the clue to my own preferred method of conducting cost-benefit analyses – a method which keeps the relative uncertainty of this or that piece of data constantly before the reader, and indeed the writer, of the analysis.

This method, then, begins by laying down the criteria against which the course of action being examined is to be judged – for example that the negative cash flow from the project must at no time exceed £x; that there must be a cumulative positive cash flow by month y; that there must be a return on capital employed, from month y onwards, of not less than z% per annum. There may be other alternative, or additional, criteria, some or all of which may not be of a directly financial nature – relating perhaps to staff employment, or to standards of customer service, or whatever. They should all, where they are critical to implementation of the course of action in question, be clearly spelled out at the outset; this is, of course, a policy-making function.

The analyst, having been given these criteria, should then begin by estimating the costs of the course in question. In the context of database, these will include the costs of:

Hardware
Software – purchased, or developed in house
Staff Training

Data Capture
Data Enhancement – by postcoding, Acorn coding, etc
Data Maintenance
System Usage – time & materials of operators & users

He should then ask, in the light of these costs, what are the *minimum* financial benefits that the system must earn in order to meet the pre-ordained criteria, and determine what likelihood there is of the system being able to produce those benefits, on the required scale. This will provide a first-order idea of whether the scheme in question is viable or not. If it does appear viable, then the analyst should go back over his figures, adjusting his anticipated costs upwards to the *highest* levels that seem probable, and ensuring that the claimed benefits really are the *lowest* that are likely to be achieved. If, on the other hand, the initial analysis seems unfavourable to the project, then the opposite course should be followed: the analyst should then consider whether his conclusions would remain the same if costs could be shaved (without straying outside the bounds of probability) and if savings above the minimum level could be achieved.

The purpose of this proceeding is to ensure, if possible, that the recommendations one makes will remain valid in the circumstances least favourable to them. At all events, if the recommendation is that the project studied should proceed, then the quantified benefits should be kept as close as common sense permits to the level required by the criteria laid down. If thereafter the analyst wishes to gild the lily, he can of course say:

> On the basis of these minimum level benefits – and assuming maximum probable costs – this project will meet its targets, and should therefore proceed. It should however be observed that certain benefits have been estimated on a deliberately conservative basis; it is reasonable to hope that a further benefit of x might, on a more optimistic view, result. Furthermore, certain other benefits will certainly occur, whose precise financial implications are wholly unquantifiable, but still real. These are ...

Of course, the difficult situation is the one where a project cannot satisfy its predetermined criteria on a fairly pessimistic set of assumptions, but can do so, perhaps with a margin, on a modestly optimistic set. Let us illustrate the point by a somewhat simplistic example.

The project is to set up a database for the Customer Care Department (better known as the complaints department) of an organisation which has to deal, by letter and telephone, with members of the public. By giving each clerk in the department immediate access via a keyboard and screen to a computerised database, it will be possible to provide a much quicker and more customer-friendly service. The criteria that have been laid down for judging the viability of this project are:

a) Capital invested must not exceed £100,000.
b) Net negative cash flow (excluding capital items) must not exceed £50,000 cumulatively at any point.
c) There must be a cumulative positive cash flow (excluding capital items) from the project within one year from its commencement.
d) During Year 2 and subsequently, net savings from the project must be sufficient to provide interest on the capital employed at the rate of 20 per cent per annum or above.

Let us suppose that our costs look like this:

Capital cost of hardware and software: £50,000 in month 1.

Other one-off costs chargeable to profit and loss: £10,000 per month from month 1 to month 4 inclusive.

Running costs: £10,000 per month from month 3 onwards.

This will give rise to a negative cash flow picture like this:

	MONTH											
	1	2	3	4	5	6	7	8	9	10	11	12
One-off Costs £	10K	10K	10K	10K								
Running Costs £			10K	10K	10K	10K	10K	10K	10K	10K	10K	10K
Cum. Costs £	10K	20K	40K	60K	70K	80K	90K	100K	110K	120K	130K	140K

Let us now suppose that we are confident of being able to generate minimum quantifiable savings (through improved labour productivity, reduction in repeat complaints as a result of faster handling, etc) amounting to

£10,000 in month 5, £12,000 in month 6, and £15,000 per month thereafter. Adding this to our cash flow, gives a picture like this:

	MONTH											
	1	2	3	4	5	6	7	8	9	10	11	12
Cum. Costs £	10K	20K	40K	60K	70K	80K	90K	100K	110K	120K	130K	140K
Savings £	–	–	–	–	10K	12K	15K	15K	15K	15K	15K	15K
Cum. Savings £	–	–	–	–	10K	22K	37K	52K	67K	82K	97K	112K
Cum. Net £	(10K)	(20K)	(40K)	(60K)	(60K)	(58K)	(53K)	(48K)	(43K)	(38K)	(33K)	(28K)

On this basis, we are failing to meet two of our criteria: there is a negative cumulative cash flow in excess of £50,000 for four months, and the arrears have still not been cleared off at the end of year 1. (On the other hand, return on capital employed, once the arrears are paid off, is at 60% per annum.)

Now assume that this is the rock-bottom position, and that we have reasonable confidence that, with some effort, the savings position could be improved, so as to start in month 4 rather than month 5, and to grow to a peak of £18,000 per month rather than £15,000. This will transform the negative aspects of the earlier picture to something like this:

	MONTH											
	1	2	3	4	5	6	7	8	9	10	11	12
Cum. Costs £	10K	20K	40K	60K	70K	80K	90K	100K	110K	120K	130K	140K
Savings £	–	–	–	10K	12K	15K	18K	18K	18K	18K	18K	18K
Cum. Savings £	–	–	–	10K	22K	37K	55K	73K	91K	109K	127K	145K
Cum. Net £	(10K)	(20K)	(40K)	(50K)	(48K)	(43K)	(35K)	(27K)	(19K)	(11K)	(3K)	5K

Further, the analyst may reasonably add that he has taken no credit for the effect on the company's reputation, and hence on its sales (and particularly repeat sales) of better customer service. Only a fool would attempt to put precise figures to such benefits – but equally only an idiot would deny their reality. What is now required is a management decision on how to balance the stringency of the original criteria against the degree of confidence in achieving the better savings target, together with the expectation of added unquantifiable benefits.

This method does not eliminate the uncertainties involved in investment decisions and project management. Far from it: by highlighting the areas of uncertainty, and trying to put high/low estimates on them, rather than attempting to clothe every guess in a make-believe garment of mathematical exactitude, it puts the difficult decisions back where they belong – in the hands of those responsible for policy, rather than in those of the technicians, who too frequently have an axe to grind.

What, then, are the areas in which one should look to achieve benefits from a database – not just in the type of example quoted above, but more generally?

a) In the context of direct mail selling, the prime benefit from a database must be the ability to secure business at a lower cost per order. Suppose the case where a company is mailing 100,000 prospects at a cost of £400 per thousand, and obtaining a response rate of 2 per cent – ie 2,000 orders, at a cost of £20 per order. It might be that database techniques would enable the user to distinguish better from worse prospects on this list, and to mail, say, 50,000 prospects only, getting a response rate of 3 per cent, or 1,500 orders, at a reduced cost per order of £13.33. Alternatively, if the total available list were larger than 100,000, it might be possible still to mail the same number, but different groupings, giving a response rate of, say, 2.5 per cent, equalling 2,500 orders at a cost of £16 per order.

b) In the context of the type of business-to-business activity where a team of salesmen is employed, the objective of database techniques is to improve the salesmens' productivity by improving the scheduling of calls, thus obtaining more calls per salesman's week and, by providing information, and by the use of direct mail back-up, to improve the effectiveness of calls. These objectives, added together, amount to more business at lower unit costs.

c) In the context of telesales – either where the telephone is being used by the seller to contact his prospects (outgoing telesales), or where ordering by telephone is a facility being offered to prospects at their discretion (incoming telesales) – a database to which the telesales team has immediate access provides a wonderfully simple basis for taking orders, checking credit, accepting credit card payments, etc, with the least possible delay and fuss. Indeed one might reasonably say that such a database is today an indispensable prerequisite of a successful telesales operation.

d) In the context of a retail operation, a database, supported by direct mail advertising, aims to increase the level of traffic in the operator's shop(s), again with the object of increasing total business while reducing the average cost per sale. Further than this, analysis of the database will enable the operator to draw conclusions, with greater precision, about the nature of his clientele, which may stand him in good stead when it comes to opening new outlets, choosing advertising media, and so on.

e) In every context, a database of customer records lightens enormously the burden of handling customer queries and complaints – both those that arrive through the mail and, even more significantly, those that come by telephone. Indeed, an on-line database makes it, for the first time, easier, quicker, and cheaper, to deal with queries over the phone than by letter – an enormous benefit (even if one hard to quantify in cash terms) for buyer *and* seller.

8

Finding Help

The advertiser who has followed the argument thus far, may have concluded that he ought to set about determining what database marketing has to offer him in his particular circumstances, and how he might embark on the task of creating and using a database. He will now wish to know how he can most economically, and with the best hope of reaching the right answers, get started on such a course.

It is a major theme of this book that neither database marketing, nor direct mail which is one of its more significant weapons, is a thing in itself: database marketing, and direct mail, are properly employed only as part of an integrated marketing strategy. This means that the review of database potential, and plans for its implementation, must be approved at that level of management, and by those persons, responsible for designing such overall strategy. This will normally mean the marketing director, and appropriate members of staff, together with their advertising agency. This in turn raises the question of whether advertising agencies in general are competent to advise on – or to assist with – database projects, and/or direct marketing. To this question there is, sadly, no simple answer.

1. ADVERTISING AGENCIES

Over the last few years, most of the major advertising agencies have found it expedient to build, or acquire by purchase, a direct marketing arm, department, or subsidiary. In some cases this represents a genuine, if late, recognition that direct marketing (and direct mail in particular) is the fastest-growing advertising medium there is, and still a long way from saturation point; in other cases it is more of a defensive reaction, to pre-empt the possible loss of restive clients who want to come to terms with these new developments.

In addition, there are agencies that specialise in direct marketing, either in the sense of undertaking nothing else, or in the sense of running an integrated all-media activity which nonetheless obtains a very large share of its total turnover from direct marketing.

Quoting names in the agency world is always a risky business, owing to the mercurial way in which agencies form, split, and reform with bewildering, kaleidoscopic rapidity. But Ogilvy & Mather is a good example of a large main-line advertising agency that has in recent years become a very significant force, worldwide, in direct marketing, having, in the UK, acquired by purchase a specialist direct marketing arm now known as O&M Direct – previously Trenear-Harvey, Bird and Watson. Contrarily, The Yellowhammer Advertising Company is an outfit presenting a single face to the world while making a very large part of its living in direct marketing. Amherst Direct Marketing, as its name implies, is about direct marketing *tout court*. (I will not tempt the libel lawyers by pointing the finger at specific outfits whose direct marketing activity consists of one man and a boy contracting out client work to other, more competent, shops. They do exist and, once warned, advertisers should have little difficulty in spotting them.)

For many advertisers the rational choice of agencies will lie between going to a specialist direct marketing agency, on the grounds that that is likely to offer the greatest direct marketing skills, and going to (or sticking with) a non-specialist with genuine skills in a variety of fields, on the grounds that this will offer the best marriage of different media. Just to complicate matters, there is another dimension to the choice.

A traditional advertising agency's role is to devise an advertising strategy for its client, to perform the creative function of translating that strategy into words and images for a single- or multi-media campaign, and to book media space. The production of print-media advertisements, or the shooting of film, will be contracted out. With direct mail, most agencies have reckoned to follow a similar path, doing the strategic thinking and the creative work, but subcontracting the printing, addressing, enclosing and despatch. The difficulty with this approach is that in direct mail, to a degree not experienced with other media, the development of new production methods for handling the 'mechanical' functions of printing etc turns these functions too into reservoirs of creative ideas, that are relevant to copy-writers and designers – and indeed to strategic planners. This means that a purely 'creative' agency, that isn't regularly exposed to production con-cepts, has rather little chance of being in the forefront of new ideas in direct mail. Naturally the good agencies are aware of the potential problem, and take care to see that their creative staff do have proper exposure to, and training in, the use of the latest production facilities. But the interface between what can often appear like two cultures isn't always a smooth one – the more so when the two are embodied in different organisations. This is one reason why some advertisers will go not just for a specialist direct marketing agency, but for a 'full-service' agency – one, that is to say, which will perform in house all of the following functions as required:

Consultancy
Creative work
List broking
Computer bureau work (including database management)
4-colour printing
Laser printing
Enclosing and despatch

Even then, of course, contracting out may be required: a shop that offers four-colour printing will not necessarily have all the relevant facilities of a specialist printer, for example. But at least within the four walls of a full-service agency there can be found all the types of skill required for a suc-cessful direct mail campaign.

The choice then can be expressed as whether to go to a specialised or a generalised agency, and if the former whether to opt for the creative house that seems to have the best possible approach to one's problems, or to choose from the small number of full-service houses that have a wider range of skills at their direct disposal – but may not necessarily be the ideal choice over every sector in question.

Of course, there is no single ideal answer. Some agencies have carved out niches for themselves in particular areas – such as financial marketing, or charity fund-raising – where they may have acquired a lead in understanding sectoral problems which would make them an almost mandatory choice for particular clients, over-riding other considerations. Or, it may be that the advertiser's need to exploit sophisticated formats, and equipment for handling such, is paramount, so that he feels the need to be with a full-service agency where complete understanding of all the factors involved may be found between one set of walls. Certainly, if he intends to get involved in database construction it will be essential to be with an agency that employs computer-literate staff who, if not themselves involved in database construction, can at least look after the client's interests adequately in this specialised field.

Where a company already has substantial advertising expenditure in conventional media, my own preference would be for appointing a single agency to handle the advertising across all media – taking care to choose an agency that has established and verifiable direct marketing skills of its own (including, where database is involved, computer expertise). I would also be anxious to know to what extent direct marketing was properly integrated into the agency's work, in terms of strategic planning and detailed creative thinking: this is still an unsatisfactory aspect of very many agency operations, where the need to have a direct mail operation has been recognised, but the need to integrate its activities has not.

2. CONSULTANCY

Where, for one reason or another, integration of direct marketing or database activity with other media advertising is not an issue, a specialist direct marketing agency is likely to be the better choice. Whether this should be a full-service agency (where the real choice is rather small) or not, will depend on individual circumstances. In any event, the advertiser may wish to consider using initially the services of a consultant to help map out an overall database and direct marketing strategy, and to assist in the choice, and perhaps the subsequent control, of one or more service houses to carry out the work. While an advertiser who is using a major agency will not require to employ a consultant as well (since consultancy is precisely part of what an advertising agency is about), an independent consultant may well be of value in guiding an advertiser through the maze of specialist houses and full-service agencies whose various activities we are about to examine in more detail. The particular activities which a direct marketing consultant should be able to perform in conjunction with his client are:

Perform a cost-benefit study of the construction and use of a marketing database.

Produce a document in the form of an invitation to tender for one or more computer bureaux.

Choose bureaux to be approached.

Evaluate bureaux tenders and make recommendations regarding the creation of a database and the subsequent activity on it.

Monitor the work of the successful bureau to completion.

Advise the client on how best to implement the agreed uses of his new database; in particuar to advise, with regard to direct mail activity, on the strategy to be employed, in terms of the products to be offered, the audiences available for them, the pricing structure likely to prove effective, and the overall results achievable.

Advise on those houses best qualified to assist in the creation of direct mail campaigns and material for this particular advertiser.

Monitor the work of the selected service houses.

Of course, not all of these functions will be required in all cases: for example, some advertisers, having determined to create a marketing database, may well wish to design and build this in house, using their existing data processing team and computer resources. We will be examining the pros and cons of this approach, so far as it is possible to do so in general terms, in Section 10. That apart, it will be seen from the above list that the consultant's function – as distinct from that of the traditional advertising agency – is to perform a series of one-off tasks, rather than to enter into a continuing long-term relationship with the advertiser; his object is to enable the advertiser to become self-supporting in a new form of enterprise, as quickly as possible.

An advertiser, then, who wishes to get into database marketing and/or direct mail, who has decided not to use a main-line advertising agency as his primary mentor, but who requires services from one or more of the specialist houses available, may consider using a freelance consultant, one of whose major tasks will be to guide his client through the choice of help-meets from the areas we will now proceed to consider.

3. CREATIVITY

The word 'creative' and its various derivatives is one of the most abused terms in advertising. Every type of operator in direct marketing needs to be creative, in the sense of finding new ways to use the tools of his trade to solve new problems, or to provide more profitable answers to old problems. Yet the 'creative department' in a full-service direct marketing agency will always be taken to mean those employed in copy-writing and design, as though they alone were possessed of this curious faculty of spinning original ideas out of the ether.

In direct marketing, as in any other form of marketing, the most important variable by far is the product on offer, and after that, the audience to whom it is offered. A host of other criteria will, or may, affect the outcome of a sales campaign – the price, incentives, such as a free premium, or a prize draw, credit facilities, and, of course, the words and pictures in which the whole package is expressed. Changing, or even just modifying, the words and pictures can significantly enhance the profits of a campaign, or even change a potential loss into a profit. And since it is usually easier to change the words and pictures than to change a product, or a target audience, and less risky than to change a price, it is frequently on the words and pictures that attention is lavished, sometimes to the detriment of more fundamental issues.

The same high profile is given to the so-called creative functions in terms of the industry's own educational initiatives. It is, I suppose, scarcely surprising that books and articles on direct marketing tend to be written, in disproportionate numbers, by copywriters, who are also among the more articulate, and entertaining, performers on the lecture circuit. But attention to words and pictures can be overdone – indeed is so habitually overdone in our industry that it is necessary to introduce any discussion of this important function by pointing out that they are neither all-important, nor even the most important feature of the direct marketing (or any other marketing) scene.

The reason for this over-estimation of one small sector of the industry, is that it is a sector which every more or less literate person believes they can understand and criticise, preferably without having to think too hard – something certainly not true of list development, or database structuring, or computerised fulfilment. This attitude can lead to a heresy the very opposite of over-estimation – that of supposing that since we can all handle the English language, basically anyone can write his own sales copy.

About this let there be no doubt: no copywriter or commercial artist will make a long-term success out of a dud product, or a good product offered to the wrong audience, or at the wrong price. Equally, the right product at the right price, facing the right audience still needs a professional copy-writer and designer to do it anything like justice, and it would be a dire mistake to attempt to avoid this process.

So, where does one go for copywriting and design services? First, it must be emphasised that copywriting for direct mail is not at all the same thing as copywriting for, say, a Press ad. No doubt it requires the same basic talents, but the experience that goes to making a skilled direct mail copywriter can only be acquired through work in that specific field. Advertisers who use an advertising agency with a direct marketing department/subsidiary should have to look no further; advertisers who are in search of a direct marketing agency will look in the first instance for one with a high creative reputation.

One of the first tasks in choosing a service house (creative or other) is to discover which trade associations it belongs to, and whether or not it is 'recognised' by the Direct Mail Services Standards Board (DMSSB) – the independent body concerned with standards in direct mail advertising, and particularly in service houses. An advertiser considering using a service house that is not recognised by the DMSSB, should take steps to find out why not – there may be quite acceptable reasons, but they should be sought. It should be expected that any service house will also be a member of the Direct Marketing Association (DMA). Some houses specialise in working for particular types of client (for example, one creative house may have substantial experience in financial services marketing); the DMSSB or the DMA may be able to help with advice in this area – although the latter's first loyalty is, naturally, to its own members.

Once one has a short list of suitable creative houses, choosing between them should be no different in principle from choosing any other supplier. Ideally, houses on the short list should be invited to study a brief prepared by the advertiser or his consultant, and to respond with a presentation. Some creative houses will only consent to give a presentation if they are paid for the work involved. This is, to my mind, deplorable – however, a house that can afford to take this attitude is clearly not one that is worried by a dearth of clients.

In addition to securing a presentation, the advertiser should visit the service house's premises. (This rule should apply to *every* service house employed, or considered for employment, on the campaign.)

The advertiser should make it clear in advance that the presentation is to be conducted by the same people who would actually work on the account: too many accounts are won by a touch of brilliance applied by some senior person who is never seen again after the presentation. Arising from presentation and visit, the advertiser should ask himself these questions:

a) Has the creative team properly understood the brief?

b) Are the creative ideas in the presentation adequate, sound, novel, or exciting?

c) Are the team members assigned to the account compatible with the operation?

d) What other clients does the creative house have that have relevance to this assignment? (One or two references should be taken up. Since it is most unlikely that the house will name as referees anyone remotely likely to give a poor reference, what one has to look for is the *degree* of enthusiasm or satisfaction expressed.)

e) Does the house have other accounts that might pose problems for it in working on this assignment – eg close competitors? (It is traditional for large advertisers not to tolerate an agency which they are using working also for a competitor – and to define competition in this context very widely. The results can be fairly ridiculous, but the problem does merit careful consideration.)

Some of the longer-established, or larger, houses will have their walls lined with certificates of award-winning feats. These are the agencies whose creative people turn out copy and art that is considered pleasing, or clever, by other creative people. (The process can be seen at work in the annual Royal Mail/DMA awards scheme.) I suppose these strings of awards do impress some clients – but it sometimes seems that their main purpose is to bolster the fragile self-esteem of those that enter for them. I suppose also that some of the award-winning items really are highly successful for the advertiser – although this is not a criterion available to the judges, and the possession of an award is no guarantee of such success. There are not too many direct mail awards hanging on the walls of Reader's Digest's creative department: that company is too busy counting the money. Personally I always feel that an award-winning direct mail piece bears about as much relation to profit as a picture hung in the Royal Academy's annual show bears to art.

It is normal (though not invariable) for the creative house, whether or not it is a full-service agency, to undertake responsibility on the client's behalf for the post-creative functions necessary to get a campaign into the mail. These post-creative functions we will now consider one by one, before going on to look at the functions, not specific merely to one campaign, that are required for the construction of a marketing database.

4. THE LIST BUSINESS

The list business has for many years been by far the most fraught, and the least satisfactory, part of the direct mail industry. For those who propose simply to create a database from their own customer records, there is no problem, since they need have no dealing with list brokers – unless and until they may wish to use list-broking services to market their database for others' use. But those who wish to acquire prospect names, with or without discriminating information, or those who wish to enhance the information on their own customer files, by reference to demographic data, or other information in the public domain, will find themselves drawn into the world of list broking. In this world there are a number of players:

a) **List owners.**   These are the people who have proprietary rights in one or more lists of names and addresses, nowadays almost invariably held on some computer-readable medium. These may be, for example, lists of subscribers to a particular publication (from which it may be possible to infer a particular occupation, or specific interest) or of persons who have bought this or that (range of) product(s) through the mail, or members of a particular society, or persons whose names appear on a public register of some kind – electoral register, list of shareholders, etc. Business lists exist, both of companies engaged in this or that trade or business, and of persons practising this or that profession; these belong to whichever party has taken the trouble to compile them from published sources.

b) **List brokers.**   Although there are companies that compile, and themselves market, their own lists, (the compilers of lifestyle lists, as discussed in Chapter 4 Section 3 being an outstanding recent example), most available lists in fact belong to owners for whom the revenue derived from list rental is strictly a side-line or by-product. Those owners find it convenient to market the use of their lists through one or more list brokers – sometimes on an exclusive basis, sometimes not – who will advertise the availability of the list, and act as a go-between for the parties involved in a list rental, in return for a commission, usually expressed as a percentage of the rental charge, paid by the list owner. Direct mail advertisers who wish to acquire the use of a list will resort to a list broker, who will produce a catalogue of relevant available lists, with a brief description of the characteristics of each, an indication of price, and a statement of the restrictions governing its use (eg most list owners prohibit rental of their lists to their direct competitors).

c) **List managers.**   In many, but not all, cases there is an intermediate party between the list owner and the list broker – namely the list manager. By this term I mean to designate (because it is not always used in the same sense) the party that actually controls the physical list, and is responsible for its maintenance, updating, etc. Frequently, of course, this will be the list owner himself; sometimes it will be the list broker; in some cases list owner, manager, and broker will be one and the same entity. But it is not unusual to find that the list owner has delegated list management functions to a computer bureau, and list broking activities to a separate list broker, creating a chain of three parties with whom the direct mail advertiser will have to do business. Indeed the three may become four: if the list broker whom the advertiser first approaches finds that the ideal list for his client is broked on an exclusive basis by another broker, then both brokers will be in on the act (and share the commission).

This division of responsibilities, together with the system whereby all intermediate parties are obtaining their fees from the list owner rather than from the advertiser, gives rise to all sorts of difficulties, running the whole gamut from dishonest practice to simple incompetence. (There are, of course, honest *and* efficient operators in the list business, but this is an area where the old adage of *caveat emptor* applies). I will try to indicate some of the more problematical issues.

Lists, in the direct mail business, are rarely, if ever, bought and sold: they are rented, usually for one-time use. Different list owners impose different conditions on the circumstances surrounding such use. On of the most common of such conditions (though not universal) is that the list cannot leave the premises of the list manager in computer-readable format: it must be reproduced onto a printed medium (eg address labels) before the advertiser, or a lettershop working on his behalf, may lay hands on it. The thinking here is that, whereas an unscrupulous person might be tempted to copy a magnetic tape, the cost of data-capturing printed names and addresses is likely to be an effective deterrent (and too many people would have to know about it). For some list owners, however, this is still not enough, and they will insist that the list, in whatever medium, shall not pass through the hands of any party they have not approved: that is to say addressing onto the advertiser's material must be carried out by the list owner himself, or a lettershop acting on *his* behalf. The list owner's final protection (for there are dubious operators on the other side of the fence as well) is to 'salt' the list with names and addresses of employees, using, perhaps, bogus initials, or some such device whereby mail addressed from that particular list can be recognised, and any unauthorised use of the list spotted.

Such caution is understandable. What advertisers must not permit is that these proper precautions might prevent them from assessing for themselves the quality of the list they are proposing to rent. It is a curious feature of the direct mail industry that lots of quite hard-headed business people, who would not dream of paying substantial sums of money for products that they couldn't inspect and check, will nevertheless take on trust – at least until disaster strikes – a wide range of services without any serious attempt to verify that they have been performed effectively, or even at all.

Consider the following true story, of quite recent vintage. An advertiser ordered a selection of names and addresses from a list broker. The names were to be selected from a specific list owner's list, for which the broker in question had no specific responsibility: his job was simply to contact the list owner, verify prices, pass on the advertiser's requirements, and take his commission. (At least, that's all he did; one question that arises is what else, if anything, *should* he have done?) The names to be selected (it was a business list) were to consist of Marketing Directors and/or Marketing Managers of European companies in a particular line of business (identified by Standard Industrial Classification, or SIC) having more than 2,000 employees.

The mailing was supposed to go out in two phases on two separate dates. The first phase duly went out – and the response was disastrous. The advertiser managed to get hold of the printed labels for the second phase, and undertook some visual study, and telephone research. The visual study revealed that many of the names did not carry the appropriate titles; in many cases a substantial number of mailings were being sent to a single company. The telephone research revealed that many of the companies did not have anything approaching 2,000 employees, and a significant number did not belong to the relevant industrial sector.

What happened after that is not important for our present purposes. Suffice it to say that the only people who made any money from the entire affair were, as so often, the lawyers. What we might ask ourselves is: how could this have been prevented? Certainly, the list manager (who was also the list owner in this case) had either misinterpreted the advertiser's instructions as relayed by the list broker, or had carried them out incompetently. (There was no question of deliberate knavery.) The advertiser's chosen remedy was to attack the list broker, who was the only party with whom he had a contract for the supply of names. The list broker in turn had a case against the list owner/manager. But all this was much too late to do any good.

So, do we conclude that the list broker should have accepted responsibility, before the accident, for ensuring that the list owner got what he was asking for – at the least so far as visual inspection could verify this? There is a feeling in some list rental quarters that some responsibility should devolve upon the list broker, but the matter is still one of considerable debate. Nor is it altogether simple. The list broker is in a position similar to that of an estate agent: he may be acting at the original instance of the buyer, but he is acting as the paid agent of the seller, from whom he receives his commission. Of course, the difference between the list broker and the estate agent is that the latter does not enter into a contract with a house buyer for the supply of a house, whereas the former will normally have a contract (written or implied) with the advertiser for the supply of a list. It may therefore be that the discussions now in progress about this issue will result in the adoption by list brokers within the Direct Marketing Association of more stringent rules of procedure regarding their responsibility for the quality of the products and services in whose supply they are instrumental.

But even if this question were resolved in favour of list brokers formally accepting greater responsibility – and it has not yet been – the question must still remain: are there not certain things that the advertiser, in renting a list can – *must* – do for his own protection, under the principle of *caveat emptor*? To which I would reply emphatically, yes. When renting a list, there are, first a number of questions that the advertiser must ask of the list broker, and second a number of actions he must undertake to ensure that he can trust the answers received. First, the questions – which any list broker *ought* to be able to answer:

i)   How was the list compiled? (Ie from what source, and by what methodology.) In most cases list compilation at some stage involves data capture by a person at a keyboard. It is important to be clear whether one can rely on a reasonable standard of accuracy. Moreover, lists composed of persons known to have responded through the mail are superior to lists sharing similar characteristics in all other respects, but not in this.

ii) How often is the list mailed by the owner, and for what purposes? If the owner is mailing frequently, and/or with expensive material, then he has a clear incentive to ensure list cleanliness (or list hygiene as it is referred to in the USA).

iii) How often is the list mailed by others, and by whom? Very frequent use, particularly by the advertiser's competitors, may erode responsiveness. On the other hand, it may indicate a trustworthy product – can references be obtained?

iv) What sort of feedback exists to the list from persons addressed from it? If it is a list of (paid) subscribers to a journal, for example, addressees have an incentive to call for correction of errors, and the list owner may be expected to make them. At the very least the 'gone aways' returned by the Royal Mail should be regularly processed against the list. (In this context, frequent list usage may be an advantage.)

v) What allowance is the list owner prepared to offer in respect of gone aways incurred by the advertiser? For some time it has been standard practice to offer to refund the postage on any gone away in excess of a given proportion (eg 5 per cent). In my opinion this doesn't go far enough: the advertiser loses much more than the postage, whereas the list owner obtains, or should obtain, a positive benefit from gone aways, which are a vital feed back to his list. It is interesting to note that one list owner at least (NDL) has for some time offered to pay a sum of money (which is greater than the lost postage) for each and every gone away returned to him. I hope that much more pressure will in future be applied by advertisers to ensure proper treatment in this respect.

vi) What proportion of the list is postcoded, fully and partly (ie outward code only)? Has the list been subjected to an automatic postcoding process? Postcoding simply copied from incoming (especially handwritten) sources of addresses is liable to a high incidence of error, and is not, on the whole, a very good indication of accurate addressing. On the other hand, the application of *full* postcodes by computer implies a very high level, among those items, of correct and viable addresses.

vii) Over what time-span has the list been compiled? What proportion of the total is more than one, more than two, etc years old? Where we are dealing with a list that implies two-way traffic – eg a list of paid journal subscribers, or club members – this question is less important; in all other cases it has a large bearing on the probability of finding particular persons at the addresses given.

viii) What proportion of the list can be personalised – that is, addressed by correct title and surname? Not every advertiser will require this facility, but most direct mail letters today do attempt to provide a personalised salutation.

ix) It can be assumed that any consumer list consists of named individuals at private addresses. But in the case of business lists, the list may consist of company names and addresses only, or of job titles at company addresses (in which case it is desirable to know whether these job titles are actually known to exist within these specific companies, or are merely presumed titles – as if one were to assume, for example, that every company on one's list had a managing director, or a sales director). Or, again, one may have a business list where each entry has a named individual, complete with a specific job title. The need is to know, for any given list, precisely what the true state of affairs is.

x) Can the list manager sort the list, prior to printing, into whatever sequence is required in order to minimise postal charges? This will normally translate into a requirement to sort for one of the three Mailsort, or two Presstream, services, and will include a requirement to produce the documentation required by Mailsort.

However, obtaining answers from a list broker is one thing; ensuring that the answers given correspond to the facts may be altogether another. This is not because list brokers, or list owners are, as a class, uniquely mendacious, but because it is absolutely standard for the possessor of any asset (in this case a list) to have a considerably rosier view of its characteristics than is justified by hard fact. (I am reminded of how many years it took for users of the Royal Mail's services to persuade the Royal Mail that the user's view of the quality of service being given was in fact broadly correct, whereas the Royal Mail's much more self-satisfied view was substantially wrong. It took an independent monitoring service by a market research agency to carry this unwelcome conviction.)

No advertiser should ever rent a list for the first time without having had sight of the actual names and addresses for which he will be paying, or a sufficient sample of them, in printed form. This inspection may have to be done on the premises of the list broker, or list manager – but done it must be. Of course, merely looking through a printed list of names and addresses will not tell you everything about the problems that may be endemic in a list, but it will suggest a good deal. Here are some of the questions to which one should be alert in looking through a printed list of addresses:

i) How have titles/initials/first names been dealt with: are titles and either initials or first names always present; has any consistent presentation been followed?

ii) If the list is a business list, is the handling of individual names/job titles as you have been led to believe?

iii) Are postcodes, full or partial, present in the sort of proportions you have been led to believe? Is there a significant number of clearly invalid postcodes?

iv) Can you spot any invalid or incomplete addresses? (Eg the omission of county names, where these ought to appear, would indicate that the list has not been through an automatic address-validation process, as would the appearance of a London address with no postal zone following it.)

v) Are there obvious mis-spellings, or other nonsenses? (Again, mis-spellings of post towns or of county names should indicate the absence of proper address-validation.)

vi) Having been satisfied so far as is possible from a visual inspection, the advertiser would be well advised, wherever possible, to test a small sample of any list being considered for rental, with an actual mailing. This has a two-fold purpose: further to ensure that the list is what it seems, but also to determine whether it can produce the results hoped for. Such list testing isn't always possible: the list may be too small to make this a sensible option, for example – but it is an option that should always be weighed up and considered.

A good list broker will be able to advise an advertiser on the full range of lists available that may be relevant to the latter's needs – will be able, indeed, to propose creative ideas on the possible relationships between available lists, or segments of lists, and the needs of a particular campaign or strategy. This creative ability is perhaps the most important quality that the list broker has to offer; the rest is simply the administrative skill necessary to any kind of broker or go-between. And, to reiterate, always remember that the broker, however willing and hard-working he may be in helping the advertiser, is actually paid by the list owner: however honest he may be, and however anxious not to alienate the advertiser, to whom it may be possible to make future sales as well, nevertheless the advertiser cannot ultimately rely on the list broker either to ask all the questions that should be asked or to be sufficiently determined to get meticulously accurate answers.

5. PRINTING

In the context of a particular direct mail campaign, the creative team may determine on their own the printing needs, and simply subcontract the work to a competent print shop, who will have the function of producing the material, possibly finishing some or all of it, (ie folding, collating, binding, stapling, etc), delivering it as required either to the lettershop that is to perform the enclosing function, or, in the case of the addressing medium (letter or whatever) to the computer bureau where the lists are held that have to be printed on this piece.

In some cases, however, knowledge of print equipment can be harnessed to the creative process to produce a new, or at any rate a non-standard, format. This is the kind of circumstance in which the creative agency with its own in-house print capacity will sometimes score, through being able to put together a multi-disciplinary team with minimum trouble.

New formats apart, the print business is normally the least troublesome of all the processes to be considered in mounting a direct mail campaign. The problems that do arise tend to be not printing problems, but problems of co-ordination; too many printers (both individuals and companies) are still possessed of the craft mentality which allows them to take all manner of trouble over the application of their particular skill, while wholly

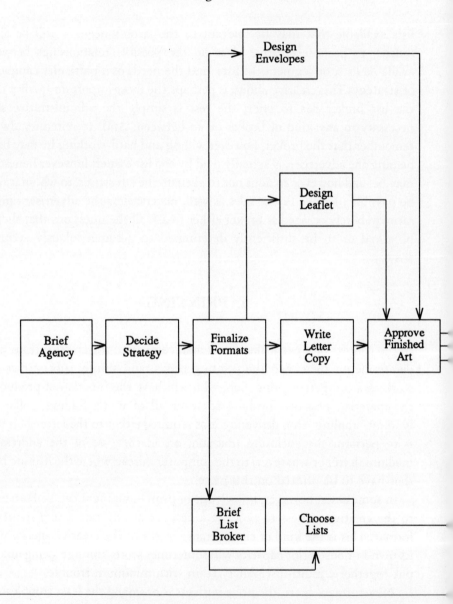

ignoring the needs of other people in the production chain – or even the dictates of common sense. Thus, attention to numbers is frequently inadequate; boxing and transportation is often careless, so that items arrive creased, or buckled (and buckled envelopes will not feed properly on an

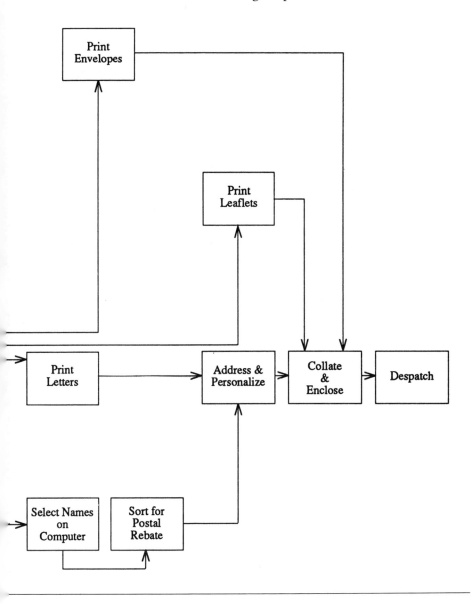

enclosing machine); boxes come unlabelled, so that they cannot be identified readily on warehouse racking; three items arrive on time for a given mailing – but the fourth is delayed. And so on. Most reputable printers can be trusted to do a respectable production job; I don't know too many printers I would trust to do all the ancillary things sensibly and competently without strict supervision.

Where the creative house is acting as agent for the advertiser, and subcontracting to a lettershop, this supervision should be its job. It is frequently (I had almost said usually) overlooked, leaving the wretched lettershop, which is at the end of the line, and has to compensate as best it can for every one else's mistakes, to pick up the pieces. Or else the creative house waits until the lettershop screams, by which time it is usually too late to mount a fully effective rescue.

The moral is a simple one. Every direct mail campaign requires a schedule of events – probably best expressed as a form of critical path diagram – showing what has to be done by whom and when. And even more urgently it requires a progress chaser (which means a person of character, and some authority, not a junior secretary) to follow the process through, to prevent delays where possible, and to foresee their consequences where unavoidable. This job *can* be done by the advertiser himself, or by his agency or creative house. Too often it isn't, and a job, which may already have suffered delays at the creative stage, arrives at the printers where it splits into its component parts and overall control is lost. Those advertisers who decide to employ consultants do so in the knowledge that a substantial part of what the latter can contribute lies in their ability to maintain control on ideas and material through the many stages, and many separate hands and heads, that they must traverse.

Pages 202 and 203 carry an example (illustrative only) of a first-order critical path diagram for this purpose. The scale along the bottom of the diagram indicates units of time; the right-hand edge of each box indicates, by its position on the scale, the earliest point in time by which the activity in the box can be completed; the 'critical' path is the one represented by the *straight* arrows – that is to say, any slippage of any of the functions on that path will cause a slippage in the whole project; limited slippage on other paths will have no such effect. In real life, many of the boxes on this chart would themselves have to be further analysed, and subdivided into component parts. For example, the process of writing letter copy will involve an iterative loop of writing, revising, re-writing, re-revising, gone through, it may be, many times; it will be necessary to check that the overall time-scale allows sufficient leeway for this.

6. SORTING

The Royal Mail, for many years past, has offered substantial discounts to bulk mailers who are prepared to observe certain terms and conditions, and to undertake some of the work that would otherwise fall to be done by the Royal Mail itself. The most important item in this context relates to the sorting of mail for convenient onward transmission through the postal system. The whole system of rebates and discounts – which had grown up over the years in a rather haphazard way – was thoroughly rationalised, after prolonged discussions between the Royal Mail and bulk user organisations, during the mid-'80s. The revised system, which goes under the generic title of Mailsort, has been outlined already in Chapter 5, Section 4.

In order to earn Mailsort discounts (which can run as high as 32 per cent for minimum weight letters, and substantially more for heavier items) qualifying mail has to be sorted according to criteria based upon the postcode. We have noted already that this requirement imposes certain constraints on the construction of databases which are to be used for mailing, and on the handling of incoming data, so as to ensure that the postcode information necessary for sorting is both present and accurate. What is important here is to recognise how the actual process of sortation has to fit into the overall business of getting an addressed mailing into the post.

Clearly the old-fashioned method of manual sortation into pigeon holes in sorting frames, as performed by the Royal Mail itself from time immemorial – and even today for certain types of mail – is inordinately time-consuming and expensive. It may still be the only available method for sorting mail which is addressed from non-computerised lists: such items will normally be sorted either after enclosing, or by sorting empty addressed envelopes immediately before enclosing. We deal with these situations below in Section 8. But the largest, and still growing, proportion of lists are now held on a computer, which renders relatively simple the task of sorting the name and address information in electronic form, prior to printing. This task of sorting, then, has to be undertaken by the computer installation that holds the database, or the list of addresses.

Mailsort allows the postal user a considerable flexibility in the choice of a sortation plan: basically, the more comprehensive the sorting that is done, the greater the level of discount that is available – but the higher will be the costs incurred, not so much in terms of computer processing, but in terms of the physical handling of the mailing subsequently, in particular at the lettershop, where, the finer the sort, the greater the labour in bagging and labelling for collection by the Royal Mail. Agreement on the level of sorting to be undertaken – and the level of discount to be expected – will have to be reached in the first instance between the advertiser (or his agent) and the lettershop; their agreement will then have to be conveyed to the computer processing house that will have to implement the required sortation.

The Royal Mail, wishing to make the original transition to Mailsort as trouble-free as possible, hired a computer bureau (CACI) to undertake the task of producing an embryo database, which is available free of charge to any computer user wishing to adopt Mailsort sortation logic. This database contains all the basic information required to enable the computer, once equipped with the necessary programming, to sort according to the Royal Mail's requirements. The database is universally available, and is certainly in use by all computer bureaux offering services in the direct mail field. Those who wish to install it on their own computer systems should experience little difficulty: it involves a small amount of once-for-all effort from a qualified programmer. (The database itself is subject to change – as new postcodes are created, etc – not more frequently than once per year, and changes are automatically notified by the Royal Mail to all users.)

Thereafter, all mailings addressed from that computer installation can be produced in whatever version of the Mailsort requirements are specified: little more computer time is normally required to meet Mailsort specifications than was needed for the previous rebate system.

In the early 90s the Royal Mail introduced a further facility, enabling mail users to apply 'final' labels to their outgoing mail which would specify not merely the destination of the bag, but also the route by which it would have to travel. Clearly the route (as distinct from the destination) varies significantly depending upon the point of origin of the bag (and even in some cases upon the time of year, owing to changes in rail timetables). Therefore, each computer installation that wishes to produce final bag labels requires to have – and can obtain free from the Royal Mail – a further database which relates data for printing on bag labels to postcodes.

The application of final labels by Royal Mail customers (who previously had to apply intermediate labels showing destination only) has relieved the Royal Mail of a task. Despite protest from some segments of the industry, there is no extra discount forthcoming from the Royal Mail for those who do apply final labels to their bags – but there is almost certainly an overall improvement in the level of service obtained, although this is hard to measure precisely.

Those who wish to mail into Continental Europe also have to sort their mail, if they are proposing to use Royal Mail International services – but the level of sortation required is very simple. If, however, advertisers wish to insert their mail (after trucking it across frontiers) into the domestic mailing systems of Continental countries, and to obtain local discount rates equivalent to Mailsort, then they will have to conform to the sorting requirements of each individual country. These vary widely, but are, in all cases, simpler than UK sorting requirements, due to the much simpler structure of Continental postcodes.

7. ADDRESSING

Determining the mode of address for a direct mail shot is an important part of the original strategic design; it is closely bound up with the question of personalisation, which we will also discuss here. Most direct mail shots are addressed to an individual person by name (or possibly by job title) either at home or at place of work. The simplest way of achieving this in bulk is to print a series of identical letters, all with the salutation 'Dear Sir or Madam', and to put the individual names and addresses on the outer envelope only. Few direct mailers would consider this adequate today, for two reasons:

a) A direct mail shot, as we have already seen, should always carry a response medium. This may be a tear-off slip on the letter, or a separate business reply card, or anything else the designer cares to dream up. Ideally the response medium should itself carry the addressee's name and address printed by the advertiser: this saves the punter from having to overcome his inertia so far as to find a pen and fill in a form; it also ensures that the advertiser's reference data apposite to this particular customer will be present when the response comes back. But this means that some response item *within* the envelope must be addressed.

b) Most direct mail letters today are personalised, at least to the extent of starting with a personal salutation: 'Dear Mr Ramsbottom'. To achieve this, the letters will have to pass through some form of computer printing which, even if it doesn't print the full letter text, will at least print the bits that differentiate one individual addressee from another.

The first of these problems was solved many years ago by the use of window envelopes: the response medium would carry the punter's name and address, which would show through the window – avoiding the problem of double-addressing envelopes and response media, not to mention the problem of correctly collating two separate individualised items.

The second problem, personalisation, could only be solved on any large scale with the advent of computers. The computer could be programmed to print a personal salutation on the letter – what a waste then to be using a second operation to put addresses on a second medium, re-introducing, incidentally, the collation problem referred to above. The most usual answer was to print the name and address at the top of each letter (this being the standard practice for business letters in any case) followed by the personal salutation; to turn the top of the letter, bearing the name and address, into a tear-off response medium, and to let this show throught the window of the envelope.

There still subsist, however, a variety of different modes of addressing, suitable for different circumstances. We will discuss here only those that involve at some stage computer printing from a magnetic tape, or disk.

a) **Cheshire label.**   In this example, the computer prints addresses onto plain continuous stationery. The address will appear with 1–4 items in parallel across the web, the number depending upon the particular type of machine to which the stationery must go after printing. This factor will also govern the depth of each label, from the top of one address to the top of the next – usually either $1''$ or $1^1/_2''$. This in turn will determine how many lines of address can be accomodated on a label. After printing, the stationery, still in fanfold and with its sprocket holes intact, will go to a labelling machine. The first machines of this type were made by the Cheshire company in America, and first used in this country by The Reader's Digest in 1964. Although Cheshire nowadays has competitors, the name, like Hoover, has become generic. The labelling machine will feed the continuous stationery, and cut it up into separate labels, gumming each one to a separately fed cut form, or envelope, or whatever, and either stacking the result or dumping it on a moving belt.

b) **Self-adhesive labels.** These can be produced in any desired size and shape, with the backing paper fanfolded and provided with sprocket holes. The computer prints the labels, as in the previous case, which can then be removed from the backing paper manually, or by a semi-automatic process, and stuck onto the required medium.

c) **Computer letters.** In this variation, either the entire computer letter, or the first sheet of each letter, is produced in continuous stationery form and fed through the computer printer, which adds the name and address, a salutation, and any other variable data in the text of the letter that the advertiser wishes to specify and that the list manager can program for. The letters will then proceed to a burster, or a guillotine, where the fanfold will be separated into individual sheets, and the sprocket holes removed.

d) **Laser printing.** Line printers on a computer are slow, and highly inflexible, compared to a printing press. Typefaces are very limited as well, and one cannot change from one to another in the middle of a letter. So computer printing is normally limited to the situation where the advertiser wants to add only a few lines to each letter. The alternative method, which is now in very wide use, is the laser printer. (The ink-jet printer offers not dissimilar facilities from a different technical starting-point; the output of a laser printer is normally considered somewhat superior to that of an ink-jet.) Different models of laser printer will accept either continuous stationery or cut sheets, and will print on them *both* a standard text *and* individual variations (including, of course, name and address) in one pass, at speeds akin to those of a printing press rather than a line printer, and with a much extended range of typefaces. These printers are computer-driven, from magnetic tape, and a wide range of computer service bureaux now have such equipment, as well as the older conventional line printers, which are now becoming outmoded so far as the production of promotion letters is concerned.

8. LETTERSHOP

The lettershop, or mailing house, is the sharp end of the direct mail business, where the sins, delays, and other shortcomings of all the previous actors in the piece must either be made good, or inexorably come to light and start to exercise their baneful effect on the results of the mailing campaign. In the early days of the direct mail industry, the work of enclosing mailing material in envelopes was almost entirely manual, and tended to be handled on a piece-work, cottage industry, basis. This mode of operation required very little working capital, and incurred very few overheads for the entrepreneur, and indeed a minimum of skills. This in turn led to a fiercely competitive situation, where margins were pared to the bone. Employees were mostly women, almost invariably non-unionised and often working part-time to earn pin-money rather than looking for a living wage. As a result, wages (or piece-rates) were held at very low levels: any departure from such a structure by one company would simply create a competitor under-cutting the rates with the minimum of delay.

The availability of service houses working to tight margins had obvious short-term advantage for direct mail advertisers – and longer-term disadvantages as well. It was the cottage industry lettershop business above all that helped to create for direct mail the undesirable image of rat-faced exploiters squeezing little old ladies, who toiled by candlelight into the small hours, to fulfil their quota of work for greedy capitalists. Worse still, the low cost of entry to the business encouraged the emergence of some dubious characters who, finding that it was easier to get started in the business than greatly to profit in it, turned to ways of improving their lot which were not within the rule-book, and sometimes not within the law – as we shall see.

Times have, to a large extent changed. The advent of computer addressing has given a great boost to all forms of mechanical handling within the lettershop. This in turn has raised the stakes for anyone who wishes to enter the lettershop game as a serious player. To date, this has not resulted in the improvement one might expect in margins, and/or levels of wages: it is still easy, especially in a climate of heavy unemployment, to set up a small manual lettershop which can erode the business of its mechanised competitors. But this will change too. There is now a sufficiency of substantial, well-run, and properly conducted lettershops to satisfy the needs of direct mail advertisers. Nevertheless, advertisers, and their agents, need to be more aware than many of them have been in the past, both of the constraints under which lettershops work, and of the damage that can be done to the prospects of a mailing if the work of the lettershop is not properly controlled and supervised.

The main functions of a mailing house are:

a) to receive the various items that constitute a single mailing from the various printers/manufacturers originating them;

b) to undertake such finishing tasks on each item as may not already have been performed – eg bursting of continuous stationery, removal of sprocket holes, folding of items, etc;

c) to collate the items required for the mailing, and enclose these in the specified sequence in whatever type of enclosing material may be required (envelopes, plastic wrapping, etc);

d) where the items bearing names and addresses have been assembled in a particular sequence – eg for postal discount purposes – to maintain that sequence through the various handling processes;

e) where two or more separate items in a mailing piece are individual to a particular customer (as, for example, where a name and address appears on one item, and a personal salutation on another) to ensure that items are correctly matched up in the enclosing process;

f) where addresses have been produced in no particular sequence, to sort mailing pieces prior to despatch to meet whatever Royal Mail requirements are laid down in order to achieve the level of postal discount agreed in advance with the advertiser or his agent;

g) to bag the final mailing pieces in accordance with Royal Mail requirements for the particular level of service and discount agreed;

h) to label all bags either to the minimum standard required by the Royal Mail, or with 'final' labels if the advertiser or his agent so requires, and to arrange with the Royal Mail for collection in such time as to meet the required mailing date;

i)   to keep an accurate count of the number of pieces mailed, and to advise the advertiser or his agent accordingly; accurately to complete the documentation required by the Royal Mail;

j)   in cases where the advertiser does not wish to pay postage directly to the Royal Mail, to pay the Royal Mail on his behalf, and to account fully to the advertiser or his agent for moneys so spent;

k)   to complete the task within the timespan agreed with the advertiser or his agent, and to provide documentary evidence that this has been done.

Enclosing may be in a conventional envelope, in a paper wrapper, or in plastic. In any of these modes, enclosing can be accomplished manually or by machine. Some items, by reason of their peculiar shape, or particularly unusual or complex make-up, may be unsuitable for machine handling, and therefore require manual enclosing. Where this is not the case, the interests of the advertiser are likely to be best served by having the task performed by machine: there is a much better guarantee of a uniform result, and proper supervision is very much easier.

The particular type of mechanical equipment employed by the lettershop manager may have implications not only for work performance, and how much is to be charged for it, but also on events both precedent and subsequent to what happens within the lettershop itself. Let us consider an example. The most common form of enclosing machine in lettershop use is the Philipsburg. This Heath Robinson-looking machine has been chugging away inserting items in envelopes for as long as anyone in the direct mail industry can remember; other manufacturers have produced comparable equipment, sometimes with modest improvements, but the standard Philipsburg remains the work-horse of the lettershop business. However, this machine, once set up to do a particular job, performs exactly the same function on every cycle: that is to say, it picks up an item from each of its four, or six, stackers that have been filled, collates them into an unvarying sequence, inserts them into an envelope, seals it, and stacks it (or deposits it on a conveyor). Each envelope will contain exactly the same contents. For some years now it has been possible to obtain 'smart' enclosing machines, which will select material from a variety of different possible stackers, according to a coded instruction printed on each master document fed to the machine. In this way, mailing pieces can be produced where the contents of each envelope vary according to the particular needs of each addressee. The number of possible variations is, of course, not unlimited, but the flexibility is substantial.

Consider the value of this in practice. An advertiser wishes to undertake a mailing to advertise a given product, but wishes, let us say, to test the effect of three different leaflets on prospects, without varying any other part of the mailing. If the mailing is to be enclosed on standard Philipsburgs, it will have to be split, prior to addressing, into three streams, corresponding to the three different leaflets to be used; each stream will be handled separately by the lettershop. This has two detrimental effects:

a) The computer installation that decided which addressee was to receive which leaflet, will have taken great care to ensure that names are randomly selected, so that the response to the three leaflets can be properly compared. But, unless scrupulous care is taken at the lettershop, it is probable that the three separate streams will be despatched in three separate lots of mail sacks – possibly even on different days. What happens to them thereafter is largely a matter of chance, and it is quite probable that unintended – and untraceable – variations in handling by the postal service may contribute to an unknowable extent to variation in response between one stream and the next, thus invalidating any conclusions that might be drawn from the test.

One can actually see this happening again and again in observing direct mail test results, where not only the quantity of response, but even the timing of response differs as between two or more test groups supposedly mailed at the same time, indicating either that the mailing house actually released them at different times, or that the Royal Mail treated them in some way differently. In order to avoid this outcome, the mailing house would require either to handle the three streams in parallel on three enclosing machines, mixing their outputs in common bags as they come off the line, or else would have to wait until all three streams had been completely enclosed (and mixed in the same bags) before any part of the mailing could be released. It is in practice totally improbable that any mailing house would do any such thing, unless someone was standing over them the while – and even then the chances of error are substantial.

b)   Splitting the mailing into three streams makes it almost certain that the quantity of Mailsort discount earned will be markedly less in total than it would be for one single stream.

Consider by contrast what happens where the mailing house has a selective enclosing machine. First, the computer house does not have to divide the mailing into three, sort each stream separately, and provide documentation that will keep the three separate thereafter. It will now sort in one single stream, thereby saving some quantity of computer time, besides making the whole subsequent control system much simpler. The computer will, in this scenario, be programmed to put one of three codes in a predetermined position on each addressed item. The enclosing machine will read this code, and choose accordingly the appropriate leaflet for this piece, and enclose it, with the other standard items, maintaining a single sorted stream. The mailing house can then put each bag in the post as its contents come off the enclosing line, secure in the knowledge that each bag contains a proper mix of the three test leaflets. The advertiser will be able to believe the results of the test, and the postal discount available will be maximised.

Rather few mailing houses have selective enclosing equipment, which is relatively expensive. For this state of affairs advertisers and advertising agencies are much more to blame than the mailing houses themselves: the short-sighted emphasis of too many of these companies has for too long been on keeping mailing costs to a minimum, instead of ensuring an optimum service at a proper price. Here too the full-service house is best placed (or should be) to meet its clients' needs, since it can objectively assess the relative merits of using a client's budget to tinker with copy, or to secure proper despatch arrangements (which, if not secured, may render 'improvements' in copy valueless). The advertiser who is not using a full-service house *must* have access to some person, either on his staff or employed as a consultant, who has an understanding of lettershop work, of the impact that its optimum performance ought to have on precedent operations, and of the need to pay a proper price for a proper job. Past experience suggests that those advertising agencies that subcontract lettershop work have neither the competence nor the incentive to deal with those issues in the way that the advertiser's interests demand.

Most lettershops have rather little opportunity to contribute 'creatively' to the planning of a direct mail campaign, partly because there is a tendency among advertisers and agencies not to commission, leave alone to consult, a lettershop until the planning is all complete, and partly because advertising agencies are frequently at pains to keep all their subcontractors well away from their clients. Probably not many lettershops employ staff who are competent to make substantial contributions in the creative area (a chicken and egg problem), but this isn't always so. The best-known example to the contrary is the building (at The Lettershop in Leeds) of the Laserlope – a machine designed and built at a mailing house, to produce a highly sophisticated type of mailing piece. The moral, which the industry has still not learned, is that the truly creative ideas which contribute to the success of a unique mailing, may come from copy-writers, from designers, from list brokers, from computer staff (whose contributions we will be examining in Section 10), and from mailing house staff – or best of all from the interaction of all of these. The task of constructing an optimum campaign demands that each of these disciplines has the opportunity – and is encouraged – to provide an input.

Having said which, most lettershops most of the time have to perform, quickly and efficiently, a fairly mundane function. In doing so, they have to take account of three parties: their client, (who may be either an advertiser, or an agency acting on behalf of an advertiser), the printers, or other suppliers, from who the materials on which they are to work must come, and the Royal Mail.

The lettershop's first concern, in handling a mailing to meet the despatch date set by the client, is to ensure that the necessary materials are delivered on time, and in good condition. Clients, and agencies, sometimes find it surprisingly difficult to recognise that, if a mailing consists of five pieces of material, and one of them is delivered late, the whole mailing, and not just 20% of it, will be delayed. Still less do they appreciate that the task of scheduling several different machine processes for a number of clients so as to make efficient use of machines in meeting scheduled dates, is a fairly complex exercise, where delays have a domino effect. There is a tendency among both advertisers and agencies to suppose that, once the 'creative' stage of a mailing is complete, and printers' proofs have been passed, the rest will happen automatically; progress-chasing tends to be non-existent, or desultory, resulting in last-minute panics where the lettershop is expected to make up for lost time by squeezing its schedules, working overtime, etc. Some delays, of course, are the fault of the lettershop itself, either directly, or indirectly because of fruitless efforts to make up for delays in an earlier job. Whichever way it happens, the result is all too often that the client receives a report about the despatch of his mailing which is, shall we say, less than the whole truth: mailings due out on a certain day will in fact go out n days late, or part of the mailing will go on time, with the rest trailing after, or a mailing due to be spread over x days will actually spread over x + y days, with a full account of the situation often not being given – even where the lettershop itself is not necessarily at fault.

Untidy despatch of this kind might be expected to show up in a peculiar pattern of response – or indeed, where the mailing list has been 'salted' with names of the advertiser's staff, in late arrival of the original mailing. In such circumstances, there is a ready scapegoat to hand – the Royal Mail. Bulk mail these days is not normally postmarked, so there is no indication on the individual envelopes of when they were received by the postal service. Quality of service has in the past had a very poor reputation (although both the reality and the reputation have improved quite dramatically in the last two or three years). There is not too much inclination, therefore, to question mailing house claims to have put material in the post on a certain date: the Royal Mail carries the blame for many peoples' faults as well as its own.

Theoretically, the answer to this problem is simple. The mailing house is required, for each posting, to fill in a postal docket (an official Royal Mail form) which constitutes the basis for postal accounting. The docket shows the quantity of items posted at each weight step, and the date of posting. The advertiser who is paying the cost of postage direct to the Royal Mail, should receive a copy of this docket from the Royal Mail to support the entry on his invoice. Where postage is being paid by the advertiser in advance to the lettershop, leaving the latter to settle up with the Royal Mail, the advertiser *ought* to receive a copy of the relevant postal docket(s) from the lettershop, as part of the accounting process.

Alas, in practice neither of these processes works too well. Many post offices are extremely slack in ensuring that they receive documentation completed properly and on time from lettershops. Dockets are frequently given to the Royal Mail late, particularly where a mailing has been spread over a number of days; the dates on them are unreliable, and the alleged quantities are rarely checked. Moreover, where the postage account is paid by the lettershop on behalf of the advertiser, it is the exception rather than the rule for the advertiser to receive a copy of the postal docket from the mailing house: this means that there is no positive evidence that the mailing has taken place at all, or in the quantity alleged – leave alone that it has happened on a particular day.

Let us be quite clear. The great majority of mailing houses are scrupulously honest. But over the years there have been a small number – and still are – that are not. Without wishing to excuse dishonesty, it has to be said that the losses sustained through it are usually the fault of idle advertisers and agencies on the one side, and the Royal Mail on the other. The industry remembers with wincing clarity the case of the major clearing bank that used a mailing house not in membership of the relevant trade association, and not recognised by the Direct Mail Services Standards Board, to deal with a privatisation issue on its behalf; a high proportion of the documents due for mailing were found part-destroyed on a skip – needless to say, the bank had done no more to verify the performance of the mailing house than it had done to check its standing in the industry. We remember, too, the mailing house (similarly shunned by the industry) that finally went into liquidation owing a seven-figure sum to the Post Office, which had been privately warned three times over the preceding two years of the company's sharp practice, without succeeding in taking any effective action.

Moreover, because the opportunities for malpractice are known to exist, the occurrence of an unexpectedly bad result on a mailing – a much more frequent happening than malpractice – will not infrequently result in an advertiser who has until then been reprehensibly slapdash, suddenly becoming paranoiacally suspicious. So let us consider just what are the opportunities for malfeasance in this area, and then ask what can be done to close them off.

a) The advertiser expects a mailing to be put in the post on a certain day, or spread in a given pattern over a number of days. The mailing house will be scheduling a number of activities for the same time-period, and the advertiser's activity may run late – either because some of the material was delivered late, causing a domino effect on the schedule, or because the job took longer than anticipated – perhaps due to poor scheduling, perhaps due to imperfect material. Whatever the reason, the advertiser requires to know what posting(s) took place when. Sometimes a lettershop will indicate that a mailing went out on the required date, when in fact a small piece (or perhaps a large piece) of it actually went out subsequently; sometimes the advertising agency that subcontracted the mailing may be aware of the true situation, but less than anxious to admit the whole truth to the advertiser (since the agency may have been the original source of the delay). The Royal Mail may then find itself carrying the blame if the mailing is observed to be delivered late.

b) Most mailing houses will, if asked, handle postal accounting for the advertiser, and some, particularly among the smaller houses, are eager to do so. This is not surprising: lettershops in these circumstances request payment of postage (usually calculated on a gross, ie pre-discount, basis) x days in advance of the projected mailing date. They then stick this money in their bank account, where it accumulates interest (or is used as working capital) until the time comes to pay the Royal Mail, several weeks later. They then account to the advertiser for the net amount, returning any excess (or deducting it from their own bill for services). This accounting may, or may not, include copies of the official Royal Mail dockets (which may, or may not, have been officially stamped by the Royal Mail) apparently confirming that such-and-such a number of items of a certain weight were mailed by a certain class of service on a certain day. Problems can occur. First, if the mailing house, between receiving the advertiser's money and completing the mailing, falls into the hands of the receiver, not only will the mailing not go out, but the postage paid in advance will become the property of the generality of the lettershop's creditors. Second, the advertiser has no means of knowing whether or not the mailing was in fact despatched at all, whether in part or in whole, unless he receives a copy of the official stamped Royal Mail docket. (Even this is not a guarantee of the accuracy of the quantity mailed, but it is a guarantee that the lettershop will be invoiced by the Royal Mail for this quantity.) There are certainly cases of lettershops performing half of an advertiser's mailing, docketing that half and paying the Royal Mail for it, meanwhile pocketing the advertiser's money intended to pay for postage on the other half. Advertisers who are dozy enough to facilitate this state of affairs in a certain sense get what they deserve. Unfortunately, the industry as a whole pays, since the response to such a campaign will only be half of what it should have been, so that the advertiser, even if his suspicions remain dormant, will be disappointed with the result, and disinclined to venture forth again.

c) It isn't only the advertiser that can be ripped off by the occasional unscrupulous lettershop: the Royal Mail too may suffer. The lettershop may take the correct money for postage from the advertiser, and indeed mail correctly – but make out postal dockets (knowing the advertiser will not see them) for smaller quantities than are actually mailed, resulting in smaller postal bills, and a surplus for the lettershop. There is always a risk that the Royal Mail will execute a random check on such a mailing, and discover a discrepancy; against this there are two defences. First, check weighings (all that the Royal Mail can reasonably be expected to do) cannot give an answer accurate within 15 per cent; there is little risk for a lettershop in ripping off the Royal Mail for, say, 10 per cent of the postage on a large mailing – provided the advertiser is not going to see the postal docket. Second, even if a discrepancy is discovered, most post offices in such circumstances will merely ring up the offender and point out that a mistake appears to have been made; the lettershop will 'discover' that this is indeed the case, apologise profusely, and correct the error – this time.

So, what can be done to enable the advertiser to safeguard himself against the effects of this kind of villainy? Really, all that is required is that both advertisers and the Royal Mail should exercise the sort of vigilance in this field that most business people regard as second nature in other areas, such as receipt of goods. For example:

i) An increasing number of advertisers are nowadays opening direct accounts with the Royal Mail (and the larger mailing houses are encouraging them to do so rather than paying for their mailings through a lettershop. Particularly for large advertisers, who may use a number of lettershops, as well, possibly, as undertaking substantial amounts of mailing from their own premises, this has numerous advantages, not least being the consolidation of total postage bills under a single account. It does also eliminate the temptation for a mailing house to be less than 100 per cent above-board in terms of postage paid, quantities mailed, and discounts earned.

ii) Mailsort has already brought in its train revised docketing procedures, which are, in principle, harder to cheat on; the Royal Mail is also proposing tighter and more frequent checks on dates, weights, and quantities. But, above all, those advertisers who will now be paying their bills direct to the Royal Mail will receive back copies of the dockets that form the basis of their payments.

iii) Advertisers need to insist that arrangements with lettershops, whether made by themselves, or by agencies on their behalf, are fully documented. In fairness to both parties, this means that the lettershop's obligation to mail on or by a given date must be balanced by an assurance of supply of materials by an agreed date. Advertisers should then insist on having the opportunity to inspect the lettershop's work while in progress, and to receive precise notification of completion. If advertisers are prepared to exercise oversight of the mailing process themselves, well and good. If they feel they can trust the advertising agency to do so on their behalf, equally OK. But if they are employing a direct marketing consultant, this is a task that functionary would automatically expect to perform.

iv) Above all, advertisers and agencies need to stop treating lettershop work as though it were some tedious afterthought to the creative process of inventing a mailing. A good lettershop can be a valuable partner in the creative process; over and above that, it has a serious job to perform which, according to whether it is done well or badly, honestly or less so, will affect the results of the campaign – very possibly to a much greater extent than anything a 'creative' agency can, for good or ill, achieve. And if a lettershop is to do its job well, and honestly, then it should be able to expect a reasonable level of profit for its work – not to be nailed to the floor by an agency, or client, that is only interested in the short-term problem of minimising costs today, regardless of the effect on tomorrow's quality of service.

9. FULFILMENT

Some further definition of terms may be called for here. Whereas the lettershop work we have been discussing consists of enabling an advertiser to get direct mail advertising material into the post, *en route* to the potential customers' letter-boxes, fulfilment work consists in handling customer-generated response to advertisers' messages. This can take a variety of forms: consumers sending in six Brand X box-tops, who must be sent a plastic daffodil each, or £1 sterling, or a clutch of discount coupons, in exchange; people applying for free samples of this or that product; people seeking further and fuller particulars of such and such an offer; people ordering, and perhaps sending money, or credit-card details, for an advertised product.

Some lettershops will undertake fulfilment work also, although rather few of them specialise in this type of activity; at all events we will discuss fulfilment houses as though they were – as indeed most are – a separate phenomenon. The basic requirements for running a successful fulfilment house are first of all the warehousing capacity for whatever items clients may wish to despatch to those responding to their offers and, secondly, a highly flexible labour force able to adapt itself to every manner of odd requirement. Nowadays a further requirement is a computer system which can be used to capture names and addresses and to print labels that will carry the fulfilment packs to their appointed destinations.

This thought raises a curious reflection. Many fulfilment houses handle hundreds of thousands of consumer names and addresses each week – a high proportion of them arising from responses to point-of-sale offers for fmcg items. Most of these names and addresses are data captured – as the simplest way of initiating the fulfilment process. Yet enormous numbers of these names, captured on a computer and recorded on disk, are never again used by the companies concerned, many of whom, if they have heard of such things as databases and direct marketing at all, are quite convinced that these have no connection with their own businesses.

Those who have travelled with us thus far will recognise this as the most terrible heresy of all: at a time when companies alive to the direct marketing process are straining every nerve to accumulate relevant data, it is a shock to find marketing dinosaurs (and many of them are giants in point of size, as well as in evident lack of cranial capacity) who blithely ignore or discard data that has already been captured.

Be that as it may, the advertiser who seeks a fulfilment house should look for one that is capturing data on computer as a matter of course, thus acquiring, as a by-product of the fulfilment operation, a quantity of invaluable data. If the list thus created can't be used in a further marketing effort, then at the very least it is a marketable asset which, through a list broker, can earn revenue.

Commissioning a fulfilment operation demands the same kind of common-sense vigilance required in commissioning a lettershop: the advertiser needs to have proper evidence that instructions have been carried out fully, and in a timely manner. In practice, far too much of this work is done sloppily, and once again this is primarily the fault of the advertiser, or his agency. This is particularly true of point-of-sale offers, where the main object of the campaign is to stimulate sales of the brand, and fulfilment of the 'special offer' is seen as a side issue, to be farmed out and quietly forgotten about.

Of course, where fulfilment is a consequence of a request from a consumer, who is therefore expecting something, failure by the fulfilment house to execute its instructions in any significant number of cases is likely to give rise to a large body of complaint to the advertiser, who will thus be alerted to the problem. Nonetheless, advertisers should, as a matter of course, set up a regular reporting structure which will enable them to know daily how many requests for fulfilment have arrived, how many have been handled, how many have been posted (supported by Royal Mail documentation) and how many are awaiting action. And they should inspect the activities of their chosen fulfilment house from time to time, either in person, or through an agency, or a consultant.

10. COMPUTER BUREAUX

In the context of the kind of activities dealt with in this book, a company may have cause to consider using a computer bureau in any of the following circumstances:

As a list manager, as described in Section 4 above on The List Business.

To build a database system, which may subsequently be run on the client's own computer in house, or by the bureau.

To run a database system.

a) List management. List management is a function required by a list owner either because he is making more or less frequent use of the list himself, and requires it kept up to date for that purpose, or because he wishes to derive a subsidiary income from renting the list to other users, and needs, through list maintenance, to preserve the quality of this marketable asset. We will examine three possible scenarios, to determine in the case of each what might be the advantages to the list owner of using a computer bureau.

i)   Consider first the fmcg manufacturer referred to briefly in the previous Section on Fulfilment. He acquires names and addresses as a result of his point-of-sale activities, and uses a fulfilment house to carry out his obligations to those persons. As a by-product of this operation he has a continuing flow of computerised consumer addresses, with a certain amount of data about each – but at this time no further use for this data in the context of his own operation. Such a person will require to find a list broker who will market his list, and a list manager (quite possibly the same person) who will maintain it on his computer, make parts of it available to clients as required, and update it in respect of any new data acquired – including, for example, gone away information resulting from mailings. For the manufacturer to perform these chores for himself would probably make little sense, diverting him from his true business into areas in which he has little experience or skill, and in which potential earnings would be a quite small proportion of his business interests. Use in such a case of outside bureau services, which provide the list owner with a continuing revenue for little ongoing effort makes excellent sense.

Nonetheless, certain precautions do have to be taken. The list owner will probably wish to specify certain restrictions as to the kinds of business to which the list can, or cannot, be rented – to exclude direct competitors, for example. He should expect to receive from the list broker each month a list of all companies who have contracted to rent the list, and he will wish either himself, or the broker on his behalf, to have advance sight of all material it is proposed to mail to names from his list. If the broker is to exercise this oversight, he will need to be supplied with a set of criteria by which he can judge what type of material is or is not suitable. And finally, the list owner will wish to 'salt' his list with a sprinkling of names and addresses which, by virtue of their spelling, use of initials, or some such, are instantly recognisable by their recipients as having emanated from this list. Such persons, on receiving a promotion from the list, will send it to a single person in the list owner's organisation, who will be able to spot any unauthorised, or otherwise unsuitable, use of the list. (It is also important that all those involved – the list broker, list manager, and indeed the list owner's own staff, all know that the list has been salted in this way – prevention is always better than cure.)

ii) Next, take the case of a small magazine publisher. He has a list of subscribers which he requires to use regularly for the despatch of copies, and for sending out renewal notices and bills. But he regards this as a fairly mechanical small-scale chore; just as he subcontracts the printing, binding, and wrapping of his publication, so he feels that it would make sense for him to contract out also the addressing, despatch and list maintenance functions, which otherwise represent a distraction from his proper skills. And if this contracted job can be handled by a company that can also earn some revenue for him by renting use of the list to non-competitive advertisers, so much the better for everyone.

iii) The company which is using its list of past customers as an integral part of its day-to-day marketing effort, cross-promoting product x to buyers of product y, is in a somewhat different position. The list – or, as surely it should in such a case become, the database – is now so central a part of the operation of this company that it is to be expected that most such operators would wish to have it managed on their own computer in house, where it can be instantly accessed, and where the company's own staff is available to react swiftly to the changing needs of the moment. But how, in such a company, does the database come to be created in the first place?

b) Creating a database. The use of computers in business and industry is today widespread; few companies of any size do not have computer equipment of some kind, and substantial installations of hardware, supported by systems and operating staff, are commonplace. Why, in these circumstances, is there still such a thriving business for computer service bureaux? And why are these bureaux occupied, for much of their time, in working for clients who already have their own, often large, computer installations?

Two reasons can be found for this curious state of affairs. First, most computer staff are neither intelligible to, nor understanding of, the businesses in which they work, and by which they are paid. There is an enormous gulf of understanding, in most computerised companies, between the professional systems staff, who have a limited understanding of what the business is about, and little or no feel for how the individual talents within it actually operate, and the company's general management, who, despite familiarisation sessions, have no gut feeling for what a computer can and cannot do, or which types of problem are simple and which difficult for a computer to handle.

Second, every computer department, regardless of its size, is always full up with work, now and for the next six months. (Although I have been a computer manager myself for some years, and experienced this phenomenon close to, I am far from clear as to the reasons for it, so I give none: I offer the observation merely as an extension of Parkinson's Law, and other such mysterious forces, like gravity, whose effects one can measure without having the slightest notion of their causes.) This means that any manager requiring systems work, whether in the form of a few hours' work, or a major project, must submit his demand to some type of evaluation system, which will either give it priority on the grounds of perceived urgency, or, more probably, will assign it to the back of the queue, to be started six months hence – always provided its place is not in the interim usurped by something more evidently important.

Faced with this dual problem, of poor communications and inaccessability of resources, the marketing director who has become convinced of the need to capture and maintain all the information he can about his customers, his prospects, their behaviour, lifestyles, and all that – and who sees this information daily escaping for want of any system of data capture – will be attracted by the idea of going to an outside bureau. This will give him access to people whose very livelihood depends on being able to communicate intelligibly, and who, if he chooses his bureau carefully, have some experience in the database field, which his own internal computer staff probably do not.

There is no single answer to the question whether this is a sensible move or not. What we can do is to consider what is the necessary – or at any rate the desirable – relationship between the marketing staff for whose immediate use the database must be designed, and the systems staff who must create it. Each marketing director must then make up his own mind whether this kind of relationship can be created – and the work done within the required timescale – with existing company resources, or whether he needs to look outside.

The most often-reiterated statement of the proper relationship between computer technician and computer user is that the user must define his requirements, which it is then up to the technician to find an appropriate means of meeting. This is the most awful piece of rubbish, which has been responsible for a high proportion of the disasters that have occurred in the computer world over the last thirty years. Most aspiring computer users don't have 'requirements' in this sense at all – first and foremost they have problems, which usually fill their horizons; secondly, when they do get a little breathing space, they have dreams, aspirations, concepts even – but requirements, no. A statement of requirements implies a prior analysis of problems, and indeed a determination of the broad means by which they should be solved. Whereas the computer user has no idea, initially, which of his aspirations is practical or impractical, easy or difficult, cheap or expensive. The ends one wishes to achieve, and the means of achieving them are simply not separable, in systems analysis any more than in philosophy.

Further, few computer users, and particularly few marketers, have the *kind* of mental equipment, or training, or inclination that would enable them to undertake a rigorous analysis on which a statement of requirements could be based – even if they had a sufficient background understanding of the technical possibilities to render this fruitful. In fact, when one hears a computer manager demanding that a prospective user should produce a clear written statement of requirements, this is normally a cop-out: the computer manager knows that no such statement will be forthcoming; if he should prove mistaken in this, he will find twenty-six questions to ask about the statement, and another twenty-six about each of the answers – this will keep things ticking over fairly indefinitely, and will postpone the evil day when he has to admit that he lacks the resources to embark on the task at any time during the next six months.

Producing a statement of requirements is a task for a systems analyst. It is moreover a wholly crucial task. It can be divided, conceptually, into four parts. First, the analyst must get to understand the way in which the part of the organisation he is looking at now functions; he must understand this in the fullest possible detail. Much of that detail will turn out to be peripheral, and will be discarded from further consideration, but some – and it is impossible to tell which in advance – may prove crucial, so everything must be absorbed in this first phase. Second, the analyst must be able to reduce the mass of material so acquired to essentials; he must be able to describe the current functioning of the entity analysed with just enough detail to render it intelligible. Third, he must be able to reconstruct this entity on paper, in a way which will minimise existing problems, and maximise opportunities, within the accepted constraints of the function itself. To do this properly, he will have to stand inside the mind of the user, and to sense problems and opportunities as the user does, only with greater clarity. Fourthly, and most importantly of all, he must not only sell this system re-design to those who will operate it; he must actually convince them that all the important parts of it were their idea in the first place. Then, and only then, can the task of implementing the system begin.

Of course, the process is nothing like as simple a series of events as the above suggests: for a start the whole procedure is iterative rather than simply serial. That is to say, the tasks of learning current procedures and reducing what one learns to essentials go on in parallel: one's 'essential model' is modified – sometimes wholly reconstructed – in the light of each new finding. Again, reconstruction is not a single uninterrupted process: each step of the process must be tested in dialogue with the user, and modified in the light of his comments; in this way the process of 'selling' the ultimate design is a continuing one, interwoven with the design process itself.

A company that has a computer systems department dedicated to this type of approach, and possessed of analysts capable of carrying it through, should not have to look to an external bureau to construct its marketing database – subject, of course, to the problem of priorities already alluded to. But a company where the systems department has no spare capacity, or where the systems manager seeks to conceal his own problems by asking for a statement of requirements, will be one whose marketing director would be well advised to see what external assistance he can acquire.

It is at this point that a company is most likely to call on the services of a consultant. There are two problems in using consultants. These may be described thus:

i) Cost: the good ones aren't cheap, and the cheap ones aren't good. (Nor are the expensive ones guaranteed to be good either.) A senior partner in any established consultancy will, in 1993, cost upwards of £1,000 a day. A freelance consultant, without office overheads to support, will usually come cheaper – but is still much more expensive per hour than most marketing directors themselves. There is no point in choosing a consultant on the strength of company reputation; first, that reputation relates to past events, and you are interested in the future; second, it is the quality of the individual working on your account that matters, not that of his or her colleagues.

ii) Adhesion: consultants are a bit like fleas: once you have them, they are very difficult to get rid of. It has been said that the first imperative of a good consultant is to work himself out of a job as quickly as possible. On this definition, there are not too many good consultants around.

Accordingly, the sensible time to use a consultant is in order to undertake a self-contained, one-off task which is beyond the scope of your current staff. Boundaries can, and should, be set to the job, and when these are reached, the consultant can go. And if they aren't reached in the expected time, the consultant goes anyway. The task of creating a marketing database is precisely such a circumstance, and the ideal type of operation for the employment of consultancy help. Broadly, the areas to which a database consultant should be able to make a crucial input are:

Specification of requirements
Evaluation of tenders for software and hardware

Choice of suppliers
Liaison with suppliers and supervision of installation

c) **Running a database.**   Only a few years ago, creating, maintaining, and running a marketing database would have been regarded as a major undertaking not only in terms of systems development (which it still is) but in terms of hardware requirements. Today this is much less true, and concern that such a development would cause overload on existing computer hardware, or necessitate acquisition of extensive further hardware, expensive both intrinsically and in terms of space, maintenance, operating, etc, can be largely discounted. Indeed, there are already two or three software offerings available in this country that enable quite large databases (say of up to 200,000 persons) to be run on a micro computer with a hardware cost of less than £5,000. And indeed these software packages are such that, once the system is designed and installed, technical computer considerations are almost non-existent, and the whole process of interrogating and using the database can be handled by the end-user – the marketing director and his staff, sitting at their own desks.

This state of affairs has greatly lessened the case for using a bureau actually to hold and operate one's database, and increased the case for putting computer power at the finger-tips of the end user, rather than centralising it in either a computer department or an external bureau. However, there remain two problems – bulk printing from the database, and data maintenance. As to the printing problem, micro computers will not at this date support fast line printers, or continuous stationery laser printers, such as are necessary for volume printing; a means therefore has to be available for transferring data in magnetic medium to a location where adequate printing capacity is available.

The second problem is somewhat harder, although it depends on the type of database in use, and the extent of new data affecting it. One thing is for sure: the marketing director may be very glad to be able to call individual items from his database to a screen in his office, and to initiate analyses or manipulations, or print-outs of the data at the touch of a button – but he will not relish the thought of having to handle large volumes of data consisting of changes of address, gone away notifications, orders, cancellations, payments, and all the other multifarious items that can impact his database. For this reason, a compromise solution may make sense, under which the database is held, and maintained, at a central location possessed of the facilities to handle all the updating chores, while the marketing department can access the database directly from one or more micros of its own, with facilities to download all or part of the database onto that micro, and there to handle it as may be required.

11. CONCLUSIONS

For those about to make their first essay into database marketing, as for those with a dawning interest in direct mail, there is a plethora of agencies of all kinds waiting to lend a hand (and to take their money). The object of this chapter has been to indicate the kinds of service that are available, the sort of circumstances that would indicate resort to each, and the pros and cons of this or that alternative. The chapter that follows attempts to indicate the sources of further information that are available, in terms of organisations, of listings, and of reading materials. What cannot be done (entertaining though it might be) is to indicate the strengths and weaknesses, skill or lack of it, of this or that operator. So, use these sources to determine what sort of facilities are available from whom; when it comes to choosing which outfit to select you are on your own – unless, that is to say, you have a good consultant at your elbow to help in choosing.

9

Other Information Sources

---

1. *Direct Mail Services Standards Board (DMSSB)* This body was set up, with Post Office funding, in 1983. Its objective is 'to encourage the achievement and maintenance of the highest standards of practice and conduct in the direct mail services industry'. To this end it runs a recognition scheme for direct mail service houses of all kinds, and publishes a list of recognised houses (currently some 200 of them). There are still quite a few companies offering services in direct mail (including database facilities) that are not recognised by the Board. However, most of the major players are recognised, and anyone contemplating buying services from an unrecognised house should, for his own protection, satisfy himself of the reasons for such non-recognition.

   The strength of the Board as a source of advice is that it is an independent body, beholden to no one. (Although it continues to be funded by the Royal Mail, it operates independently and at arm's length. Moreover, it has no obligations to its recognised houses – who are not 'members' as in a trade association, and who pay no fee for their recognition.) It is run on a day-to-day basis by a Chief Executive (Mr Michael Goodrich) and an Assistant Director (Miss Priscilla Titford). Its governing body is a Council (whose Chairman is Mrs Kate Foss) composed of prominent members of the industry, and independent persons. The Board has always worked closely with the Advertising Standards Authority. Its address is shown overleaf:

DMSSB
26 Eccleston Street
London SW1W 9PY
Tel: (071) 824 8651
Fax: (071) 824 8574

2. *Trade Associations*
    a) *The DMA*   One of the major weaknesses of the direct marketing industry in the UK has always in the past been the plethora of overlapping trade associations it contained. Many attempts have been made to rationalise the situation, and at last, one such attempt has borne fruit. The result has been the formation of the Direct Marketing Association (UK) Ltd, or DMA for short, founded by the previous members of the Association of Mail Order Publishers, the British Direct Marketing Association, the British List Brokers' Association, and the Direct Mail Producers' Association all agreeing to pool their identities in the new DMA. The aim of this body is to bring together in one powerful and united organisation all those who have a vital stake in any form of direct marketing, so that the industry can speak with one voice – to consumers, to the media, to Whitehall and Westminster, to Brussels and Strasbourg – knowing that that voice will be heard, respectfully.

    The Acting Chief Executive of the DMA is Mr Colin Fricker, and its address is:

The Direct Marketing Association (UK) Ltd
1 Oxendon Street
London SW1
Tel: (071) 321 2525
Fax: (071) 321 0191

Membership of the DMA doesn't come cheap. This is because so much work has to be done to correct the image of direct marketing that has developed over those years during which its protagonists were too busy tilling their own gardens to observe what was going on in the world outside. Every company which seeks to benefit from direct marketing has a duty, to its own long-term future, to be a member of the DMA.

b) *Promotion Handlers' Association (PHA)* This is a relatively recently formed trade association; it consists of companies with a substantial interest in fulfilment work – the handling, that is, of coupon response from advertisements. The chairman of the PHA at the time of writing (there is no full-time staff) is Mr Alan Crossman, who may be found at:

PHA
c/o Mailcom plc
Snowdon Drive
Winterhill
Milton Keynes MK6 1HQ
Tel: (0908) 675666
Fax: (0908) 668801

c) *Incorporated Society of British Advertisers (ISBA)*   This organisation has a very large membership of advertisers. It also runs a small direct marketing committee; this has been in existence for some time, and rendered useful service to its members, but its continuing relevance is in some doubt with the advent of the DMA. ISBA's full-time director is:

Ken Miles
44 Hertford Street
London W1Y 8AE
Tel: (071) 499 7502

d) *Institute of Practitioners in Advertising (IPA)* The IPA is an organisation for agencies. It too has in the past run a direct marketing committee. However, most of the IPA's members who have a serious direct marketing interest have joined the DMA, and the continuance of this committee is in some doubt. The address of the IPA is:

44 Belgrave Square
London SW1X 8QS
Tel: (071) 235 7020

e) *Mail Order Traders' Association (MOTA)* This is a very small grouping, basically consisting of the large mail order catalogue houses (with the exception of Great Universal Stores). The director of MOTA is:

Keith Tamlin
25 Castle Street
Liverpool L2 4TD
Tel: (051) 227 4181

f) *Advertising Association (AA)* All the above Associations belong to the AA. This body used to take very little interest in direct mail, but this attitude has changed radically in the last few years — indeed the recent Director-General was an important catalyst in bringing together a number of key direct marketing figures in order to set up the DMA, which effectively replaced a number of overlapping bodies. The Advertising Association now has a direct marketing committee, which serves to provide a forum in which all the various parties with interests in direct marketing can meet. It also has a data protection committee, which has done invaluable work, in debating controversial issues with the Data Protection Registrar; in gaining industry agreement to detailed self-regulatory procedures; and in co-ordinating the industry's lobbying efforts directed at Brussels and Strasbourg. The full-time Director-General of the Advertising Association is:

Andreas Brown
Abford House
15 Wilton Road
London SW1V 1NJ
Tel: (071) 828 2771
Fax: (071) 931 0376

3. *Mailing Preference Service (MPS)*   This body was also set up with Royal Mail help in 1982. Its object was to enable consumers to register, with a single body, their desire to receive, or not to receive, direct mail advertising of particular kinds – ie in particular to act as a safety-valve for disgruntled consumers. The service collects details of all consumers who write to it, and forwards these, in computerised media, to its subscribers.

It is extremely important to the health and reputation of the industry that all those who own consumer mailing lists should use the facilities of the MPS. It is also highly desirable that advertisers should only use lists that are regularly 'cleaned' against MPS lists; it may shortly become mandatory on list brokers to ensure this in respect of any consumer lists that they broke. Since the MPS is now financed through the Mailing Standards Levy (see below under Advertising Standards Board of Finance), the MPS list is freely available to all-comers.

The Chairman of MPS at time of writing is Mike Hawker, of Freemans. Its full-time Chief Executive is:

Kay Beckett
MPS
1 Leeward House
Square Rigger Row
Plantation Wharf
London SW11 3TY
Tel: (071) 738 1625

4. *Data Protection Registrar*   The duty of this personage is to ensure compliance with the Data Protection Act, which has been dealt with at length (Chapter 5, Section 2). Once the Brussels Directive on Data Protection has finally been passed, there may need to be further legislation in the UK, to bring British data protection into line with the requirements of the Directive. However, these new requirements, whatever they may be, will continue to be overseen by the Registrar. The present incumbent is shown on the next page:

Eric Howe
Office of the Data Protection Registrar
Springfield House
Water Lane
Wilmslow
Cheshire SK9 5AX
Tel: (0625) 535777

5. *The Royal Mail*   Direct mail is the fastest growing component of letter traffic handled by the Royal Mail. For this very sufficient reason, the Royal Mail is eager to act in concert with – indeed as part of – the direct mail industry. A number of schemes are available for the assistance of direct mail users; those not well acquainted with them already can find out more from Streamline – the Royal Mail service for handling bulk mail – which may be found at:

Royal Mail Streamline
Beaumont House
Sandy Lane West
Oxford OX4 5ZZ
Tel: (0865) 748768

6. *The Advertising Standards Authority (ASA) & The Committee of Advertising Practice (CAP)*   These two bodies are the main machinery of self-regulation in the UK advertising world; they were set up in their present form in the 1970s, in the context of a growing groundswell of hostility, among public and politicians, to some of the excesses of advertising.

    The CAP is a committee of advertising industry representatives. It is responsible for writing, and keeping up to date, the industry's Codes of Practice (ie the British Code of Advertising Practice [BCAP] and the British Code of Sales Promotion Practice [BCSPP]. These Codes cover all forms of advertising which are not covered by legislative initiatives (ie all except radio and television). The CAP is also responsible for dealing with intra-industry disputes on advertising matters. It has a staff which it shares with the ASA. This staff provides an advice service for advertisers or agencies who may have queries about acceptability of copy, or other aspects of an advertisement.

The ASA has a Council of independent members, and a staff, which it shares with the CAP. Its function is to monitor compliance by all concerned with the Codes of Practice, and to deal with complaints about advertising from all quarters, publishing their findings.

Until recently the ASA, like the Advertising Association, paid scant attention to direct mail – and indeed to other forms of direct marketing, apart from direct response advertising in print media. This has changed completely; the ASA has now agreed to incorporate the industry's Code of List and Database Practice into the BCAP, and to monitor compliance with it.

The current Chairman of the ASA is Sir Timothy Raison. The current Director-General is:

Matti Alderson
Advertising Standards Authority
Brook House
2–16 Torrington Place
London WC1E 7HN
Tel: (071) 580 5555

7. *The Advertising Standards Board of Finance (ASBOF)*   The ASA, very properly, advertises its activities to the public. This costs money, as does its significant staff and premises. The industry finances these necessary expenditures by a levy on advertising. The levy on above-the-line advertising (from which radio and TV advertisements are exempt) is paid, at the rate of 1% of the advertising cost, to ASBOF by all advertising agencies, and charged out by them to their clients. The levy on direct mail is collected by the Royal Mail as a charge of 0.25% levied on Mailsort postage bills, and paid by the Royal Mail to ASBOF. This Mailing Standards Levy pays not only for the work done by the ASA on direct mail, but also for the MPS.

The current chairman of ASBOF is Brian Nicholson. The current Secretary is shown on the next page:

John Robinson
ASBOF
74–77 Great Russell Street
London WC1B 3DA
Tel: (071) 580 5871
Fax: (071) 580 7057

8. *Listings* Nobody has yet succeeded (although several have tried) in producing a wholly comprehensive and effective guide to direct marketing services. The latest, and most nearly comprehensive entrant is British Rate and Data with *Brad Direct Marketing*. This consists of a list of mailing lists available for rental, and a list of companies offering services of all kinds, with appropriate indices. It is compiled by Mardev, itself a notable player in the list-broking game. The first edition was published in September 1989, and it is the best of its kind to date.

Earlier ventures in this field include the *Direct Mail Databook*, published by Gower Press. The fifth edition came out in 1987, and is for all practical purposes superseded by Brad. (Benn Publications had an earlier entry in the field *Direct Marketing Services* published in 1980.)

From time to time *Direct Response Magazine* publishes a booklet giving details of companies offering services in this or that capacity. The information given in these listings is substantially greater than in Brad (or Gower), and they are therefore useful. The difficulty with these booklets is, firstly, that they are very far indeed from being comprehensive and, secondly, that the description of each company's facilities is written by the company, which imparts a variable degree of credibility – or sometimes intelligibility – to each.

9. *Bibliography* Useful books on direct marketing, or on database, are not numerous; books that you can actually *read*, without going to sleep, are few and far between. The traditional direct marketing picture has been one of a number of heavyweight American tomes, some of which contain valuable material if one knows where to find it, but all of which are so totally indigestible as to render their practical value of considerable doubt. British books have been in shorter supply, and have avoided the temptation to give encyclopaedic coverage to what is,

after all, a potentially immense subject. The British are catching up now in the numbers game, and thankfully have not forgotten that books are there to be read, not simply to provide impressive office furniture.

9.1   *U.S. Books*   Let us start with the blockbusters:

Dartnell Direct Mail and Mail Order Handbook, by Richard S Hodgson. 3rd edn 1980, pub by the Dartnell Corporation.

Direct Marketing: Strategy – Planning – Execution, by Edward L Nash. 2nd edn 1986, pub by McGraw Hill.

The Direct Marketing Handbook, ed by Ed Nash, 1984, pub. by McGraw Hill. (A collection of articles by leading US practitioners.)

Elements of Direct Marketing, by Martin Baier, 1984, pub by McGraw Hill. (Also in paperback)

Profitable Direct Marketing, by Jim Kobs, 1980, pub by Crain Books.

Successful Direct Marketing Methods, by Bob Stone. 3rd edn 1984, pub by Crain Books.

Then there are a number of American books that I would describe as primarily academic studies:

The Business-to-Business Direct Marketing Handbook, by Ljungren, 1989, pub by Amacom.

Direct Marketing, by K Retzler, 1988, pub by Scott Foresman.

Response Marketing, by W Cohen, 1984, pub by Wiley.

Direct Marketing Management, by Mary Lou Roberts and Paul D Berger, 1989, pub by Prentice-Hall. (It covers the ground, and gives some useful further reading – all US however.)

And a few recent American titles that are perhaps rather less hard going, and less didactic, than the preceding:

The Direct Marketer's Workbook, by Holtz, 1986, pub by Wiley.

Integrated Direct Marketing, by Ernan Roman, 1988, pub by McGraw Hill.

Selling by Direct Mail, by Graham & Jones, 1985, pub by Piatkus.

The Solid Gold Mailbox, by Walter Weintz, 1987, pub by Wiley. (An anecdotal book, for those that like that sort of thing, about successful direct mail campaigns. Personally I always feel there is much more to be learned from failures than from successes, but people are strangely reluctant to write about these.)

And one hybrid book composed of articles by American and European practitioners:

Handbook of International Direct Marketing, ed by J Dillon, 1976, pub by McGraw Hill.

9.2 *British Books* Still few on the ground, but with some note-worthy recent additions. None of them will break your wrist, and some of them are actually interesting:

Advertising That Pulls Response, by Graeme McCorkell, 1991, pub by McGraw Hill.

Commonsense Direct Marketing, by Drayton Bird, 3rd edn 1993, pub by Kogan Page. (A succinct, frequently witty, book by one of the industry's foremost copywriters.)

Cost Effective Direct Marketing, by Christian Brann, 1984, pub by Collectors Books. (The author has now retired from his eponymous company, which he created and built into one of the most respected full-service direct marketing agencies in the country. He is still one of the best lecturers on the circuit, particularly on the fundamentals of the business. This is an ideal introductory book.)

Database Management, by F R McFadden and J A Hoffer, 1985, pub by Benjamin Cummings.

Database Marketing, by Shaw & Stone, 1988, pub by Gower.

Databases in Theory and Practice, by J A Jones, 1986, pub by Kogan Page. (A good deal stronger on theory than practice, but a good theoretical introduction.)

Direct Mail Handbook, ed. by Les Andrews for The Royal Mail. 2nd edn 1988, pub by Exley. (A collection of articles by leading UK practitioners; a very useful introduction.)

The Essential Guide to Database Marketing, by John M Davies, 1992, pub by McGraw Hill.

The Secrets of Effective Direct Mail, by John Fraser Robinson, 1989, pub by McGraw Hill.

Total Quality Marketing, by John Fraser Robinson, 1991, pub by Kogan Page.

Index

Index

Index

negative cash flow 181–2
Newcastle University 118
News of the World readers 66
newspapers 40
Nicholson, Brian 237
NOP (National Opinion Polls) 113
NRS (National Readership Survey, 1982)
    107–8

O&M (Ogilvy and Mather) Direct 186
offers 45, 163–4
    point-of-sale 221
    premium 47
    special 222
OFT (Office of Fair Trading) 115
Ogilvy, David 67–8
OPCS (Office of Population Censuses and
    Surveys) 99–100

PAC (Pinpoint Address Code) 112
PAF (Postal Address File) 95, 116, 117,
    136, 149, 155, 157, 178
periodical journals 32
personalisation 82, 86, 147–51, 207, 208
persuasion 21, 24, 29, 68
PHA (Promotion Handlers' Association)
    233
philatelic market 33
Philipsburg enclosing machine 212–13
Pinpoint Analysis Ltd 112–14, 120–1
point-of-sale activities 223
population groups 99, 100–2, 123
Porsche buyers 126
positioning 37, 45
Post Office (UK) 22–3, 32–3, 95, 110,
    198, 217, 231
    Blue Books 156
    bulk mailing system 96
    Direct Mail Handbook 161n
    see also Mailsort; MPS; PAF
Post Offices (European) 158
    Dutch 145, 158

postage 35, 50, 151–8, 199, 216–20 *passim*
    European 157–8
postcodes 104–5, 108, 152, 154–7, 178
    clearly invalid 200
    computerised services 113, 116
    Continental 144, 207
    data for printing on bag labels to 206
    enumeration districts and 102–3
    full 198, 200
    inaccuracies 112
    partial 200
    safest system for avoidance of
        duplication 95
    separating, according to Acorn codes
        110
    software for 156, 164
premia 46, 47
Presstream 151, 152, 199
printing 201–4, 208
    bulk 177
    capacity 175
product planning stage 44
products 59–60, 71, 83
    affinities 81
    fmcg 130
    new, to old customers 80
    old, to new customers 80
    positioning 45
    related 80, 81
    undifferentiated 69
    see also collectibles; consumables
profiles 113, 117, 119, 133
    readership 40
profit 15, 16, 20, 36
    powerful tools for improving 47
promotions 40, 74, 82
    book 150
    cost 35
    direct mail 79
    promotions information about 80
    material relevant, targeting 77
    maximising response to 99

Index

Index

Wade, Richard 234
weaknesses 28, 30
wholesale trade 76–9
Williams (J D) 32

women 210

'Yes/No' stamps 50
yuppies 126